17.20

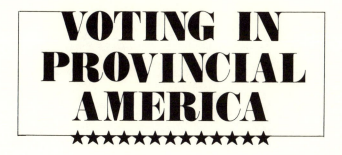

VOTING IN PROVINCIAL AMERICA

★★★★★★★★★★★★★★★★

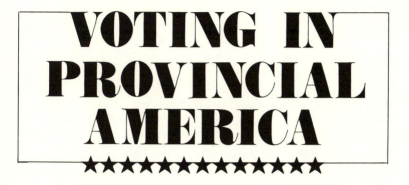

VOTING IN PROVINCIAL AMERICA

★★★★★★★★★★★★★★★

A Study of Elections in the Thirteen Colonies, 1689~1776

Robert J. Dinkin

Contributions in American History,
Number 64

GREENWOOD PRESS
Westport, Connecticut · London, England

Library of Congress Cataloging in Publication Data

Dinkin, Robert J.
    Voting in provincial America.

    (Contributions in American history; no. 64)
    Bibliography: p.
    Includes index.
    1. Elections—United States—History. 2. United States—
Politics and government—Colonial period, ca. 1600-1775.
I. Title.
JK97.A3D56   329'.023'7302   77-71861
ISBN 0-8371-9543-8

Library of Congress Catalog Card Number: 77-71861
ISBN: 0-8371-9543-8
ISSN: 0084-9219

First published in 1977

Greenwood Press, Inc.
51 Riverside Avenue, Westport, Connecticut 06880

Printed in the United States of America

Contents

★★★★★★★★★★★★★★

60872

Tables

★★★★★★★★★★★★★★★

Preface

★★★★★★★★★★★★★★

It is an interesting quirk of our historiography that despite all the scholarly and nonscholarly concern about the subject of voting today, no modern writer has ever attempted to reconstruct the beginnings of the American voting system. It is the intention of the present work to fill this gap in our knowledge and provide the first comprehensive analysis of voting in provincial America. Although numerous and lengthy surveys of early American politics have long been in print and several books and essays dealing with voting in individual colonies have been written, no single volume concentrates on all thirteen. I have tried to synthesize the extensive secondary materials, combining them with many previously unused primary sources, to present some new and challenging overviews, as well as to investigate each separate part of the voting process.

This book focuses initially upon the general nature of provincial elections. Then it explores the extent of the franchise, the characteristics of the candidates, the manner of nominations, the methods of electioneering, and the forms of balloting. Finally, I have tried to estimate the number who actually voted and to examine the various patterns of voting behavior of this era. Because of the relative absence of data concerning local contests—municipal, parish vestry, and so forth—my emphasis is chiefly on colony-wide elections. For much the same reason, the elections I treat here are primarily those for the years 1689 to 1776 rather than from earlier.

I hope that this study will foster a better understanding of the origins of the nation's voting system and how it evolved prior to the Declaration of Independence. By looking at the roots of current election practices, perhaps we can gain a greater appreciation of the development and importance of our democratic political institutions.

Every piece of historical scholarship is the result of the cumulative labors of an almost infinite number of people. Especially in a work of partial synthesis such as this one, the author has enormous obligations, most notably to those persons whose names appear in the notes and bibliography. For my part of the process I would like to thank my teachers at Brooklyn College for encouraging me in the study of history, and the members of the History Department at Columbia University, particularly Richard B. Morris, for providing excellent training and much inspiration. I am indebted to the American Philosophical Society and the Research Committee, California State University, Fresno, for financial assistance in the gathering of data. The staffs at the many libraries and archives I visited were extremely helpful in locating materials. Numerous scholars across the country courteously answered my many questions. Several of these individuals, including Professor Gary B. Nash of UCLA and Professor Edward M. Cooke of the University of Chicago, generously shared their latest research with me. My colleagues at California State University, Fresno, have given me continuous support in my endeavors over the past nine years. Professor Patricia U. Bonomi of New York University and Professor Chilton Williamson of Barnard College, Columbia University, read the entire manuscript and made many suggestions for its improvement. My editors at Greenwood Press have worked diligently to enhance the quality of the book. Mrs. Elsa Taylor of the University Research Office, California State University, Fresno, expertly typed the first draft of the manuscript, the secretaries of the Department of History, Shirley Kaser, Necia Warren, and Diana Rude, cheerfully typed the revisions, and a graduate student, Rebecca Caskey, helped with the index and proofreading. Lastly, I would like to thank my children, Sam and Leslie, for their love and patience throughout the many years I have been working on this project.

Robert J. Dinkin

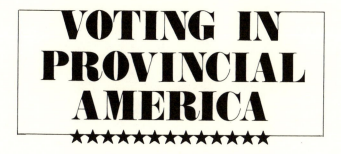

VOTING IN PROVINCIAL AMERICA

1

Provincial Elections

★★★★★★★★★★★★★★★

It may be difficult for a person living in the twentieth century to visualize
the election and voting practices of the provincial period. To the present-
day American, the term *election process* brings to mind images of smoke-
filled rooms, noisy nominating conventions, national parties with conflicting platforms, long and lavish campaigns, rallies, speeches, parades, radio
and television announcements, giant billboard and newspaper advertisements, colorful buttons, and catchy slogans. But to the average colonist,
an election meant almost none of these things. Since there was no national political system, the entire proceedings took place on a much smaller
scale. Each colony created its own distinctive forms and styles, which
contained few modern trappings. Candidates were rarely nominated in
smoke-filled rooms or at conventions. Party development and platform
appeals were still in an embryonic stage. Campaigns were not at all lengthy
and seldom involved oratory, and the communications media played only
a minor role in the majority of contests. To be sure, many of our current
procedures had their roots in these early times, but most of them were
just in a formative state and did not really evolve and take on familiar attributes until after the new nation was established.[1]

In many areas, especially New England and the lower South, elections
on the provincial level were conducted in a rather low-keyed manner. More
often than not, they went completely uncontested. Even when a contest
did occur, it usually lacked the excitement of those in subsequent eras.
Because public office was not highly sought after and electioneering was
rather limited in scope, few settlers gave any thought to who was running

for a particular position, much less to participating in the event. This absence of strong interest or enthusiasm was evident to numerous contemporaries. Elections, declared a South Carolinian in 1765, have "hitherto been regarded as a matter of little or no consequence."[2] "We should not make so light a Matter of it, as we too too often do, and be so indifferent about it," exclaimed a gentleman in Massachusetts on the same subject.[3] The citizens of several towns and parishes in these colonies showed such a lack of concern that on many occasions they declined to choose any provincial representatives at all.

The relative indifference toward elections in these locales can be attributed to a number of factors. For one, a sizable percentage of colonists accepted prevailing political conditions and expressed little desire for change. Recent historians writing about New England have emphasized the large degree of consensus found in most communities. Unanimity was considered a highly valued goal by the majority of the inhabitants. Conflict over public issues was something to be avoided or at least played down as much as possible. Local leaders, in seeking to preserve harmony and unity, frequently attempted to resolve differences before the town meeting took place. As a result, an election often became a means of sanctioning decisions already reached, which made the formal event seem relatively unimportant and unnecessary to attend.[4]

Even in regions where consensus was less in evidence, certain ecological conditions prevented the growth of an active and informed electorate. The primitive state of communications made it difficult for many people to know what was happening in public affairs. Roads were few and often impassable; travel on them, especially in winter, was irregular. Thus, news from the main centers did not usually penetrate too far into the interior. Particularly along the frontier, people often had only a vague knowledge or understanding of the political developments of the time. When a controversy arose in Massachusetts in the early 1720's over the eligibility of a certain gentleman for the provincial Council, one resident of the distant town of Woodstock wrote: "I hear so many different stories about it, that I don't know what to make on't. They say the Truth of it is in the Votes [the legislative journals], but we Country Folks, very few of us at least, can get a Sight of 'um."[5] Communications were so backward in western South Carolina that the Council of Safety in 1775 had to send two emissaries into the backcountry to "explain to the people at large the nature of the unhappy public disputes between Great Britain and the American Colonies."[6]

Indifference was also a result of the lack of institutions such as political parties that traditionally have been responsible for stimulating large numbers of persons to vote. In this period when such organizations had not yet fully developed, people in many areas felt less of an attachment to the electoral process. The potential voter was not so much an integral part of the political picture as he has since become. With no permanent parties, he was often without any means for clarifying issues or distinguishing among opposing candidates. Therefore, he frequently found himself baffled by the situation confronting him and tended to stay away from the polls. This was especially true among the non-English population, who had always played a passive role in their European homeland and had difficulty adjusting to the new system in America.[7]

In addition, some persons may have remained at home on election day because they thought their vote would not have much bearing upon who governed them. They had some reason to believe this because they had little voice in the selection of their highest officials. The inhabitants of each colony lived under the rule of a provincial governor who was in all but two cases designated by a proprietor or by the British Crown. The upper house of the legislature and most administrative and judicial posts were not generally subject to the people's choice either. Rhode Island and Connecticut were unique in having popularly elected governors, upper houses, and other high officers. Elsewhere, just the members of the lower house and certain local officials were chosen by the people, though in the southern colonies, many of the local magistrates were appointed too. The parish vestries in Virginia, for example, often became self-perpetuating bodies over the years, filling their own vacancies when they occurred.[8]

Another limiting aspect of voting in the provincial period was its circumscribed function within the eighteenth-century system of government. According to the prevailing Whig theory of checks and balances, each elector played a fairly narrow role in the overall process. His duty was to choose from among rival candidates the men he believed to be the best leaders and to keep them in command. If the incumbents abused their power during their tenure, it was his responsibility to oust them from office. Hence, voting was primarily a defensive mechanism, a means by which to "call to account and punish the Instruments of . . . Oppression."[9] As James Wilson, the noted Pennsylvania lawyer, explained it, "The people can make a distinction between those who have served them well, and those who have neglected or betrayed their interest."[10] But this was as far as popular influence was to extend. The electorate was not supposed to initiate policy, to translate political views into political action, or to force its will upon the rulers. Only later did voting come to mean a mandate for government programs and policies. In the provincial era, the major concerns of the state were confined to providing defense against external enemies and keeping internal order.

Notwithstanding these limitations, the purpose of voting was still considerable. As a check against undesirable candidates or possible tyranny, it was no small function. The American colonists, in electing their assemblymen and numerous local officials, were one of the few peoples in the eighteenth century to possess any authority over those who governed them. Certainly many provincial leaders recognized the importance of the franchise and sought to make their constituents aware of it too. William Penn, the founder of Pennsylvania, emphasized the fact that it was a most "valuable privilege," one that should be exercised wisely and with great caution.[11] A gentleman in proprietary Maryland called the "free Choice of proper Persons," "the great Bulwark of British Liberty."[12] The right to vote was a significant one and not available to everybody. As a writer in the *South Carolina Gazette* declared: " 'Tis a glorious privilege! and methinks every one of you should be fond of all Opportunities to put in your Claim to it, and shew what a Right you enjoy beyond some others of your Fellow Subjects."[13] Yet as one New Yorker sadly lamented, "The Liberty of Voting is a Treasure possessed by Multitudes who have no Idea of its real value."[14]

If the prospect of voting did not inspire a great deal of enthusiasm and excitement everywhere, it did in some places bring about quite a stir at times. At the very least it provided a welcome break from the monotony of colonial existence. "We have dull Barbecues and yet Duller Dances," wrote John Kirkpatrick of Virginia. But an election, he added, invariably "causes a Hubub for a Week or so." During those few days the "flame of burgessing entered every heart," and the impending struggle took up the "whole talk."[15] This type of spirit was also exhibited in pre-Revolutionary Rhode Island where the relentless factional competition each year kept the people in a constant "Rage," according to John Brown of Providence.[16] Much the same situation was observed in parts of Pennsylvania by the Reverend Henry Muhlenburg. Election day, said Muhlenburg, "is the most turbulent day in the whole year . . . the towns are crowded and noisy."[17] The postelection calm offered a striking contrast to the vigorous activity surrounding the entire event. After a particularly lively contest in Lancaster, Pennsylvania, one bystander remarked: "The Borough is restored to its former Quiet, & the Inhabitants have again resumed their Senses."[18]

Such activity at election time, however, was not very common during the earliest years of colonization. Only after the new dominions had grown and matured did competitive politics become possible. The first elections for the Virginia House of Burgesses in 1619, and those of several decades thereafter, were, as far as can be determined, uncontested.[19] The same can be said for the initial voting efforts in Plymouth, the second British settlement in the New World. Following the death of John Carver in 1621, William Bradford was annually chosen governor for the major part of the next thirty-six years, in many instances without opposition. The deputies to the legislature were also periodically reelected in most cases.[20] New Netherlands, founded in the mid-1620's, had no genuine competition for office in the period of Dutch rule, as representative government was nonexistent beyond the local level. Even under the English, New York, as the colony became known, was not provided with an elective assembly until 1683. Massachusetts, which was chartered in 1630, had a small number of contests during its infant stages as a result of some disagreement with the policies of Governor John Winthrop. But once the early disputes were resolved, the chief magistrates were generally returned to their posts each year until their retirement or death. Connecticut and Rhode Island also had some internal quarrels shortly after being established, yet usually these did not extend to conflicts at the ballot box. Many of the other provinces, such as the Carolinas and Pennsylvania, were not settled until the latter part of the seventeenth century; since it took time for a political system to become organized, contention at the polls was scarcely known in these places before 1689. Thus, the first seventy years of elections in America produced few real encounters and generated little sustained interest among the populace.[21]

By the 1690's, and certainly after 1700, however, more and more elections were becoming competitive. The homogeneity and closely knit leadership that had characterized some of the early settlements was beginning to break down. For the first time challenges were being raised against traditional authority. Newly emerging interests began clashing with older, established ones. Influential colonists, unhappy with certain aspects of English rule and unable to gain satisfaction from the Crown, started appealing to the local populace for support.[22] Moreover, increasing numbers of individuals now had the affluence and leisure to participate in politics and stand for public office. Young men seeking to rise in the social scale often looked to a seat in the legislature as a means of enhancing their position. All these factors opened up new possibilities for much greater activity at election time. If in parts of New England widespread involvement and vigorous contests did not occur until the 1730's and 1740's, elsewhere it had already begun to happen nearly a half-century earlier.

The basis for contested elections varied. In some instances competition stemmed from a particular type of local conflict—for example, a difference over the division of land, the apportioning of taxes, or religious questions.[23] In others, colony-wide matters tended to overshadow local disputes. The demand for paper money, the amount of military spending, the Great Awakening in religion, and the crisis with the mother country each led to serious struggles at the polls in certain provinces. But in probably just as many cases, neither local or provincial issues were of much consequence because the outcome hinged primarily on the competing candidates' background and personality. As Lucille Griffith has written about contests in mid-eighteenth-century Virginia: "It seems not to have been so much a question of *what* as *who*." For example, when George Washington first ran for public office in 1755, he stood for the same things as both of his opponents.[24]

At times competition at the ballot box resulted from a personal feud of some kind, for instance, where one individual challenged another because of a slight upon the former's reputation. One of the more amusing incidents of this sort occurred in Cambridge, Massachusetts. When John Vassal, a wealthy gentleman who had come to Cambridge from the West Indies, was chosen to the legislature in 1739, Deputy Sheriff Samuel Whittemore announced publicly that Vassal "was no more fit to discharge the said trust than the horse that he, the said Samuel then rode on." The following day, Vassal brought suit against Whittemore for £1,000 sterling, claiming that he had been much "damnified" by the statement. Whittemore was held for lack of bail, but the court soon ruled that his words were "not actionable" and ordered his release. The deputy promptly sued Vassal £290 for damages and then attempted to stir up opposition to the latter at the next election, but Vassal was reelected by an overwhelming majority.[25]

A more important source of competition than feuds between two individuals was the widespread factional rivalry that developed over the course of this era. Contests in many towns and counties, and indeed on a provincial scale, were often based upon the quest of various groups of men for power and place. Most of these factional squabbles were relatively short-lived, though a few continued for generations. Sometimes these conflicts centered around great families such as the Livingstons and the DeLanceys in New York, the Otises and Hutchinsons in Massachusetts, or the Wards and Wantons in Rhode Island. Usually the two sides differed very little in their basic ideology and clashed mainly over personal interests and the desire for office. The world, said James Otis, was divided between winners and losers, "between those who are discontented that they have no Power, and those who never think they can have enough."[26] When one side ousted its opponents from positions of influence, no fundamental change in policy resulted, just a change in personnel. Because of their essential similarities, contemporaries like Thomas Hutchinson frequently referred to such groups as the "ins" and the "outs."

To be sure, not all factional rivalries with their consequent battles at the polls grew out of simple power struggles. A great number of clashes were the result of deeply rooted economic differences or religious and ethnic distinctions. Some of these quarrels could split a colony to such a point as to shake it to its very foundations. Numerous partisan alignments were closely related to the tug of war between the provincial governors and the lower houses of the legislatures.[27] A governor bent on retaining the dominance of the Crown or proprietary interest would usually attempt to rally those persons sympathetic to his cause into a court faction. Meanwhile, members of the house who opposed the prerogative and sought greater local autonomy would form a group known as the country faction. The court versus country conflict in America took its name from a similar division in England, where a country party had emerged in the House of Commons to check the influence of the King and his court favorites. On this side of the Atlantic, contests between the two adversaries revolved mainly around control of the purse strings and authority over political appointments as the Assembly desired to take these powers out of the chief executive's hands. But in some encounters the country leaders were motivated less by the principles at stake than with promoting their own private concerns.

Generally, the most heated contests in this period took place in those colonies whose political struggles were multifold, that is, where the fight between the governor and the Assembly was combined with various economic, religious, and personal controversies. Probably the best examples of such complex division could be found in New York and Pennsylvania. In these two provinces the idea of party, which was anathema almost everywhere else, had gained some degree of acceptance, and the opposing sides at times organized large-scale campaigns.[28] It should be noted, however, that factionalism even in New York and Pennsylvania was not always continuous on the same basis over long periods. As was true elsewhere, factions here comprised temporary and shifting alliances. Moreover, the competing groups did not usually contest every single election. A report issued by the Pennsylvania legislature in 1753 emphatically stated that "there had not been for some Years, nor was there expected to be, nor has there since been, any Contest at Elections between the [two] interests."[29]

Indeed, the frequency of contested elections was not in all cases connected to factional development and widespread internal dispute. Parties in the provincial period were essentially legislative parties, which competed primarily within the Assembly chamber and only to a limited extent outside.[30] The leaders of such groups often felt no need to mobilize voters or saw too many obstacles involved in doing so. They thought that their ends could best be achieved by using their persuasive powers over the other representatives during the legislative sessions rather than out on the stump. Several of the court factions, not being popular among the electorate, commonly held such views and made little effort to provide a perennially combative force on election day. Thus, Massachusetts, which endured a vast amount of factional hostility over the years, engaged in few heated contests. On the other hand, Virginia, which was relatively free of such strife by the middle of the eighteenth century, because of certain peculiarities continued to witness a great deal of competition at the polls. Yet, as the following survey of all the colonies will show, the degree of contention at election time was often closely related to the extent of political, economic, religious and ethnic division in a particular province.

In the southern colonies, political conflicts and accompanying election struggles were quite extensive in the upper part of the region and gradually less so toward the lower part. Overall the predominantly rural environment and relative homogeneity of those within the political community made for much less strife than in the middle colonies. Only in Virginia were heated contests commonplace throughout most of the pe-

riod. Maryland and North Carolina saw considerable skirmishing at the
polls from the mid-1720's onward, yet in neither did it occur with overwhelming frequency. South Carolina experienced little competition after its formative years, while Georgia's rather late settlement (it was not
founded until 1733) prevented much factional development and election
furor there.

In Georgia, which had no representative assembly until shortly before
it became a royal colony in 1753, competitive elections were few and far
between. Not many actual contests took place except in the capital, Savannah, where four House seats were at stake.[31] Prior to the first provincial
polling in 1754, opponents of the new Crown-controlled administration,
led by the adventurer Edmund Gray, organized an active campaign among
the town dwellers in order to obtain a strong foothold in the legislature.
According to one observer, Gray "us'd all wicked Means to enflame the
Minds of many weak People" and formed them in a "Party" to "blacken
and distress" the government. Yet, in spite of such "sinister dealings,"
the Gray faction was defeated in the voting for three of the four spots,
to the "great Mortification" of Gray and his friends.[32]

Outside of the capital, rivalry during this initial election was almost
unknown. Many of the neighboring districts did not have any willing candidates. In fact, leaders in three parishes appealed to the same gentleman
in Savannah to represent them. Moreover, in the Midway district to the
south, no formal contest was even held. The Congregational church in
the area merely summoned its members to a meeting, designated a delegate, and sent his name on to the central authorities. Throughout the new
colony's existence, it often proved difficult to find anyone in the rural
locales who would accept a seat in the Assembly.[33]

The lone contest in the short history of provincial Georgia to extend
beyond Savannah occurred in 1768 amid the growing crisis with Great
Britain. Governor James Wright, trying to uphold the position of the
Crown, used all the influence at his command to have assemblymen sympathetic to his cause chosen, but he was no match for the so-called Liberty party. These Sons of Liberty managed to convince the populace at
large that there was "a distinction between the Interest of the People
and the Interest of the Crown and Mother Country." They spread rumors that Parliament was planning more oppressive measures, which
could be resisted only by representatives devoted to preserving local
rights. In the voting that followed, the Liberty party achieved a resound-

ing victory: eighteen of the twenty-five men elected were "avowed Sons of Liberty." The winning margin was, in fact, so great, that the Governor and his supporters never again made any real attempt to promote candidates to the lower house.[34]

South Carolina had a political configuration somewhat similar to Georgia's. Some spirited elections occurred in the capital, Charleston, but few happened elsewhere until the Revolutionary era.[35] The only heated contests before the 1760's were held in the early years of settlement when the province stood under proprietary rule. Conflict between Anglicans and Dissenters, as well as economic differences, caused a great deal of factional strife at the turn of the eighteenth century. Charleston, which served as the polling place for the entire colony at this time, often became a "scene of riot, intemperance, and confusion." After the tally was made in 1701, Governor James Moore, an Anglican, was accused of fixing the results in order to have an Assembly of his "own complexion."[36] The Dissenters also claimed that many aliens and other unqualified voters had been allowed to participate. The next election, they asserted, was even more fraudulent, as "Jews, Strangers, Sailors, Servants, Negroes and almost every French Man in Craven and Berkly County came down to elect, and their Votes were taken and the Persons by them voted for were returned by the Sheriff, to the manifest wrong and prejudice of other Candidates."[37] Such excitement subsided for a while but resumed in the following decade under proprietary officials Nicholas Trott and William Rhett, who tried to govern in an arbitrary manner. Finally, beginning in 1716, steps were taken to reduce tensions. Election districts were created whereby the balloting would be conducted in each parish rather than in Charleston. In 1719, the proprietorship was taken away and the province placed under the direct control of the Crown.[38]

During the royal period, interest in elections began to wane. The earlier conflicts were resolved. New problems were more or less confined to the legislative sessions and did not lead to divisions at the polls. Apathy soon became the norm, not only among the voters but among the prospective candidates as well. As one commentator noted: "Many Persons of Property and Figure" refused to serve in the lower house even if they were elected to it.[39] On some occasions it would appear that anyone willing to accept a seat would be welcomed, and certain spots were never filled. In 1747 and 1749 the Assembly was unable to obtain a quorum and had to be dissolved by the Governor without ever having met officially. A writer in the *South Carolina Gazette* remarked: "we have very lately seen an Assembly called but not Members enough meet even to make a House, tho 19 of the 44 Members are sufficient for that purpose."[40] Although there were many more men available for office in South Carolina than in Georgia, few were inclined to give up any part of their business or social life for public service. The one place that proved an exception to this rule was St. Philip's Parish (Charleston), but its residents did not show the same degree of enthusiasm for politics as did those of the other leading cities of America. Not until the 1760's and the emergence of deep conflict with England was there any rebirth of competition at election time in this province.[41]

North Carolina's elections followed a pattern somewhat the opposite of South Carolina's. While contests in the latter colony began to decline after the establishment of royal government in 1719, contests in the former, which also switched to Crown rule, started to rise. Factional disputes developed from time to time on a court versus country basis, over the land question, the payment of quitrents, and various sectional differences.[42] The most divisive issue in the first decade and a half was the desire by the Crown to increase quitrents, which soon triggered strong opposition to administration supporters at the polls. "Burgessing," complained Governor Burrington in the early 1730's, "has been for some years a source of lyes and occasion for disturbances, which has deterred good men from being Candidates or entering the lists of noise and Faction."[43] Political conflict continued on an even greater scale during the reign of Gabriel Johnston (1734-1752). Not only was the rent question still undecided, but fresh controversies emerged over the allotment of representation and the location of a permanent capital. The new chief executive sought to reduce the number of opposition northerners in the House (each of the Albemarle counties had five members, the others but two) by moving the capital to the south. He believed few delegates from the upper part of the province would be willing to travel long distances to attend the legislative sessions. When this step was taken, the Albemarle men reacted by boycotting the Assembly for many years, especially after the regular five-man delegations were refused their seats following a new election in 1747. This situation was not ultimately resolved until after Johnston's death and Arthur Dobbs's succession to the governor's chair in the mid-1750's.[44]

The north-south clash eventually proved to be minor so far as contested elections were concerned compared to the sectional split between east and west in the decade before independence. By the late 1760's, almost half of the colony's population lived in the six western counties. Yet this section was allowed fewer than one-third of the seats in the legislature. Moreover, the men in the frontier communities were dissatisfied with the corrupt administration provided by the Governor's appointees in the region. In response, they organized a group known as the Regulators, who were intent upon changing the manner of government in the area. Although they were primarily interested in removing unscrupulous appointed officials, they also realized the need for replacing dishonest elected officials as well. Thus, in 1769, they undertook a major campaign to oust the incumbent Assemblymen in several counties, many of them nonresident court favorites. In the voting that followed, four solid Regulator delegations were chosen, showing that the people in the Carolina backcountry were beginning to play an active role in politics.[45]

Virginia's provincial election history had two distinct phases: one extending down to the late 1720's and the other continuing from that time until the Revolution. In the first period, contests were usually part of a court versus country division, pitting the royal governor and his supporters against the defenders of local interests within the House of Burgesses. In the second, contests were primarily personal in nature as factions declined and issues were left to be debated inside the legislative halls.[46]

The elections of the early eighteenth century were probably the most bitterly contested of any held in the province. Despite the fact that the governor's salary question had long been settled, many issues facing the chief executive and the lower house remained unresolved. As one authority on Virginia has written, problems relating to land grants, tobacco, finances, Indians, church government, pirates and privateers, boundaries, trade, militia, and security from foreign encroachments during Britain's wars with France and Spain continued to plague several administrations for a number of decades. Local leaders often refused to go along with the imperial position on many of these matters and did everything possible to defeat the court candidates at the polls.[47]

Election intensity reached its highest peak during the reign of Governor Alexander Spotswood (1710-1722), who actively sought to build a powerful court party. In 1715, his plans met with little success, however, as most of his friends were soundly beaten. Afterward, Spotswood lamented the people's "Mistaken choice" of representatives and sarcastically remarked that the voters seemed more interested in ringing the noses of errant hogs than in the quality of their burgesses. Three years later, the Governor was even less successful. At least thirty-four members from the previous hostile Assembly were reelected and many of the new men chosen were staunchly opposed to his administration.[48]

The sharp friction between the governor and the Assembly, which had long caused uneasiness in the colony, eventually began to subside. Neither Hugh Drysdale (1722-1727) nor William Gooch (1727-1749) attempted to establish a court party, and eventually factions died and relative harmony emerged within the government. As the Speaker of the House, Sir John Randolph, told Gooch in 1736: "You have shew'd how easy it is to give universal satisfaction to the people. . . . You have not been intoxicated with the power committed to you by his Majesty, but have used it as a trustee for the public good."[49]

After this time, heated elections continued in Virginia but on an entirely different basis. With the competing bodies fully removed, factional politics soon gave way to personal politics. Why contests were still strenuously fought in the absence of organized groups is difficult to explain, though there are a few possibilities. Perhaps the long tradition of competitive elections was so firmly entrenched that men continued to clash in spite of the disappearance of factions and issues. Then, too, the prestige, power, and other benefits that accrued to members of the House of Burgesses may have kept many individuals vying for a seat. Possibly the rivalry between great families in some counties was seen in people's minds as a factional conflict. Whatever the reasons, contests persistently flourished in the Old Dominion, giving future statesmen like George Washington and Richard Henry Lee their first taste of political fire.[50]

Maryland's politics was continuously filled with controversy beginning with the Glorious Revolution and Coode's Rebellion in 1689. However, elections in the province did not become competitive on a broad basis until the mid-1720's. At that point, the enduring conflict between the proprietary government of Lord Baltimore and its numerous opponents became increasingly manifest in a struggle for control of the Assembly. The administration's adversaries, known as the country party, who had traditionally dominated the lower house and wished to limit proprietary power, now saw their interest threatened by the emergence of a highly active court party. Generally, in the decades that followed, the court, composed of the proprietor's family, friends, and appointees, found it impossible to win more than a third of the seats in any one contest. This was largely due to the overall unpopularity of their position and their lack of organization. Nevertheless, the court members often managed to exert a great deal of pressure when battling against the country party at the polls.[51]

The two groups differed on several issues, such as tobacco inspection laws, military spending, and the rights of Catholics. But the underlying problem at all moments was the extent of the proprietor's ruling power. During the 1730's and after, country leaders in the Assembly sought to restrict the proprietor's veto, more closely regulate fees, make the sheriff's position elective, and choose their own agent in London. Court candidates who opposed these measures or defended such positions as leniency to Catholics were frequently sent down to quick defeat. In the mid-1750's, when Daniel Dulany, Jr., the noted lawyer, took a stand against the confiscation of lands held by the Catholic clergy, anti-Catholic sentiment among Dulany's constituents reached such proportions that he could not even appear in public on voting day.[52]

The biggest clashes involving the two protagonists occurred in the capital city of Annapolis, where many of the proprietary officials resided and the competing groups were most evenly matched. No fewer than seven of the elections held there after 1728 resulted in disputes that had to be settled by the legislature. But Annapolis was not the only place in which heated contests were frequent. Anne Arundel, Baltimore, Calvert, Cecil, Dorchester, Frederick, Kent, and St. Mary's counties also had their share of chaotic struggles. Baltimore, in particular, was sharply divided between court and country, with the upper part of county supporting the latter and the lower part backing the former.[53]

The conflict between the two factions at the polls continued unabated down through the late 1760's. Until that time, the court usually won a number of seats and always seemed optimistic about its future chances. However, circumstances had begun to change, causing the ardent competition to subside. The court had become completely discredited as a result of its close identification with the recently enacted British measures that many people perceived as a threat to their liberties. In most places, country candidates now ran unopposed. Only in Annapolis did the proprietor's friends make a final bid in 1773, but their standard-bearer, Anthony Stewart, found so many voters committed to his adversaries even before the polls opened that he "thought it prudent to decline."[54]

The middle colonies—Pennsylvania, Delaware, New Jersey, and New York—had much greater political conflict than the South did. An increasingly heterogeneous population surely played an important part in laying the background as more non-English elements settled in this region than in all other places combined. Factions formed early and were generally more cohesive than elsewhere. The perpetual power struggles between the governors and assemblies along with family rivalries, economic, and ethnic-religious divisions often made this area a hotbed of controversy at election time.

In Pennsylvania, opposition quickly arose against the proprietary government of the Penn family. Court and country factions emerged at the beginning of the eighteenth century, the former led by the proprietor's secretary, James Logan, and centered in Philadelphia, the latter led by lawyer David Lloyd, and supported chiefly outside the city. Disputes developed over various issues related to the desire by the Lloyd-dominated lower house to limit proprietary power. Factionalism continued on a somewhat similar basis during the 1720's as Lloyd joined forces with Governor William Keith against the authority of the Penns.[55] By the late 1730's, however, politics began to take a new direction. The Quakers, who had largely comprised both of the earlier factions and had generally run the colony over the first half-century, now found themselves declining in numbers and influence. In response, they busily erected a united Quaker party for the purpose of maintaining their preeminent position. Yet, no sooner had they formed their organization than they came into contention with a newly established Proprietary party, composed mainly of Anglicans and some backcountry Presbyterians, who hoped to put an end to Quaker rule.[56]

During the early 1740's, with the British empire at war, the Proprietary group, under the direction of William Allen, made a strong attempt to remove the pacifist Quakers from control of the Assembly. Allen and his supporters pointed especially to the military weakness of the province, which, they said, exposed it to hostile attack. The Quakers took up the challenge and sought to ally themselves with the colony's large German population, claiming that only their continued leadership could prevent excessive taxation, loathsome militia service, and tyrannical rule. The Quakers proved more effective as political organizers for, in spite of all the efforts by their opponents, they won practically every seat in the House for several years. The Proprietary party was so disheartened by these results that for more than a decade it did not even bother to enter candidates in the elections. In the mid-1750's, competition resumed, and at a more intense level than before. The outbreak of the French and Indian War on the western border made the question of frontier defense even more pressing than earlier, creating immense problems for the Quakers who displayed little enthusiasm toward military preparations. In these years, the Proprietary forces made some inroads, but the Quaker party was still able to preserve much of its strength. The pacifist elements were persuaded to step down and non-Quakers, such as Benjamin Franklin and Joseph Galloway, moved in to take over the organization.[57]

The Proprietary side, or New Ticket, as it was later called, initiated its greatest effort to gain ascendancy in the election of 1764, attempting to counteract a move by Franklin and others to make Pennsylvania a royal province. But despite a sweeping victory for the New Ticket in and around Philadelphia, the Quakers managed to retain their mastery of the House by winning elsewhere. Then, in the following year (1765), after another hard battle it regained many of the seats that it had lost. By 1767, the Proprietary interest had all but given up at trying to defeat the Quakers.[58]

Over the next few years, as difficulties with the British increased and the old factional alignments began to break down and disappear, so too did most discord and rivalry at the ballot box. But starting in 1774 when the imperial crisis came to a head, new groups solidified and elections once more became extremely competitive. Radicals or Independents led by Thomas Mifflin and Charles Thomson, hoping to push Pennsylvania toward a more vigorous stand against Britain, worked to oust Moderates such as John Dickinson from office. Although they achieved some gains in the rural areas, they were not too successful in Philadelphia. As late as May 1, 1776, the Moderates still found it possible to win a majority in the special city elections held on that date. Yet these results could not, of course, turn the tide against separation from the mother country, which occurred a short time afterward.[59]

Very little is known about elections in Delaware except for the earliest years of settlement and for those immediately preceding the American Revolution. From 1682 to 1704, the area that comprised Delaware was officially united with Pennsylvania and often took part in the same political conflicts. As the three Delaware counties were accorded an equal amount of representation with the three from Pennsylvania in the combined legislature, the stage was set for some extremely hard-fought contests.[60] Even after 1704, when a separate legislature was provided for the three lower counties, Delaware's politics tended to follow Pennsylvania's, especially since both colonies still shared the same chief executive. During the administration of Sir William Keith, who turned against the Penn family in the late 1720's, there was a great deal of campaign activity. Quite frequently the Governor tried to set up his supporters for the Assembly in New Castle just as he had done in Philadelphia. Caesar Rodney, father of one of the signers of the Declaration of Independence, noted in September, 1729, "People Very Busey Now about ye Election Being Ney at hand." Besides the struggle with the proprietor, paper money was a major issue here as it was in other colonies at this time.[61]

Some competition probably occurred in Delaware elections as a result of problems at the time of the French and Indian War. But the most ardent contests in the province took place in the few years just prior to independence. As in neighboring Pennsylvania, the inhabitants of the lower counties displayed considerable sentiment against any precipitous break with the mother country. This compelled the staunch patriots to take vigorous measures to eliminate the more cautious members from the Assembly. In 1774 and 1775, the radicals, led by Thomas McKean, scored significant victories in New Castle, but in Sussex, the moderates, led by Thomas Robinson, still won a number of seats, which helped maintain some balance in the legislature until separation occurred.[62]

Many major election battles took place in New Jersey, as religious differences, paper money, and land problems often caused considerable conflict. Unlike most other colonies, which saw factional strife reaching its highest point toward the end of the provincial era, New Jersey was more politically divided in the early and middle years of the period. During the first decade and a half of the eighteenth century there was a sharp split between the Scotch or Scottish-Quaker faction in East Jersey and the Anglican faction in West Jersey. Hard feelings ran so high at the polls that on one occasion Governor Robert Hunter had to dissolve an Assembly just after it was chosen "in order to give the Country one opportunity more of a Free Choice, having heard many Complaints of undue practices and Artifices Used in the last Election."[63] The Scottish-Quaker group managed to remain in control of the lower house until 1716, when opponents led by Daniel Coxe staged an intensive campaign in West Jersey to gain the upper hand. Nevertheless, the Coxe faction was ousted from its position of influence soon afterward, eventually bringing peace to the province for a time.

Elections were rarely competitive in the 1720's and early 1730's but became so on a much bigger scale than ever before during the governorship of Lewis Morris (1738-1746). Several Assemblymen who disliked Morris's high-handed methods, extravagent expenditures, and executive vetoes began organizing against him and his backers. Morris, meanwhile, did everything possible to counter this thrust but to little avail, as most of his detractors were reelected each time. Upon hearing the results in 1739, Morris complained that it was becoming a maxim in politics "that such men are only fit to be chosen representatives as will most Strenuously oppose their governours."[64]

Perhaps the most tenaciously fought elections in the colony's history occurred in the late 1740's and early 1750's in the reign of Jonathan Belcher (1747-1757), a time of economic crisis and rent rioting. The election of 1749, for instance, was marked by four times the amount of turnover in House members as the previous one. Many of those who had supported harsh measures against the rioters wound up losing their seats. Five years later, contests were even more impassioned. One newspaper reported that in "several Parts [of] New Jersey, . . . there has been lately the greatest Struggles in electing Representatives, in some of the Counties, that ever were known."[65]

By the late 1760's, however, many of the older problems had been resolved, and a sharp reduction in the number of fierce clashes had taken place. For example, in 1768, the two members from Burlington and the contingent from Hunterdon were all elected unanimously. Even where contests continued to flourish, a decline in the fervor exhibited in previous times could be observed. After Hendrick Fisher and John Berrien were declared the winners in Somerset County, one witness exclaimed: "The election was carried on with the greatest coolness and good order: no reflecting nor abusive words were heard during the whole election." This pattern continued into the 1770's. Conflict at the polls was generally absent in most parts of the province, as supporters of Tory Governor William Franklin were easily defeated.[66]

New York was the scene of almost constant political turmoil during the provincial era. Clashes between imperial and local interests, various merchant and landed groups, plus ethnic and religious differences among English and Dutch, Anglican and Dissenter, made this colony a natural spot for factional controversy and a veritable battleground at election time.[67]

Factionalism and hard-fought contests occurred from the beginning of the period. The revolt in 1689 against British authority, known as Leisler's

Rebellion, soon created a deep division between Leislerians (principally the long-established Dutch) and anti-Leislerians (the newly rising English). This split was primarily responsible for the high feelings and several irregularities at the first few elections, a situation that remained throughout the 1690's and early 1700's.[68] Relative peace was finally secured for a time through the efforts of Governor Robert Hunter (1710-1719), but this tranquillity proved to be somewhat short-lived. Although the old factions eventually died out, new ones began to appear in the late 1720's and early 1730's, which quickly stimulated activity at the polls once more. Some of the most exciting encounters in the colony's history happened in the 1730's during the administration of William Cosby (1732-1736). Cosby's arbitrary political actions and corrupt financial policies alienated numerous groups in the province, setting the stage for vigorous campaigns against his supporters in many locales. Perhaps the biggest single election took place in Westchester County in the fall of 1733. The formidable Lewis Morris, whom Cosby had removed from the post of Chief Justice, managed to achieve a measure of vindication by defeating the Governor's nominee in the Assembly race.[69]

A sharp division between the court and country elements continued through the 1740's and early 1750's, especially during the reign of Governor George Clinton (1743-1753). Clinton's disagreements with Chief Justice James DeLancey over several civic and military matters at the time of King George's War led to some extremely bitter election struggles. In these contests, DeLancey, the head of a powerful mercantile family in New York City, soon emerged as the most efficient political organizer the province had ever seen. He and his allies in the Hudson River counties, using various tactics both above and below board, were generally able to win a majority of seats each time, and they dominated the Assembly for many years.[70]

When James DeLancey died in 1760, New York politics remained in a state of flux for a time. But another rivalry soon developed as a revitalized DeLancey faction was challenged by a new group centered around the prominent Livingston family and supported by several influential lawyers and a number of dissenting religious sects. This challenge formed the basis of the two hardest fought elections in the history of the province: those of 1768 and 1769. Especially in New York City, more people campaigned, more heated words were exchanged, and more printed matter was distributed than in any other pair of contests. The DeLanceys were

attacked for not taking a strong stand against Britain during the Stamp
Act crisis, while the Livingstons were accused of being "artful, designing,
ambitious men . . . grasping at power, solely to aggrandize themselves and
their families, without any view to the public interest." In the end, the
better-organized DeLanceys with their cry of "No Lawyers, No Presbyterians" struck a more responsive chord with the voters. The Livingstons
suffered major defeats on both occasions, bringing to a conclusion the
long series of election quarrels in the province.[71]

In New England, where the population was most homogeneous, competitive elections on a broad scale were rather late in developing, considering the early dates of the first settlements. To be sure, there was a good
deal of political conflict in the era of the Dominion of New England
(1686-1689) and its immediate aftermath, but this involved few tussles
at the ballot box. Except for a few brief flurries from time to time, widespread contests at the polls did not generally become part of the region's
politics until the 1730's and 1740's. Only then did changing conditions
lead to the breakdown of earlier harmony and the appearance of fairly
coherent factions in each of the area's four colonies. In addition to typical power struggles, various religious and economic questions were becoming major issues. The fact that the people of Connecticut and Rhode
Island were allowed to choose their own governor and upper house merely heightened election enthusiasm in these provinces as it gave rise to
colony-wide races.[72]

Before 1740, Connecticut politics were probably the most peaceful
in New England. The province was often referred to as the "Land of
Steady Habits." Competition for public office in the early eighteenth
century was at a minimum. The records reveal almost no trace of electioneering or disputed elections. Few issues were ever divisive enough to
disturb the political equilibrium. In general, the people, as part of their
Puritan inheritance, still unhesitatingly accepted the authority and
decision-making power of their chosen rulers. Magistrates who did not
veer too far from traditional lines of policy were sure to be reelected.
As the observant New Yorker Cadwallader Colden noted: "Seldom are
their officers changed while they strictly support the government and
execute their laws, and the offices for the most part continue in the
same families from father to son."[73]

In the years following 1740, the number of contests gradually began
to rise. The religious revival known as the Great Awakening divided the

colony into factions of Old Lights and New Lights, the former favoring the old church establishment, the latter desiring change. This disruption of traditional institutions made many more people concerned about who governed them. As a consequence numerous persons were no longer willing to acquiesce in the continuation of certain magistrates in office as they had in the past. They began movements, first local, then provincial, to oust officials with whom they were not satisfied: New Light towns dropped Old Lights from their lists, and vice versa. If most high officeholders still gained reelection, it was not with the same ease as in previous generations.[74]

During subsequent decades, hard-fought elections became even more frequent as new issues and deeper divisions emerged. Quarrels resulted over the advisability of a large-scale speculative venture by a group known as the Susquehanna Company, which intended to obtain land in the Wyoming Valley of Pennsylvania. This dispute became intertwined with the question of the proper response to the British tax measures of the 1760's. By that time, the eastern section of the colony, predominantly New Light and favoring the Susquehanna scheme, was engaged in an all-out political battle with the Old Light western counties, whose leaders opposed the speculative enterprise and did not react very forcefully to the Stamp Act. The latter argued that strenuous pursuance of New Light policies would lead to the loss of the colony's charter privileges. Over the next few years, election controversies reached their highest level. As Reverend Samuel Johnson declared after the balloting in 1767, "Never were there such struggles as have, and will be, at any elections here."[75] Both sides used all sorts of machinations in their attempt to obtain power, some of them not always legal. Although the New Lights led by William Pitkin won the governorship several times in succession, the Old Lights under Thomas Fitch kept trying to regain the top post. Not until after the election of 1774 did the Old Lights acquiesce in New Light leadership, which by that juncture had passed to Jonathan Trumbull, thus putting an end to vigorous contests in pre-Revolutionary Connecticut.[76]

In Massachusetts there was a curious development: great factional duels inside the legislature but few real battles at the polls outside the city of Boston. The province was, to be sure, often a "theatre of parties and feuds," as John Adams later remarked, yet only in a few isolated instances did such controversy lead to widespread factional competition at election time. For example, during the early 1700's there was a great deal of conflict between Governor Joseph Dudley (1702-1715) and his foes in the Assembly over several political, military, and financial matters. The Governor, however, did not seek to organize popular support for his cause so that the anti-Dudley forces in the House did not encounter much adversity at the ballot box.[77]

The situation changed to some degree in the administration of Samuel Shute (1716-1722). For the first time, a court faction competed actively with country members for votes, at least in the vicinity of Boston. The merchant Thomas Lechmere, describing conditions in the capital at this time, stated: "No news stirring here only factions and divisions, party writing against party."[78] At issue was the monetary problem, the Governor's followers defending a hard-money policy, the opposition calling for heavy paper emissions in a period of rising inflation. The defeat of the court faction and continued wrangling over the currency eventually caused Shute to leave the province.

After Shute's departure, contested elections gradually declined in number. Most of the outstanding issues were ultimately compromised in the reign of Jonathan Belcher (1730-1741), who seemed more concerned about remaining in office than in upholding the royal prerogative. But one important matter was still unresolved: the currency question. As economic hardship reached crisis proportions around 1740, paper-money advocates became convinced that the only solution lay in the creation of a Land Bank. In order to obtain legislative approval of their scheme, the Land Bankers engaged in an all-out campaign to oust the hard-money men from office. As a result of their efforts, a majority of the bank's opponents in 1741 were swept from their seats. So many Land Bank enthusiasts were elected, recalled the historian Thomas Hutchinson, that this Assembly later became distinguished by the name "Land Bank House."[79]

The Land Bank crisis eventually passed. The bank was declared illegal by the British government but a fairly workable money policy was instituted by the new Governor, William Shirley (1741-1757), bringing relative peace to the province. Although some factionalism remained in the legislature, partisan election activity soon died down. For the next quarter of a century, contests, where held, grew primarily out of local and personal differences. Only one measure, the excise tax of 1754, aroused much interest on a large scale, and even this issue probably did not prod too many people to go out and vote.[80] The passage of the Stamp Act in 1765, however, and the subsequent difficulties with the mother country soon led to the greatest election struggle in the colony's history. While the act itself had become a dead letter by the spring of 1766, numerous pro-British sympathizers still retained their places in the Assembly. The "popular party," headed by Samuel Adams and James Otis, hoping to remove these individuals from power, called for a purge of the alleged "friends" of the Stamp Act. In the voting, the Adams-Otis forces triumphed by a large margin, sending most of their opponents down to swift defeat. Over the course of the next decade, the patriot side met with little trouble at the polls, as few persons loyal to the Crown bothered to vote on election day.[81]

New Hampshire, despite external problems, had internal harmony during the first half-century of the colony's existence so that there is little evidence of contested elections in the years prior to 1730.[82] But a volatile dispute between Governor Jonathan Belcher (1730-1741) and Lieutenant-Governor David Dunbar in the early 1730's soon led to the emergence of factional politics and stormy elections, which lasted for almost two decades. Dunbar, an ambitious royal official who hoped to take the governorship away from Belcher, claimed that the chief executive was negligent in his duties, allowing his favorites to encroach upon valuable lands and timber rights.[83] Belcher denied this charge and consolidated his forces in order to meet the challenge. Before the Assembly election of 1732, the Governor wrote to one of his key supporters: "I believe the struggle will be great, our friends therefore must exert and bestir themselves the more diligently."[84] Bestir themselves they did, for Belcher and his followers stayed in power for the remainder of the decade.

Eventually, in 1741, Governor Belcher was removed from office by adversaries in London and replaced by Benning Wentworth (1741-1767). This action was resented by many of the previous administration's sympathizers, who carried on a relentless attack upon the new Governor for several years. On the whole, Wentworth proved even more adept than Belcher in controlling elections. Perhaps his greatest victory came in 1744 at the outset of King George's War, when he sought to gain House backing for the erection of new military installations. Despite the vigorous effort against him led by former Belcher lieutenant, Richard Waldron, Wentworth and his followers won a majority of seats for the first time and began to consolidate their position. In the elections of 1748 and 1750, Waldron and his associates made a final effort to reassert their control of the Assembly. Yet Wentworth managed to stave off the attack and emerge with an even greater margin of support than before. Subsequently the court faction was in complete command, and the country opposition began to disintegrate.[85]

During the years between 1750 and the passage of the Stamp Act in 1765, New Hampshire elections were rarely contested. Wentworth's friends tended to dominate the House without much difficulty. In the few towns where competition persisted, such as Londonderry, the results generally hinged on local issues. However, the crisis with Britain in the 1760's and 1770's rekindled widespread interest at the polls. The Wentworth family's adherence to the new British policies led to the rise of a new and determined opposition. John Wentworth, who replaced his uncle in the top post in 1767, was unable to influence the outcome of elections as his predecessor had done. Although many pro-administration men retained their seats for several years more, ultimately the Governor's allies were sent down to defeat. By the year 1775, the Assembly was dominated by the patriot faction led by Meshech Weare and Matthew Thornton.[86]

Rhode Island elections were generally peaceful during the early eighteenth century. Samuel Cranston was chosen to the governor's post twenty-nine consecutive years (1698-1727), usually without opposition. But after 1730, this pattern changed. Conflict over various economic issues plus the rivalry that developed among a number of great families in the province kept elections extremely competitive for many decades thereafter. The colony's small size and its sectional division between north and south further encouraged heated campaigns.[87]

Factionalism first developed in the early 1730's over the currency issue. Governor Joseph Jencks, who opposed the circulation of large amounts of paper money, was ousted from office in 1732 by a pro-inflation group led by William Wanton of Newport. Wanton's victory did not bring any semblance of peace as "Ill Designing Persons," he said, continued "to create Divisions and Make parties amongst the Inhabitants."[88] Political controversy remained in vogue during the governorship of John Wanton who served for the six years prior to 1740. After the latter's death, however, hostilities disappeared for a while. Richard Ward of Newport, the former secretary of the province, and William Greene of Warwick, forged an alliance against the Wantons, which held sway over Rhode Island politics down to the mid-1750's. Ward stayed in the governor's chair for just a few years (1740-1742), but Greene took over and won election to that spot in eleven of the next thirteen contests.[89]

The dominance of the Ward-Greene faction did not continue indefinitely. By 1755, it was being overtaken by a new and more powerful organization as the Wantons had aligned themselves with Stephen Hopkins and the wealthy Brown family of Providence. For the next decade and a half, this Providence-based group, headed by Hopkins, took part in a long series of hard-fought contests with the Ward faction, now led by Richard Ward's son Samuel and centered in Newport. The protracted political battle between the Ward and Hopkins camps did not involve any great differences in principle. Primarily each side was engaged in a power struggle aimed at securing control of the government in order to promote its own economic and political interests.[90]

During the Ward-Hopkins controversy, the most organized large-scale election campaigns held anywhere in early America took place. Every year the party chieftains made immense efforts to achieve a major victory. No area of the province was ignored, no expense was denied. Despite the fact that the Wards captured the governorship just three times in a fifteen-year period, the races were unusually close and the leadership always remained optimistic. "We could undoubtedly obtain the Election this Year," Samuel Ward told one of his backers in 1764, "if our Friends in the Country will but exert themselves. They may depend upon all proper Support and Assistance."[91] This heated factional competition persisted down to 1770 when the Hopkins group finally overwhelmed its opponents and created an organization that eventually became acceptable to the whole province.[92]

From this summary of election activities, one may draw several conclusions. Although provincial elections were often uncontested or lacking in fervor, many areas experienced vigorous struggles at the polls. Generally the most heated campaigns took place where internal division was greatest and fairly stable factions emerged. In a few provinces, the competition was relatively continuous throughout the era; in most, it tended to be more intermittent. Some colonies were sharply split in the early years; others divided later on. But everywhere, over the course of the period, elections became increasingly significant as a means of enabling the colonists to control their own destiny and achieve greater self-government.

2

The Electorate

★★★★★★★★★★★★★★

The electorate in provincial America comprised a considerably smaller part of the total population than it does today. Several important segments of the community were excluded from the franchise by a system heavily laden with rules and regulations. Requirements for voting were far more numerous than at present and were related not only to age, residence, and citizenship, but also to race, sex, religion, and the holding of property.[1]

Most of the suffrage laws framed in early America followed English precedents. In fact, certain specific enactments in some provinces, such as the property qualification known as the forty-shilling freehold, were reproduced in exactly the same form as they had existed in the mother country. Nevertheless, not all British rules were directly adopted in the New World, where conditions fostered several departures. Moreover, in the cases where the colonists did not adhere to the Old World example, they were not generally compelled to make any alterations. Except on the question of property holding, the Crown did not interfere too much with the voter standards established, allowing most of them to remain unchanged.[2]

The voting qualifications created in the thirteen colonies were usually based upon one of two fundamental principles: either the right of certain individuals to vote or the interest of the state. Suffrage laws were instituted either to secure the right that was proper for some people to have or to enhance the welfare of the state. Under the first idea, it could be asserted that one should possess the franchise merely for being a freeman or inhabitant of a particular locale. To a few theorists, such factors were of overriding significance in determining eligibility. These were thought to be more important than the possible effects that a voter might have on the well-being of the community.[3]

According to the second idea, eligibility was more dependent upon one's relation to the society. Some persons should be permitted to vote because they would benefit the public interest by contributing to the good of the community. At the same time, others should be excluded from the suffrage because they could not be counted upon to do so. The participation of indifferent or irresponsible elements, many people believed, would be dangerous to the commonweal. This latter notion of restricting the ballot to those having a positive stake was asserted explicitly in the comprehensive election law passed by South Carolina in 1716. The preamble declared: "It is necessary and reasonable, that none but such persons who have an interest in this Province should be capable to elect . . . members of the Commons House of Assembly."[4]

The importance of each of these views changed over the course of the era. The first concept was probably more influential in the earliest years of settlement; the few regulations that were enacted followed this manner of thinking. Within a short time, however, the good of the state became the dominant motif. When riot and disorder started to occur at the polls the authorities thought it necessary to set up laws that would keep away all undesirables. Only by taking such steps did it seem possible to safeguard the welfare of the community. Thus, they introduced qualifications that were designed to determine a voter's capacity to take an intelligent interest in public matters. Factors such as race, sex, age, religion, residence, citizenship, and property holding were increasingly scrutinized before any individual was admitted to the suffrage.[5]

Probably the most universal restriction established in the colonies was the one imposed against women. The exclusion of women, regardless of rank, was customarily based upon the alleged differences in the character of the two sexes. Men alone were said to have the ability to make the hard-headed decisions required in political affairs. Women were thought to be unsuited both by temperament and background to exercise the franchise competently. According to the outspoken John Adams, females did not possess the essential qualities to take part in such worldly activities. "Their delicacy," he said, "renders them unfit for practice and experience in the great businesses of life, and the hardy enterprises of war, as well as the arduous cares of state. Besides, their attention is so much engaged with the necessary nurture of their children, that nature has made them fittest for domestic cares."[6]

The tradition of male suffrage was so much taken for granted that just one colony, Virginia, enacted a statute specifically stating that women were to be barred. Several others, however, including South Carolina, Georgia, and Delaware, had laws stipulating that electors must be male, while the pronoun *he* appeared in the laws of some of the remaining colonies. Furthermore, the term *freeman*, which was used to designate voters in New England and certain other areas, can be interpreted to prohibit females.[7] Nevertheless, scattered evidence indicates that not all women were deprived of the ballot in the provincial period. Records from a few Massachusetts towns show that a number of widows who owned substantial property did exercise the franchise on occasion.[8] Moreover, the *New York Gazette* reported in June, 1737, that at the recent Queens County election "two old Widdows tendred, and were admitted to vote."[9] But outside of these examples, it seems doubtful that women were allowed to vote anywhere in early America. When a woman attempted to hand in a ticket in South Carolina in 1733, the entire contest was rendered null and void.[10]

Almost as common as the exclusion of females was the exclusion of males under the age of twenty-one. If each of the colonies did not always establish a minimum age in its election laws, it is probable that such a restriction was still customary.[11] The rationale for barring young men was similar to that employed in rejecting women. "Children," declared John Adams, echoing numerous eighteenth-century thinkers, "have not judgment or will of their own." "But why set the standard at age twenty-one," asked Adams. "What reason should there be for excluding a man of twenty years eleven months and twenty-seven days old, from a vote," he continued, "when you admit one who is twenty-one? The reason is, you must fix upon some period in life, when the understanding and will of men in general, is fit to be trusted by the public."[12] To Adams and others steeped in Old World traditions, this "understanding" was reached only after a man passed the age of twenty-one. Some colonials obviously thought that even this was too early an age. In the late seventeenth century, both Massachusetts and New Hampshire raised the level to twenty-four years for a brief time.[13]

Despite the laws against minors, some record of their having participated in certain elections in North Carolina, Pennsylvania, New Hampshire, and

Massachusetts can be found. Several petitions to the legislatures of these provinces list complaints of voting by unqualified "boys" or "youths."[14] In most cases these votes were subsequently voided, but not always. At a disputed election in Sheffield, Massachusetts, in 1751, both a nineteen year old and an eighteen year old successfully cast ballots. The vote of the latter young man was accepted by the presiding officials on the grounds that he possessed his deceased father's estate and was a "town born child," thus making him eligible as a freeholding inhabitant.[15] In Hampton-Falls, New Hampshire, during a local dispute in 1770, four lads were objected to as being below the proper age, yet their tickets were allowed to be counted.[16] However, such occurrences were quite uncommon. With the possible exception of militia elections in New England, where minors were sometimes eligible, no one under the age of twenty-one was ever legally permitted to vote for public officials, and few tried to circumvent this regulation.[17]

Religion was another important factor in determining a voter's eligibility, especially in the seventeenth century. Those persons who did not belong to the established church in a particular colony were often considered to be a threat to the existing government as well as to the dominant faith. Therefore, men who were not bona fide members of the Congregational church were denied the vote in early Puritan Massachusetts, while certain minority Protestant sects, such as Quakers, Baptists, and Presbyterians, were frequently barred in the Anglican colonies. But because of increasing toleration of Dissenters after the accession of William and Mary in 1689, many of these restrictions were lifted or amended, allowing previously excluded groups to exercise the franchise. The religious ban in Massachusetts was completely removed by its new charter in 1691. Dissenting elements in Virginia were voting without hindrance by the middle of the eighteenth century. Quakers, who had been deprived of the vote in some places because of their scruples against oath taking, were allowed to participate after affirming certain principles.[18]

While voting disabilities were being removed from various Protestant groups, restrictive legislation started to be enacted against Catholics and Jews. As a reaction to the French-Catholic threat following the Glorious Revolution and also to the so-called papist activities in Britain in behalf of the Jacobite pretender around 1715, several American provinces excluded Catholics or "popish recusants" from voting. This began with Virginia in 1699 and eventually included New York (1701), Maryland (1718), and Rhode Island (1719). Some decades later, South Carolina added its name to the list.[19] Maryland, which had the largest number of Catholics, took their vote away, lest they make a "party," which "would tend to the Discouragement and Disturbance of his Lordship's Protestant Government."[20] Other colonies claimed similar fears even though they each contained relatively few Catholics. The enactment of these restrictions is an indication of the xenophobia and religious prejudice that sometimes surfaced in early America and took a strong hold of the populace.

In response to the alleged danger from Catholicism and in the interest of defending Protestantism, a number of colonies also disfranchised Jews. According to the leading authority on early American Jewry, at least seven colonies eventually denied the suffrage to that group.[21] It is not clear, however, whether the laws against Jews were as strongly enforced as those against Catholics. Although legally deprived of the vote, several Jewish names appeared on the poll books for New York City in the elections of 1768 and 1769, and it is likely that this pattern occurred in many other places as well.[22] But the lack of enforcement did not extend to Rhode Island. Despite its tradition of religious liberty, Jews were definitely excluded from the ballot in this colony. After 1762, they could not even become naturalized freemen. The reasons for this are uncertain, yet probably the factional struggles of the 1760's prevented the acceptance of Jews as each side feared that this new group would use the vote against them.[23]

Just as voting restrictions against religious minorities were not all encompassing, so too were those instituted on the basis of race. Suffrage laws excluding Negroes and Indians were far from universal. In the southern colonies, where the majority of the black, red, and mulatto population resided, disfranchisement came rather late, while farther north no statute ever eliminated nonwhites from the ballot.[24] That Indians could vote in parts of New England is evident from an inquiry regarding the disputed election in Stockbridge, Massachusetts, in 1763. The investigating committee sent out by the General Court found that all thirty-seven Indian males were qualified electors and that twenty-nine of them had actually voted.[25] Local custom probably kept most free blacks and mulattos from participating in the northern colonies, but it is possible that persons from these groups exercised the suffrage on some occasions (although there is no record that they ever did so).

If there is no evidence showing that free blacks cast ballots in the North, the same is not true for the South. Petitions from Berkeley County, South Carolina, in 1703 and 1704 state that "free Negroes were received and taken as good Electors as the best Freeholders in the Province."[26] Documents from North Carolina and Virginia in the same period indicate that Negroes were accepted in those colonies too. Not until 1716 did the South Carolina legislature limit voting exclusively to whites. North Carolina had forbidden Negroes, mulattos, and Indians from taking part a year earlier, but this law was repealed in 1734 and never reenacted. Thus, in theory, at least, these minorities had the right to vote during the last forty years before independence.[27] In Virginia, Negroes were permitted to come to the polls until 1723, when, in response to fears of a black insurrection, a law was passed excluding them from the franchise. When this statute was reviewed in England, Attorney-General Richard West declared, "I cannot see why one Freeman should be used worse than another, meerly upon account of his complexion."[28] This was not the first time that British officials questioned the barring of voters for racial reasons. In defense of his actions, Governor William Gooch told the Board of Trade that it was necessary to disfranchise the blacks in order to preserve a "decent Distinction between them and their Betters" until they were educated and reformed. As a result, the law removing Negroes from the suffrage was allowed to remain on the books.[29] The colony of Georgia, which was first founded in the 1730's, placed no restrictive measures against voting by nonwhites until 1761 when the legislature provided that only a free white man "and no other . . . shall be deemed a person qualified for Electing a Representative."[30]

White servants were also kept from voting in most colonies either by custom or statute. Legislation in Virginia in 1742 and 1752 on laborers in various trades stated that no servant could be enfranchised just on the basis of his being an inhabitant or resident of a town. Such a man had to be duly apprenticed within the town for five years and certified as a householder in order to be acceptable. Servants in South Carolina cast ballots in the early years of the eighteenth century but were specifically excluded under the election act of 1717. The middle colonies of New York and Pennsylvania also passed laws denying the suffrage to those in any condition of servitude. An apprenticed tradesman in New York, however, could obtain the franchise after completing his years of apprenticeship. Connecticut was the sole colony where "hired servants" could be admitted as "inhabitants" of a town and allowed to vote in local affairs, provided that they met all other requirements, which included being a person of "honest conversation."[31]

Citizenship was a significant qualification in some colonies. New Hamp-

shire, Pennsylvania, North Carolina, and Delaware explicitly excluded
aliens or "foreigners" from the polls. Their election laws stipulated that
a voter had to be a natural-born subject of Great Britain or naturalized
in England or in his particular colony. Elsewhere in America, the barring
of non-British subjects was merely customary.[32] Actually, few problems
ever developed in regard to alien voting except in South Carolina and
Pennsylvania where there were a considerable number of continental European emigrants. In the former province, the participation of newly arrived
French Huguenots, who had come to Carolina following the revocation
of the Edict of Nantes (1685), was strongly objected to by the English
inhabitants. Many of the latter asked, "Shall the Frenchmen, who cannot
speak our language, make our laws?" The Huguenots insisted that they
had already been naturalized as a result of their temporary residence in
England, but this argument was unacceptable. Political activity by the recent French settlers stirred up considerable resentment even beyond the
turn of the century. Not before the passage of the permanent naturalization act of 1704 and the gradual assimilation of the newcomers did the
question ultimately die down.[33]

Some decades later, during the 1740's and 1750's, the heavy involvement of recent German immigrants in support of the Quakers in Pennsylvania stirred up similar opposition. Spokesmen for the proprietary interests sharply condemned the manner in which the Germans were being
quickly naturalized just prior to election day. At times the certification
process had not even officially taken place when, according to William
Allen, "unnaturalized Moravians and other Germans" were permitted to
vote on the same basis as bona fide citizens.[34] The most outspoken critic
of this practice, Reverend William Smith, insisted that the Germans were
unqualified and demanded that their suffrage rights be suspended for
twenty years "till they have a sufficient Knowledge of our Language and
Constitution." "What can be more absurd and impolitic," he asked, "than
to see a Body of ignorant, proud, stubborn Clowns (who are unacquainted
with our Language, our Manners, our Laws, and our Interests) indulged
with the Privilege of Returning almost every Member of Assembly?"[35]
However, despite the efforts of the Proprietary party to outlaw Germans
of questionable status, the latter continued to make their presence felt
at the ballot box.

Perhaps more important than the citizenship qualification was residence.
Several provinces eventually established residence requirements for voting,

although such laws were unknown in England. Many persons believed that only a full-fledged resident of a community should partake in its political affairs because he would be more concerned with its welfare than a non-resident would be. Strangers and new arrivals were less attached and less acquainted with a colony's best interests than someone who had lived there a considerable time. Residency laws also helped prevent the shuttling of voters to elections in other towns or counties. The period of residence necessary to achieve eligibility varied from place to place. In Georgia and North Carolina, a six-month minimum was established, in South Carolina, one year, while in Pennsylvania and Delaware it was two years.[36]

Virginia, New Hampshire, and New York had no definite residence qualifications, and in New York this lack resulted in several major disputes. Factional leaders in closely contested races would pursue the questionable tactic of bringing in persons from beyond the town or county limits to cast ballots for their favorites.[37] One of the most notorious incidents of this kind occurred in 1737 in New York City, when numerous out-of-towners were brought into the north ward to support Adolph Philipse in his bid for an Assembly seat against Cornelius Van Horne. Despite Van Horne's vehement objections, the votes were upheld by the lower house as being in accord with English practice.[38] During the famous elections between the Livingston and DeLancey factions in 1768 and 1769, twenty-seven outsiders went to the polls the first year and six the second, as both groups accused each other of illegally employing nonresidents. Here again the votes were sustained. Subsequently, after considerable debate, the New York legislature passed a law eliminating nonresidents from the suffrage, but the measure was disallowed by the Crown the following year.[39]

In provinces where formal residence was not stipulated, such as New York and Virginia, a man otherwise qualified had only to meet the property requirement in the county he wished to participate in. It was agreed that to deny a taxpaying property holder franchise rights would result in taxation without representation. Under such an arrangement, wealthy landowners who possessed estates in several counties were permitted to vote in each of them. This was facilitated by the fact that in most cases the election in each county took place on a separate day. Nevertheless, even with the existence of plural voting, it is doubtful whether more than a handful of persons were eligible in more than one county and whether any of these men regularly exercised all their privileges.[40]

Among adult white males, the most significant factor separating voters from nonvoters was the property qualification. Property qualifications had been common in England for hundreds of years and were upheld by most of the advanced thinkers of the seventeenth century such as James Harrington, Algernon Sidney, and John Locke. Locke believed that government should be primarily concerned with the protection of property and implied that only property owners had enough of a "stake in society" to be allowed to participate in its governance.[41] Later writers emphasized that the possession of a considerable estate was necessary for a man to be free and independent. This would enable him to withstand the pressures that might be placed upon him for his vote. Election statutes, wrote the French philosopher Montesquieu in *The Spirit of the Laws* (1748), should exclude those who "are in so mean a situation as to be deemed to have no will of their own."[42] Sir William Blackstone, the famous English jurist, agreed with Montesquieu and noted that the landless could easily be coerced by those stationed above them to vote as they were told.[43] These views were fully endorsed by most American leaders. James Wilson of Pennsylvania echoed the same thoughts when he stated that those "whose poverty is such, that they cannot live independent . . . must therefore be subject to the undue influence of their superiors." It was improper, he wrote, "that they should vote in the representation of a free state."[44] John Adams added the notion that men in every society "who are wholly destitute of property, are also too little acquainted with public affairs to form a right judgment." "If you give to every man who has no property, a vote," he asked,

> will you not make a fine encouraging provision for corruption, by your fundamental law? Such is the frailty of the human heart, that very few men who have no property have any judgment of their own. They talk and vote as they are directed by some man of property, who has attached their minds to his interest.[45]

Not everyone in the thirteen colonies accepted this line of reasoning. A writer in the *Pennsylvania Gazette* in the late 1730's, possibly young Benjamin Franklin, satirically questioned the notion that a person possessing material wealth was any better qualified to vote than a person lacking it:

A PECUNIARY Gratification is offered to any of the learned
or unlearned, who shall Mathematically prove, that a Man's
having a Property in a Tract of Land, more or less, is thereby
entitled to any Advantage, *in point of understanding* over
another Fellow, who has no other Estate, than "THE AIR . . .
to breathe in, THE EARTH . . . *to walk upon,* and ALL THE
RIVERS OF THE WORLD . . . *to drink of.* "[46]

Yet if these sentiments had much public support, there was little open
expression of it before the Revolutionary era. Not until the years just
before independence did movements emerge anywhere to extend the vote
to men without property.[47] Prior to that time, few people protested against
the disfranchisement of those without any wealth. The vast majority of
the populace apparently acquiesced in the view that a "stake in society,"
preferably land, was necessary for admission into the voting class.

Under the influence of the "stake in society" theory, property qualifications of one kind or another were gradually adopted throughout colonial America. Provinces that had allowed all freemen to vote in the earliest years of settlement, such as Virginia and Maryland, soon began restricting the electorate to property owners. The Virginia statute of 1670 asserted that

. . . whereas the laws of England grant a voyce in such election
only to such as by their estates real or personal have interest
enough to tye them to the endeavour of the publique good;
It is hereby enacted, that none but freeholders and house-
keepers who only are answerable to the publique for the levies
shall hereafter have a voice in the election of any burgesses in
this county.[48]

All the other colonies ultimately passed similar legislation.

While property requirements became universal in the eighteenth century, their forms varied from place to place. In Rhode Island before 1724,
the suffrage law was indefinite, stating merely that electors be persons of
"competent estates."[49] At least half of the colonies, however, eventually
insisted that voters must be freeholders. This movement was encouraged
by the Crown, which instructed the royal governors to exclude nonland-
owners from the ballot. "You shall take care," said the order, "that the

members of the assembly be elected only by freeholders, as being most agreeable to the customs of this kingdom."[50] Yet the landowning provision was not always easy to implement. Some provinces, such as the Carolinas, which had a long tradition of freemen or taxpayer eligibility, vigorously opposed the change. When Governor George Burrington of North Carolina attempted to limit the franchise to freeholders in the early 1730's, he found that it "occasioned a great deal of heat among the people," though subsequently they were persuaded to acquiesce.[51] South Carolina fared better and was able to resist this type of pressure and retain the option of a taxpaying qualification through virtually the entire period.[52]

Although the British government sought to obtain conformity to the freehold regulation, it did not stipulate any exact provisions, so they tended to differ in specific terms from one colony to the next. For a long time, Virginia had no minimum size or value established. Nevertheless, most other provinces soon instituted standards, either compelling a definite income from land or by setting a particular size or value to the freehold. Massachusetts and Connecticut required a forty-shilling freehold, that is, land producing forty shillings in rent annually. In practical terms, this meant real estate with a yearly rent equivalent to twenty-seven days wages for a common laborer or one month's pay for a private in the militia. According to one authority on Massachusetts, almost any farm with a house, barn, and five acres of land qualified its owner for the franchise. Rhode Island allowed men to meet the property requirement in the same manner or through the possession of a freehold rated at forty pounds. New York had the same forty-pound standard but also permitted those with a lifetime lease on a forty-shilling freehold to vote. New Hampshire, on the other hand, had only one criterion: an estate worth fifty pounds.[53]

For the colonies south of New York, freehold qualifications were expressed in terms of acres rather than in value of land or its income. Land tended to be cheaper in cost toward the south, so that it would have taken an inordinately large amount of land to satisfy a forty- or fifty-pound requirement. In Pennsylvania, Delaware, Maryland, Georgia, and the Carolinas, possession of fifty acres was established as a minimum for voting. Virginia, which was slow to set down any specific amounts, eventually decided on a hundred acres of unsettled land or twenty-five acres of improved land with a house upon it.[54] What constituted a house was originally left open to question and often depended on the whims of the election officials. In 1762, William Skinner of Elizabeth City County moved a structure measuring ten feet by eight feet onto his land and was allowed to participate. Another man, Thomas Payne, placed a "House" standing less than five feet square on his property, but it was considered unacceptable. Eventually, a law was passed stating that the dwelling must be at least twelve feet square to qualify.[55]

Six of the colonies had alternatives to the real-estate qualification in the form of personal property or the payment of taxes. In addition to forty-shilling freeholders, Connecticut and Massachusetts permitted the owners of forty pounds "personal estate" to vote. Items accepted as personal estate varied from one to the other. Before 1771, Connecticut allowed only horses, oxen, and cows to be included under this heading, whereas Massachusetts followed a more liberal interpretation of the term. However, it is doubtful that this substitute was much utilized in either place since most people possessing a good deal of personal wealth usually held sizable amounts of land as well. In the town of Waterbury, Connecticut, only one of the seventy eligible voters in 1730 met the personalty standard but not the one for real estate.[56] Maryland also had a forty-pound personal property alternative, and here it probably did make a difference since many landless individuals were able to qualify only through this method. Pennsylvania established a fifty-pound personal estate as a substitute, and this was of considerable significance, too, especially in the city of Philadelphia, in which men found it almost impossible to acquire fifty acres of land.[57]

Besides the general alternatives to the real-estate qualification, some colonies established special requirements for those living in the major towns and cities where it was more difficult to meet the minimum property standard. These additional regulations were often very similar to the English borough franchise. Williamsburg and Norfolk in Virginia, Burlington and Perth Amboy in New Jersey, and Annapolis in Maryland all permitted householders to vote. A number of towns in North Carolina even accepted tenancy of a house as adequate enough for a man to qualify. Wilmington, for example, gave the borough franchise to the tenant of a brick, stone, or frame house twenty feet long by sixteen feet wide, who inhabited the house on the day of election and had done so for the previous three months.[58]

Residents of New York and Albany could secure the franchise by becoming freemen of the corporation, another practice common to English boroughs. This alternative was available not only to skilled craftsmen but to artisans and tradesmen of all types. Wishing to improve their town's economic life by encouraging workingmen to remain, the leaders in both communities allowed laborers to obtain their "freedom" for just a few shillings. At times the Common Council in New York City even permitted those too poor to purchase their freedom to be admitted without charge. Freemanship bestowed full political rights, enabling a man to vote in both municipal and provincial elections. Usually a great number applied for this status immediately prior to an important contest.[59]

In many areas, especially in New England, the suffrage requirements for colony-wide elections were not the same as for local ones. Massachusetts, for example, established a twenty-pound rateable estate in provincial currency as the standard for selecting town officials, while keeping the forty-shilling freehold or forty-pound property qualification for choosing representatives to the Assembly. This variant led some early writers such as James Truslow Adams to conclude that there was a major difference between the size of the two groups of electors. Adams believed that while practically all male inhabitants possessed the town franchise, very few persons were able to qualify for the more crucial kind of election.[60] Actually, in considering all the possible meanings of the terms in the law and the differences in styles of currency, the disparity among the varying amounts is not too great. More important, it would appear from the records that with the exception of Watertown and Weston, the legal distinction between the voting franchises was not rigidly enforced. As a rule, the writs of election for most towns in Massachusetts, Connecticut, and New Hampshire merely called for "freeholders" or "freeholders and other inhabitants qualified to vote," with no mention of the type of contest or the value of property needed. Since provincial elections were often just one small part of the business at a town meeting, it probably seemed fruitless to make any distinctions.[61]

The number of provincials who were able to fulfill all the voting requirements, especially the property regulations, is difficult to determine. The relative scarcity of tax lists and census reports in certain colonies makes any definitive statement impossible. Moreover, many of the contemporary estimates of the extent of the suffrage are sharply contradictory. Thomas Jefferson, for example, thought that the total number of electors in Virginia was quite small. "Non-freeholders," he believed, "compose the majority of our free and adult male citizens."[62] On the other hand, Robert Dinwiddie, Governor of the province in the 1750's, declared that "most of the people are freeholders, in course have votes for choosing assembly men."[63] In New England, the Reverend Ezra Stiles stated that only one-ninth of the people in Connecticut possessed the franchise, which would have meant a maximum of just 55 percent of the adult males.[64] Meanwhile, several other observers, including Benjamin Franklin, mentioned that most New England men, even the poorer ones, were generally entitled to full political rights.[65]

These differences of opinion among contemporaries have been reflected in the works of later historians of the suffrage. J. Franklin Jameson and Albert E. McKinley, writing at the turn of the twentieth century and presenting only limited amounts of statistical material, claimed that the vote was generally widespread among adult men.[66] A few years later, Carl Becker strongly challenged this view. Although offering no more data than Jameson or McKinley, Becker insisted that fewer than 50 percent of the adult males were eligible voters in the province of New York, and he soon extended his estimation to include all the settlements. "In most colonies," he wrote, "a majority, and in all cases a considerable minority, of the adult male citizens were disfranchised."[67] Despite the lack of much supporting evidence, the idea of a severly limited electorate in early America prevailed among many authorities for almost a half-century. As late as 1953, the late Clinton Rossiter, in his prize-winning study, *Seedtime of the Republic,* declared that no more than one man in four could participate in provincial elections.[68]

In recent years more rigorous methods of investigation have been applied to the colonial suffrage question and have yielded some vastly different results. Led by Robert E. Brown and B. Katherine Brown, a number of historians have found the franchise to have been extremely widespread despite the qualifications imposed upon prospective electors. The Browns claimed that at least 90 percent of the adult males were eligible to vote in Massachusetts and that more than 85 percent could do so in Virginia. Further scholarship by Richard McCormick, Milton Klein, and David Lovejoy produced similar findings for New Jersey, New York, and Rhode Island, respectively.[69] Yet subsequent inquiries by Chilton Williamson and others seem to indicate that some of the conclusions of the broad suffrage disciples must be revised downward. In several cases it appears that the actual figures are closer to Becker's implied estimate of 50 to 60 percent than to the Browns' 85 to 90 percent.[70]

Dr. Brown's own Massachusetts figures reveal that in some coastal communities the percentage of adult males possessing the franchise was not impressively high. He demonstrates that Gloucester had 59.6 percent,

Ipswich 55.1 percent, and Marblehead only 53.5 percent.[71] Newburyport had about 60 percent, according to a study by Benjamin Labaree,
while Boston had little more, judging by the increasing number of property-
less persons in 1771 noted in an analysis by James Henretta. Moreover,
data from several country towns indicate that the proportion of qualified voters in these areas was far more varied than Brown would have
us believe. In fact, some of the percentages were even lower than those
of the seaports and a far cry from the 90 percent he claims for the interior agricultural regions. For the year 1760, the village of Raynham,
containing 136 adult males, had 74 provincial voters (54 percent), whereas Southborough, with 138 men, had but 60 eligibles (43 percent). Furthermore, Kenneth Lockridge, after comparing landholding patterns in
the early period of the Bay Colony's history with those of the later part,
has concluded that the degree of ownership was declining as time went
on, which would mean that suffrage was on the downgrade too.[72]

In New Hampshire, only 209 freeholders could be counted among a
population of more than 4,000 in the year 1679, a mere 25 percent of the
adult males. The number gradually increased over the course of the next
century to a point where a majority of the men could vote. Yet just how
large this majority became is not quite clear. There were 52 freeholders
among the 67 polls in the town of Plymouth in 1774 and 103 freeholders
among the 140 polls in Hamstead, though whether all held sufficient
acreage is unknown. The more exact figures on eligibility imply a much
broader range, especially on the lower side. Although records indicate
that as many as 90 percent could qualify in Hollis, only 51 percent were
listed as voters in Dunstable and 50 percent in Dublin.[73]

Connecticut also displayed a good deal of disparity. Probably no more
than half of the adult males could qualify in the larger seaports such as
New Haven and New London. Yet it seems evident that in most country
towns, a substantial majority of men could satisfy the minimum property requirement. A tax list from Waterbury in 1730 indicates that seventy
out of one hundred (70 percent) possessed at least a forty-shilling freehold; a valuation for Salisbury has thirty-three of forty-four (75 percent)
with a forty-pound rateable estate, while one for Groton in 1734 shows
177 out of 240 (73.8 percent) could reach that standard. The question of
voter eligibility in Connecticut is complicated by the fact that to become
a participant one first had to take a freeman's oath, and many of those
otherwise qualified never bothered to do so. As the late Charles S. Grant
demonstrated in the frontier town of Kent, only about 50 percent of the

adult males, just two-thirds of those eligible, chose officially to become freemen. Similarly, in the town of Woodstock, which became part of the colony in 1749, only eighty-three persons, not more than a third of the male inhabitants, took the freeman's oath at that time to become legal voters.[74]

Oath taking presents the same problem when trying to determine the size of the voting class in Rhode Island. Lovejoy's examination of tax assessment lists in the year 1757 for the towns of Providence, Cumberland, Gloucester, Smithfield, and Little Compton indicates that 75 to 84 percent (an overall average of 79 percent) of the adult men could qualify for the freemanship. At the same time the official membership rolls for these five towns disclose that only 62.5 percent were bona fide freemen (see table 1).[75] Actually, certain factors suggest that Lovejoy's eligibility figures may not be fully representative and are very likely to be inflated. First, he fails to account for Newport, the largest city, where probably not more than half of the adult males were enfranchised. Second, he bases his entire findings on the presumption that adult males were substantially the same group as "rateable polls," when equating these two is highly questionable. A local census for Providence taken in 1767 contains 530 men over twenty-one but just 453 rateable polls.[76] If this proportion were typical of the entire colony, 67.5 percent rather than 79 percent would be a more accurate estimate of those persons able to become freemen.

New York's percentage of enfranchised was probably somewhat lower than any in New England (at most, 60 percent) due to the prevalence of

TABLE 1

Certified Freemen in Five Rhode Island Towns, 1755

Town	Adult Males	Freemen	Percentage
Providence[a]	747	565	75.6
Cumberland	230	135	58.7
Gloucester	332	183	55.1
Smithfield	448	221	49.3
Little Compton	244	147	60.2
Average			62.5

[a] Includes North Providence which was incorporated as a separate town in 1765.

tenant farming in several areas. In contrast to most other colonies where rural voters outnumbered urban ones, here the latter were more numerous. This was most evident in New York City where it was relatively easy to obtain the freemanship. By 1771, according to a modern study, 68.6 percent of the adult white males were eligible to take part in elections in the capital. The degree of eligibility was much smaller in the outlying regions where large landholdings and tenantry flourished. Suffolk County had only 328 freeholders among 1,345 adult males (24.4 percent) in 1737, while Dutchess County had just 235 among 982 adult males (23.9 percent) in 1740.[77] For populous Westchester, a recently discovered document has shown that only 801 males (22 percent) could satisfy the sixty-pound requirement for jury duty in 1763, which indicates that not too many more could meet the forty-pound regulation for voting. It has been argued that numerous tenant voters with life leases swelled the county's electorate to a majority. Yet judging by the number of men who cast ballots in the crucial contests during the 1760's, it appears that not as many persons qualified in this fashion as has been believed. Only 14 to 18 percent of the adult males participated in the provincial elections of 1761 and 1768, less than half the number tallied in many of the other counties. Assuming that the size of the turnout was roughly the same throughout the province, no more than 50 percent were eligible in Westchester.[78]

Although the fifty-acre property requirement made it somewhat easier to qualify in Pennsylvania than in New York, no more than a bare majority of the male inhabitants in the Quaker colony were legally eligible to vote. Tax records from the pre-Revolutionary years show only 56 percent of the adult males were freeholders in Chester County, 60 percent in Lancaster County, and just 48 percent in Philadelphia County. A somewhat higher percentage probably owned an adequate amount of land in the more newly settled frontier regions. About 65 percent had enough acreage in Bedford County, while up to 73 percent were acceptable freeholders in Northampton County. However, these areas were much smaller in population than the older, established centers. Theoretically, the most difficult place in the province to comply with the standards was the city of Philadelphia where few owned much land and not too many more had fifty pounds of personal property. But, according to several authorities, a liberal interpretation of what constituted taxable property may have allowed 50 to 75 percent of the taxpayers to vote in the crucial years before independence.[79]

Probably more men could vote in New Jersey than in either Pennsylvania or New York. The studies made by Richard McCormick and others conclude that practically everyone who possessed a freehold was able to qualify, and a considerable majority of males in the colony owned a freehold. For example, in part of Somerset County, records from 1735 show that among the 125 persons taxed, 80 (64 percent) held more than a hundred acres. Documents from the 1750's demonstrate that 70 percent of the adult males could fulfill the property requirement in Essex County, though only about 50 percent could do so in Middlesex County. A dozen assessment lists for the 1770's examined by Chilton Williamson indicate that 50 to 75 percent could satisfy the minimum needed, a span that includes all of the earlier samples.[80]

For Maryland, a recent study of landholding in four large counties has disclosed figures that are among the lowest in provincial America. David Skaggs, after studying the land question in Baltimore, Prince George's, Queen Anne's, and Talbot counties, claimed that fewer than half of the free adult males in the colony owned land in the middle of the eighteenth century. Moreover, landownership, he asserted, was growing more and more restrictive toward the end of the provincial period. In 1756, about 44 percent of the freemen held land in these four counties, but fifteen years later in 1771, just 37 percent were landowners. Although Queen Anne's and Baltimore counties were still above 40 percent, Prince George's County fell to 31.6 percent and Talbot County to 27.3 percent. Even with a considerable number of men added to this total by qualifying through a "visable estate" of forty pounds sterling, Skaggs concluded that anywhere between one-third and two-fifths of the white freemen were without the legal right to vote in pre-Revolutionary Maryland.[81]

Studies of Virginia by Lucille Griffith and also by Robert and B. Katherine Brown have shown the number of qualified voters to be much higher than in Maryland, perhaps because of the more lenient landholding regulations. Griffith, working primarily from the list of freeholders compiled in 1763 by the royal official James Blair, has estimated that 55 to 60 percent of the white tithables age sixteen or over (that is, 80 percent of the adult males) were potential voters. After intensive study of several counties, the Browns have claimed an even higher percentage. They argue that not only freeholders but many tenants, apprentices, and artisans "either had or soon acquired" enough property to meet the voting requirements. Using lists of tithables and payers of quitrents, as well as polling records, they declared that more than 85 percent of the white males in Virginia were eligible to participate in provincial elections. Yet the Browns' conclusions are at great variance with those of Jackson T. Main, who authoritatively demonstrates that no more than half the males in post-Revolutionary Virginia were landowners.[82]

The percentage of eligible voters in North Carolina is difficult to calculate given the absence of abundant tax lists for the provincial period. However, Main's landholding studies for this colony have shown that approximately 70 percent of the adult white males in the eastern commercial counties and 75 percent of the men in the backcountry were landowners. At least half of those in the latter section held a minimum of a hundred acres, twice the amount needed to be an elector. It is interesting to note that the Regulator movement in the late 1760's, which focused upon the frontier farmers' grievances, did not include suffrage reform as a goal. This tends to indicate that a majority of men in the region could go to the polls if they so desired. Yet there is little evidence that more than 60 to 70 percent of all North Carolinians could vote, with the exception of those living in the few eastern towns and boroughs.[83]

In South Carolina and Georgia, the lack of census data plus the paucity of land records make it impossible to measure accurately the size of the electorate in most counties. Nevertheless, since only about one-seventh of the white males were without land and suffrage requirements were extraordinarily lenient, probably not too many individuals were excluded in the former province. Royal officials, including Governor James Glen and Indian agent Edmund Atkin, firmly attested to this in their description of the ease of qualification and their constant effort to raise the standards. In the city of Charleston, where many persons of limited property resided, at least two-thirds of the white men were voters.[84] Georgia's available lands and minimum requirements probably did not exclude too many white males either, for, according to Governor James Wright, "by far the great number of voters, are the most Inferior Sort of People."[85]

One may thus conclude that the suffrage right in provincial America among adult white males was fairly extensive, though by no means universal. If in some colonies like Virginia the degree of eligibility may have run as high as 80 percent, in others, such as New York, it was closer to 50 or 60 percent. Many regions, especially parts of Maryland and New England, saw the number of property holders, hence voters, declining toward the end of the period. Generally the largest percentages of electors could be found in those areas where new settlements were opening up and land was most easily available. The smallest occurred in older, established communities as wealth became concentrated in fewer and fewer hands. With the exception of New York City and Charleston and those towns with special borough requirements, the large urban centers containing numerous artisans and day laborers had by far the greatest amount of disfranchisement.

Many writers, both contemporary and modern, have argued that the legal requirements for voting were virtually meaningless, claiming that they were never enforced. Qualifications were rarely scrutinized, insisted Thomas Hutchinson of Boston. "Anything with the appearance of a man," he said, was allowed to vote.[86] Oaths taken by persons attesting to their having satisfied the minimum standards had little effect in Philadelphia, according to Thomas Paine. "The only end this answered was, that of tempting men to forswear themselves," he declared.

> Every man with a chest of tools, a few implements of hus-
> bandry, a few spare clothes, a bed, and a few household
> utensils, a few articles for sale in a window, or almost any-
> thing else he could call or even think his own, supposed him-
> self within the pale of an oath, and made no hesitation of
> taking it.[87]

To be sure, on some occasions the number of people permitted to poll depended less on the provisions of the election laws than on the discretion of the officials present. During a contest in Puritan Boston, when George Craddock, an Anglican, sought one of the vacant Assembly seats, "the town became alarmed at it," reported one British observer, "and cried that popery had come upon them like a scarlet whore." The moderator, Dr. Elisha Cooke, "passed some votes rejected others but accepted all those who voted against Mr. Craddock."[88] In an episode that occurred in Granville County, North Carolina, Reuben Searcy, one of the clerks recording the names of the voters, was said to have "shewed great Partiality therein and Acted in several Instances in a manner subversive of the rights and Freedom of Elections."[89]

Yet the fact that incidents occurred where oaths were inadequate and eligibility depended upon the whims of a few officials does not necessarily signify that suffrage restrictions were meaningless and that every male in provincial America could vote. If the standards were relaxed on some occasions, on others they were adhered to very strictly. In crucial contests involving important issues, property qualifications were rigidly enforced and voter eligibility carefully scrutinized. This can be seen by examining the abundant records of disputed elections for the colonies.[90] Since a heated contest was often a possibility, it would seem doubtful that the casual enforcement of election laws had much effect on the number of individuals at each turnout. The majority of small farmers and laborers who could not meet the minimum property level probably would not have risked traveling a long distance to the polls when there was a distinct chance that their vote might be rejected. In addition, the various attempts to change the requirements throughout the period indicate that the statutes must have been meaningful and for the most part obeyed. Thus, the evidence suggests that a considerable body of persons was excluded from this important function.

Besides the exclusion of those people unable to satisfy the legal requirements, many others were effectively barred even if they could legally qualify. Persons who lived in the backcountry often had no real access to the ballot box, and therefore could not exercise their suffrage right. As Richard Hooker has written about the frontiersmen in provincial South Carolina:

> Although they were technically within parishes and had the right to vote for members of Assembly, most of them were in fact without the franchise. When the parishes were first surveyed, the lines that divided them had been extended only a short distance in a northwestwardly direction beyond the then existing area of settlement. As the western areas became populated, only theoretical, unsurveyed lines divided the parishes so that . . . the settlers wandered "in the Mazes of Supposition." Even settlers who knew their parish could not vote without a long trip to the parish churches near the coast where the balloting took place.[91]

Similarly, in a large part of New England, many people were never able to use the franchise. New townships that did not have a minimum number of families settled could not hold provincial elections until they reached the enumerated requirement. Even older towns, which were too poor or too unconcerned to send a deputy to the General Court, went without representation. The system in Massachusetts whereby all seats in the house were allotted to towns and none given to counties seemed "anti-constitutional" to the Scottish-born physician, William Douglass, an admirer of the British style. In the mother country, he declared, everyone, even residents of tiny hamlets, had county representation. On the other hand, many persons in the Bay Colony of "good estates" were in no manner represented, "as if they were aliens, servants, and slaves."[92] Among the 168 incorporated towns in existence in the year 1763, at least sixty-four did not hold any Assembly elections. Thus, for the inhabitants of 38 percent of the communities, being qualified to vote had little meaning on the provincial level.

In New Hampshire, the situation was even more inequitable. Here many of the new towns desiring representation were denied the privilege by the Wentworth government, which allowed only areas sympathetic to its policies to obtain House seats. By the early 1770's, some 101 of the colony's 147 towns, including 44 percent of the total rateable polls, were unable to participate in Assembly elections. As colonial spokesmen had already questioned the lack of American representation in Parliament, some New Hampshire residents began to wonder about the related problem within their own borders. Political representation, one writer asserted, existed more in theory than in practice. Although this was "the Birthright of every Englishman; yet we annually see this very Right violated and infringed upon." "The town of Nottingham," he added, "has never had this Privilege; and it is now one of the primary Towns in the Province. The whole County of Grafton (which consists of several Thousand Inhabitants, and daily greatly encreasing) and in short near one Third of the Province is unrepresented."[93]

Certainly, possession of the suffrage in many parts of early America did not guarantee that one could vote in provincial elections. Those individuals without representation, along with those isolated from the polls, were as effectively disfranchised as, perhaps even more so than, persons who could not meet the minimum qualifications. Adding all these groups together, at least one-fifth to one-half of the adult males—a considerable percentage—were unable to exercise the right to vote. Of course, one should always remember that despite the limitation upon the size of the electorate in America, it was still much larger than in England or anywhere else in the world at the time. According to the historian J. H. Plumb, just 15 percent were qualified in early eighteenth-century Britain, a figure that firmly underlines the difference.[94] The fact that about 50 to 80 percent of the adult men could vote in the colonies is surely more important than the fact that fewer than half of them could not. Several of the obstacles facing the disfranchised, moreover, were beginning to come into question in the years prior to independence, which set the stage for a significant broadening of the number eligible to vote later on.

3

The
Candidates

★★★★★★★★★★★★★★

The candidates were, of course, the primary focus in an election. Even at that time they were the main object of the electorate's attention. In examining those who stood for public positions in the provincial period, one should study the qualifications for office, the difficulty in meeting them, the class background or occupation of the office seeker, the reasons these people sought office, and the length of time that they remained in their posts. In addition, it is necessary to find out whether the colonial candidates were similar or dissimilar in background and motive to the men in eighteenth-century England who stood for Parliament. Finally, it is important to ask whether the elected official in America could obtain fulfillment, as did most members of Parliament, or whether his situation was wanting in terms of wealth and power.[1]

Like qualifications for electors, qualifications for officeholders were influenced by English precedent, although the mother country exerted little direct pressure toward the adoption of specific requirements. From the beginning, the colonial legislatures had created their own standards for membership. Inevitably, some royal governors interfered in the process as they sought to take measures to prevent their adversaries from gaining office. Indeed, down to the end of the period they tried through various forms of subterfuge to circumvent existing customs and statutes. With their power to create constituencies, determine the frequency of elections, and personally involve themselves in disputed contests, they could make it difficult for the Assembly to enforce its own rules. But just as the House of Commons in England had acquired the privilege of establishing the qualifications of its members without intrusion from the Crown, so the lower houses in the New World obtained for the most part similar authority during the eighteenth century.[2]

The requirements for holding elective office in the colonies were several. Some of them were exactly the same as for potential voters; the candidate had to be a white male and at least twenty-one years old. There were other criteria, though, many of them more severe. Religious tests were more frequently and stringently applied to prospective office seekers than to prospective voters. It was one thing to allow a Catholic, a Jew, or a dissenting Protestant to vote; it was another to permit him to hold office because officeholders were considered far more crucial to the public welfare. In 1715, North Carolina, while enacting no religious restrictions against voters, specifically forbade Quakers from holding elective positions. A number of other provinces, either by law or custom, eventually followed suit, if they had not already done so before, excluding Catholics, Jews, and certain Protestant dissenters from office.[3]

Property qualifications for officeholding were also more difficult to meet in many cases than they were for voting. Since being employed in a public position involved much more responsibility than the single act of casting a ballot, it was believed that an elected official should have a greater financial stake in society than a voter. North Carolina enacted a 100-acre landholding minimum, twice as high as the suffrage standard. Assembly candidates in New Hampshire were called upon to own real estate worth £300, six times the fifty-pound electoral qualification. South Carolina established 500 pounds or 500 acres as its requirement, ten times the amount needed by a voter. New Jersey stipulated that its Assemblymen own 500 pounds in lands and personal property or 1,000 acres, also ten times the voter level.[4]

The colony of Georgia created the most unusual qualification in its early years. Its election law of 1751 stated that a deputy must have "one hundred mulberry trees planted and properly fenced, upon every fifty acres he possesses," and one female in his family had to be instructed in the art of reeling silk. These inclusions were primarily related to one of the original motives for Georgia's settlement as the founders had hoped to promote the cultivation of silk and other exotic items. Soon afterward, this regulation was dispensed with as impossible to meet, and the criterion was simplified to 500 acres of land. To be sure, even this more traditional landholding restriction was not always met with or always enforced.

Governor Henry Ellis noted in 1757 that there were not ten men in the province worth 500 pounds, yet nineteen men were members of the legislature. However, it seems certain that here and elsewhere the higher property standard at times acted as a barrier against the unqualified.[5]

Citizenship qualifications enacted in several colonies were usually more strictly enforced against prospective officeholders than against prospective voters. Few, if any, unnaturalized foreigners ever obtained an elective post in America, and persons of questionable status who managed to secure one often had trouble maintaining it. German-born Hendrick Fisher of Somerset, New Jersey, for example, was expelled from the Assembly in 1740 because his election was said to have followed too closely upon his naturalization. In New York, a major controversy arose in 1725 concerning the eligibility of Stephen DeLancey, who had been born in France and naturalized in England. At first, it was argued that DeLancey could not be seated in the House since he was an alien. Subsequently, however, he was ruled acceptable on the grounds that other prominent individuals in the province had gained their citizenship in a similar manner. Maryland was also deeply involved in the controversy over political rights of naturalized foreigners, long excluding those of foreign birth from holding office. The election of Jonathan Hager, a man of German origin, in Frederick County during 1771 finally caused the legislature to pass a naturalization law that permitted foreign-born citizens to be chosen to public posts. Yet this measure was not fully enforced until after independence.[6]

Although no statutes excluded people born in America of non-English extraction from holding office, it was customary in most places to choose mainly those of English ancestry. In Pennsylvania, prior to 1764, it was very unusual to have a German sitting in the Assembly, even though Germans made up at least a third of the colony's population. While few Germans sought election due to a desire to remain aloof from politics, those who did were deemed unacceptable because of their foreign background and alleged incapacity. By the 1770's, a handful of Germans was being elected but the total was comparatively small. Similar rejection was experienced by the province's Scotch-Irish. Considered "lawless and shiftless" by many, they were looked upon as an element to be barred from positions of power. Outside the frontier counties inhabited by the Scotch-Irish themselves, few of their kind were ever chosen before 1776. Only in South Carolina and New York were men of different stocks designated by the voters in any numbers, as descendants of French Huguenot and Scottis Presbyterian immigrant families frequently found their way into the leg-

islature. Yet even in New York certain nationalities were not completely accepted. The Dutch, for example, were elected primarily in areas
heavily populated by other Dutchmen and often condemned in predominantly English locales as persons of "Ignorance & mean spirit."[7]

Residence requirements for officeholders were generally nonexistent
in the earliest years of settlement, but a substantial number of provinces
eventually established them, beginning with Massachusetts in 1693. Increasingly, many colonists became convinced that an Assemblyman residing among his constituents could be held more accountable for his
actions than would be the case otherwise. Such a qualification, it was
thought, would reduce the possibility of executive influence and corruption. If a representative were closely involved with his constituents, he
would be less likely to have a strong attachment to the governor. Of
course, the residency principle contained a certain drawback since it deprived many of the most qualified individuals, who lived in the larger
towns, from serving in the legislature. Doctor William Douglass of Boston insisted:

> a gentleman of good natural interest and resident in the [city],
> a man of reading, observation, and daily conversant with affairs
> of policy and commerce, is certainly better qualified for a leg-
> islator than a retailer of rum and small beer called a tavern
> keeper, in a poor obscure country town remote from all busi-
> ness.[8]

Despite such arguments, residence restrictions were on the rise during the
eighteenth century. By the end of the provincial period, nine of the thirteen colonies had by law or custom excluded nonresidents from elective
positions. In this manner Americans rejected the British practice of virtual representation for a system of actual representation.

In the colonies where they were legally established, the term of residence for prospective officeholders was usually the same as for voters.
Thus, New Jersey set a one-year requirement, Pennsylvania and Delaware
a two-year requirement. North Carolina, however, made the time period
for Assembly candidates twice as long. The statute of 1743 clearly stipulated that while electors need be a resident for six months, "no Person
shall be deemed qualified or admitted to sit and vote in the General Assembly, unless he hath been One Full year an Inhabitant of this Province."[9]

Another requirement aimed at preventing outside control of the legislature, one that went beyond the regulations applied to potential voters, was that an Assemblyman not be a placeman appointed by a royal or proprietary governor. The latter officials had often increased executive power by conferring posts of profit among numerous representatives. In response to this practice, laws were passed, especially in the southern colonies, disqualifying officers in many categories from sitting in the lower house. As early as 1717, South Carolina outlawed revenue collectors. Virginia removed sheriffs beginning in 1730 and, six years later, eliminated tobacco inspectors. Subsequently, North Carolina excluded commodity inspectors, while Maryland enacted measures against the seating of various types of proprietary appointees. For a time, the latter province also barred tavern keepers, who were dependent upon the government for their license, and ministers, who had traditionally been kept out of Parliament. Among the middle colonies, New Jersey was the most stringent, rejecting anyone who by reason of "office, pension, or salary from the crown" would be excluded from the House of Commons. Interestingly enough, of all the statutes relating to the qualifications of members, only the ones involving exclusion of placemen were strongly objected to by members of the English Board of Trade. Obviously they thought it very important to retain as much influence in the legislatures as possible.[10]

Besides restrictions according to age, race, sex, religion, property holding, citizenship, residence, and executive connection, several provinces also established moral qualifications that went beyond the minimal requirements for voters. The Charter of Privileges issued in Pennsylvania called for the choice of persons "of most note for Virtue-Wisdome-and Ability." New York statutes specified that a representative be a "fit and discreet inhabitant," North Carolina's ordered that each burgess chosen be a "prudent & Substantiall" freeholder, and the laws of Virginia directed that those elected to the Assembly be "most able and fit men." New Hampshire typified New England attitudes in stipulating that a deputy be "not vicious in life but honest and of good conversation." How these characteristics were to be evaluated was always left unstated, but their inclusion in the election laws shows that such qualities were undoubtedly of considerable importance to the people of that era.[11]

Although many of these membership requirements were quite stringent and aimed at keeping a check against corrupt and tyrannical government, they indicate at the same time relative satisfaction with rule by an elite group. This is most readily seen in the enactment of high property-holding and moral qualifications. These measures clearly illustrate that the majority of lawmakers and probably the American colonists in general did not expect to be governed by the average citizen. Such a view is reinforced by the fact that very little pressure was ever exerted toward reducing these standards, certainly less pressure than in regard to the franchise. A few of the statutes noted here may have reflected a desire to contain the actions of the upper classes to some degree, but none showed a wish to replace its members with the common man.

The persistence of elite rule can perhaps be better understood after examining the prevailing attitudes about class and rank. Most persons in the provincial period believed in a hierarchical ordering of the population and had no concept of the modern democratic theory of equality of men. They took for granted a stratified society in which deference to one's betters was the accepted norm. The concept of deference was associated with the traditional Protestant doctrine of the calling. Since the Middle Ages society had been seen as being comprised of several estates, such as yeoman, artisan, and gentleman, in which individuals should be satisfied with the place they had been given. Down to the end of the colonial period it was agreed that to preserve order in the community each man should remain in the same station to which God had called him and should respect those in others. John Winthrop had told the original settlers in Massachusetts in the 1630's that "in all times some must be rich, some poore, some highe and eminent in power and dignitie; others meane and in subjeccion."[12] Over one hundred years later in an election sermon delivered in the Bay Colony, Charles Chauncy of Boston still insisted " 'tis no ways fitting that men cloathed with honor and power should be brought down to a level with vulgar people."[13] The following year (1748), Reverend Daniel Lewis reiterated this theme of distinguishing the governing magistrates from the common folk. The citizenry, he stated, should "behave deitifully toward [their] rulers, and treat them with reverence."[14]

The general acceptance of upper-class dominance is further demonstrated by the tone of practically all the election literature of the time. Not before the mid-1770's did more than a few writers question the concept of gentleman rule. During most of the provincial period scarcely any items in the press referred to the desirability of direct rule by the common people or mentioned other democratic ideas. Even critics of certain aspects

of the governmental system in America (the members of the various country factions) did not condemn the socioeconomic background of the individuals in power. A great many of the pamphlets and newspaper articles on the subject emphasized certain notable qualities that a candidate
should embody, and the primary ones could be found only among representatives from the elite.[15]

The two most important and frequently mentioned characteristics were
wealth and education. "ABLE in ESTATE, ABLE in KNOWLEDGE and
LEARNING" were the attributes to look for in an Assemblyman, said
one Marylander.[16] Only a person with such a background would have the
ability, training, and leisure to perform the duties of office in a proper
manner. An essayist in Massachusetts asked "whether the men of best
knowledge, reason, and virtue, as well as estates are not more likely to
serve us in the General Court . . . than men of different characters?"[17]
A man of wealth would be less apt to violate the sacred trust between a
public servant and his constituents. He would be less easily swayed or
influenced than a man of limited financial means. "A clear Estate and
Independency of Fortune is no unnecessary Qualification," another Bay
Colony inhabitant declared, "as it frees a Man from those Temptations
which attend a State of Poverty."[18] An individual who owned a large
amount of property in a community would be more solicitous about its
welfare than someone who had relatively little at stake, it was reasoned.
Surely, as one New Yorker pointed out, a gentleman with "considerable
Interest in the Property of this Colony" would for his own sake, "consult and promote the Means that shall preserve both."[19]

In addition to financial independence, many writers stressed the need
for legislators who could maintain political independence. Considered
especially noteworthy was a person who displayed patriotism and a deep
concern for the public good, someone free from executive influence. Militia officers, tax collectors, and other servants under the power of the
governor or Crown were to be rejected. "Choose no Man that has been
a reputed Pensioner," warned William Penn. "The Representatives of a
Province ought to consist of the most Wise, Sober and Valiant of the
People; not Men of mean Spirits, or sordid Passions, that would sell the
Interest of the People that choose them, to advance their own, or be at
the beck of some great Men, in hopes of a list to some good Employ."[20]
Elaborating upon Penn's remarks, a contributor to the *New York Weekly
Journal* stated: "We must therefore not chuse . . . the Covetous Man; he

that is fond of high Places, grasps at Power, or is greedy at Gain, is unfit to be trusted."[21]

An ideal candidate was not only to be independent of government influence but independent of all factional influence. Party or faction during the provincial period was looked upon with disdain by most commentators. Someone who belonged to a political faction, it was believed, would act solely for private ends and could never benefit the public interest. He would always follow the party line and never act on his own. A party member, wrote one New Hampshire resident, was a "Tool," who "blindlessly and thoughtlessly on all Occasions gives his Voice on one Side only, [and] is but a Machine to be moved at the Will of others."[22] A pamphleteer in Pennsylvania strongly advised the people against voting for anyone restrained by "party connexions," since such a man rarely displayed cool, dispassionate judgment. "Let Persons of Merit and Virtue," he stated, "who have always shewn themselves warm and active in their Country's Service, entirely free from all immoderate Party-Zeal, and remarkable for their Calmness in the midst of the most violent Factions and Divisions, be the Objects of your Choice."[23]

Besides being free from all forms of outside influence, the ideal candidate was supposed to be void of all traces of political ambition. A true patriot did not actively seek office. He was neither forward nor aggressive. He was someone who had the office thrust upon him by the citizenry. Such a man did not campaign vigorously or try to influence the electorate's views. That a person needed to publicize his worthiness to attain support showed a lack of confidence in his own abilities. As William Livingston of New York warned in the *Independent Reflector:* "To ask a man for his vote is a confession in the candidate that he is suspicious of his own merit. 'Tis a proof of his apprehensions that the sense of the public is against him."[24]

The ideal candidate was expected to be honest and courageous. "We wish when you come to a new Choice, that you will a little consider of these Things and chuse those that are Men of Probity, Courage and Ability," said one New Englander.[25] Another declared: "Let us choose Representatives . . . Men of establish'd Characters for Honesty and Integrity, Lovers of Liberty and their Country."[26] A New Yorker added that a "poor honest man" was "preferable to a rich knave."[27] Along with courage and honesty, diligence was another characteristic highly valued in an elected official. As William Penn advised: "Choose Men of Industry

and Improvement: For those that are Ingenious, and Laborious to prop-
agate the growth of the Country, will be very tender of Weakening or
Impoverishing it."[28]

Finally, many essayists emphasized the importance of electing a na-
tive son rather than a recent arrival since the former would probably have
a deeper sense of local commitment. The best candidate came from a
family that was well known to everyone and had long been prominent
in the public affairs of the community. As one journalist insisted:

> A Person born among us may, ordinarily, be suppos'd to have
> a stronger Affection for the best Interest of the Country than
> a Stranger. And I think a Man of family, whose Ancestors have
> distinguish'd themselves in the Service of their Country, sup-
> posing him equally qualified in other Respects, may very fair-
> ly be preferr'd to a new Man.[29]

Complementing this idea, a South Carolinian stated: "Choose not *those*
who live a great distance from you, and whose *abilities, probity* and *fortunes* are not well known to you; for afterwards it will be too late."[30]

Not all the candidates lived up to the standards expected. Not only
were some office seekers probably lacking in honesty and courage but in
wealth and learning as well. The refusal of leading gentlemen to serve or
the low level of affluence in a particular area sometimes provided opportunities for the "middling sort." Especially in the northern colonies there
were frequent reports of uncouth plowmen and tavern keepers vying for
seats in the legislature. During the early 1720's, Governor Shute of Massachusetts claimed that many of the colony's representatives were people
of "small fortune and mean education." New Jersey's Assembly was said
to be "chiefly composed of mechanicks and ignorant wretches."[31] Even
in Virginia numerous candidates for the Assembly lacked a genteel background. Within those areas where several men stood for a poll, not more
than a few of them were members of patrician families. As the Browns
have concluded, "The candidate might be the wealthiest man in the county, or he might be a man of relatively modest means."[32]

Robert Munford's early comedy about Virginia elections, *The Candidates* (1770), gives a glimpse of the various types of individuals who competed for a spot in the House of Burgesses. When one of the former delegates, Worthy, an impeccable gentleman, announced his desire not to

stand for reelection with his colleague, Wou'dbe, a number of questionable characters rushed to enter the contest. Among them were Sir John Toddy, "an honest blockhead" with little ability except in consuming large amounts of liquor, and Smallhopes and Strutabout, middling fellows of doubtful virtue, the latter of whom it was claimed, "he'll promise to move mountains. He'll make the rivers navigable, and bring the tide over the tops of the hills for a vote." Eventually, Worthy reconsidered his original decision to retire and joined the fray, and the undesirables were sent down to ignominious defeat.[33]

But by and large in every colony the candidates for public office were men of substance from the upper layer of property holders. Even where the less affluent were not excluded by law, it was primarily persons of wealth and leisure who wished a place in the legislature. The average farmer, who formed the bulk of the provincial population, was, as the Reverend Edward Holyoke of Massachusetts observed, not usually concerned with holding an important post. "There are men," said Holyoke in 1736, "who because of their occupations, cannot get Knowledge which fits them for public position," such as one who "holdeth the Plough, and that glorieth in the Goad, that driveth Oxen and is occupied in their Labours, and whose Talk is of Bullocks."[34] In most areas, a candidate coming from the lower or middle classes was a rather uncommon occurrence. When a tradesman in Philadelphia named Robert Kennedy announced his intention to stand for county sheriff in 1770, he noted that he was "the first Mechanic who, for a Series of Years has applied for this office."[35] Moreover, an artisan was not necessarily felt to be the most desirable candidate even by persons of his own background. When Amos Dodge, a carpenter by trade, ran for the Assembly in New York City in 1768, he finished last in a field of seven and received a smaller percentage of the mechanic vote than any of the other aspirants, who were all men of estates and professional standing. In the New World where economic opportunity was so widespread, perhaps an affluent man inspired more confidence in the political sphere than a less affluent one.[36]

If the candidates for office sometimes came from outside the gentleman class, the vast majority of successful ones were invariably drawn from the group of the rich and well-born. This was especially true in the latter part of the provincial era when few observations about "plowman legislators" can be found. More typical were descriptions of the kind made by William Eddis, the London-born placeman stationed in Annapolis, regarding the men chosen to the Maryland legislature in the early 1770's. "The delegates returned," he said, "are generally persons of the greatest consequence in their different counties."[37] Figures for the pre-Revolutionary period in this and several other colonies compiled by Jackson T. Main bear out this conclusion.

In New Hampshire, though the vast majority of the population were common farmers, no more than one-third of the representatives chosen were from this group. Merchants, lawyers, doctors, millers, and small manufacturers comprised the bulk of the remainder, one-third being wealthy (owning more than £5,000) and two-thirds well to do (owning more than £2,000). New York, a more affluent colony than New Hampshire, drew more than 85 percent of its Assembly members from the class of the wealthy or well-to-do. Merchants and lawyers made up half of the membership, while the rest consisted of large landowners. The lower house in New Jersey possessed similar characteristics. Merchants and lawyers were predominant; about 80 percent of that body were well to do or wealthy. Maryland and Virginia differed in that their legislatures were controlled by tobacco planters rather than merchants and professional people, who comprised less than 20 percent of the total. Naturally, these planters were men of means; four-fifths were at least well to do, perhaps half were wealthy. South Carolina's lower house followed the northern pattern more closely than that of Virginia and Maryland. Although the colony had large numbers of plantations, the great planters in most areas were not very willing to serve. Because there was no residence requirement, almost half of the members were merchants, lawyers, or doctors from the one urban center, Charleston. Approximately two-thirds of them were wealthy and the remainder well to do.

In these six legislatures, approximately 85 percent of the Assemblymen were wealthy or well to do despite the fact that the economically affluent represented no more than 10 percent of provincial society. Most of the persons elected were large landowners, though about one-third were lawyers, merchants, or members of other professions. Besides wealth and frequent professional status, many of these individuals came from prominent old families. More than one-third of the New York and Maryland assemblies and about half of the Virginia and South Carolina bodies were comprised of men from the colony's elite.[38] Even in New England, where the proportion of wealthy officeholders was somewhat smaller than elsewhere, the principal offices usually went to members of the long-standing, established families. John Adams later observed:

Go into every village of New England, and you will find that
the office of justice of the peace, and even the place of representative, which has depended only on the freest election of the
people, have generally descended from generation to generation,
in three or four families at most.[39]

Main has demonstrated that more than 50 percent of the Bay Colony
representatives in 1765 owned property worth £2,000, while 17 percent
had estates valued at more than £5,000.[40]

On the local level in New England, there was a similar alliance between
wealth and office. Selectmen, clerks, treasurers, and moderators of the
town meeting "were almost always a significant cut above the average
townsperson economically." According to Bruce Daniels, three-quarters
of the highest officeholders in three of the largest Connecticut towns
(Hartford, Norwich, and Fairfield) were in the top 10 percent in terms
of property held.[41] Also, a survey of the printed tax lists for Massachusetts indicates that the position of selectman, the most important town
office, invariably went to the rich and prominent citizens in each community. The only available valuation for the town of Oxford (1771)
shows that among 238 polls, two of the three selectmen were ranked
in the top five, with the third member standing seventeenth. In Cohasset
for that same year, two persons on the board placed second and third;
the other, a doctor, was rated twenty-fourth. Generally a selectman somewhat further down in the assessments was still part of the local hierarchy,
either as a churchman, a professional, or a military officer. For example,
Ephraim Tucker of Milton, designated sixty-sixth, was a deacon in the
church; Theodore Danforth of Billerica, one hundred thirteenth, was a
physician; and Abraham Knowlton of Hardwick, one hundred twenty-
fifth, was a lieutenant in the militia. To be sure, a number of the other
town offices such as fire warden and tithingman were held by some of
the less affluent individuals, but the major posts were usually the domain
of the gentleman. Thus, on all levels there was a close connection between
high status and officeholding.[42]

The periodic election of the most economically and socially prominent
citizens to public office, however, did not mean that such choices were
automatic. The members of the ruling elite came to realize that their being elected implied fulfillment on their part of certain minimum obligations to the populace. In many places, these men acknowledged that
their power inevitably rested upon the approval of the electorate, who

could easily drop a person from a high post who did not please them. A classic example was the wealthy Thomas Hutchinson of Boston who was in the Massachusetts House of Representatives for a dozen years before he was ousted from that body in 1749 for favoring a hard-money policy against the wishes of his constituents. He later admitted that despite the sympathy for him among the upper classes, "we are governed not by weight but by numbers."[43] Those in Hutchinson's position discovered that in their political actions there were bounds beyond which they could not go and that ultimately they were dependent for reelection upon the continued support of the lower orders.

Why persons sought office in the provincial period is a difficult question to answer. In recent times, some political scientists have attempted to create a general model for understanding why men have become active in politics that can readily be applied to the more narrow category of office seekers. One such construct by Robert Lane postulates six basic reasons for men's participation in politics.

1. Men seek to advance their economic and material well-being, their income, their property, their economic security through political means.
2. Men seek to satisfy their needs for friendship, affection, and easy social relations through political means.
3. Men seek to understand the world, and the causes of the events which affect them, through observing and discussing politics.
4. Men seek to relieve intrapsychic tensions, chiefly those arising from aggressive and sexual impulses, through political expression.
5. Men seek power over others (to satisfy doubts about themselves) through political channels.
6. Men generally seek to defend and improve their self-esteem through political activity.[44]

These motives are probably applicable in some respects to persons living in the eighteenth century. However, given the absence of concrete information about individual motivation in past eras, it is almost impossible to deal with every one of these hypotheses in a meaningful manner. The available data do not allow for a determination of whether large numbers of men entered politics to obtain power over others, improve their self-esteem, relieve intrapsychic tension, and so forth. It might be that these observations best be left for scrutinizing twentieth-century politicians. Perhaps a more relevant model to work with is the one provided by the late Sir Lewis Namier in his classic study of eighteenth-century English political life. Namier's survey, which focuses upon certain major types, enables us to see important similarities as well as differences between potential officeholders on each side of the Atlantic.

Namier's analysis in *The Structure of Politics at the Accession of George III* shows eight different kinds of men seeking election to Parliament. First of all, Namier listed predestined or "inevitable Parliament men" for whom membership in the House was "a duty whatever were their individual predilections." This group consisted primarily of the eldest sons of politically active peers. Second were the country gentlemen to whom the House of Commons was not a means to ulterior aims. "What mattered to them," said Namier, "was not so much membership of the House, as the primacy in their own 'country' attested by their being chosen to represent their county or some respectable borough." Third, he mentioned the politicians, those persons who aspired to the highest positions of state, men such as William Pitt. Fourth were the social climbers, those who wanted social advancement, especially a seat in the House of Lords. Fifth were placemen and purveyors of favors, those coveting various forms of patronage in an era when sinecures were still quite common. Sixth were those in the civil and military service or the law who wished to advance their professional career. Seventh were merchants and bankers who hoped to obtain lucrative government contracts, domestic and foreign, chiefly for supplying the army and navy. Finally, he included those "robbers, muddlers, bastards, and bankrupts," who desired a place in the Commons for the purposes of immunity from creditors and the law.[45]

In general, "robbers, muddlers, bastards, and bankrupts" notwithstanding, eighteenth-century Englishmen sought a place in Parliament for positive ends. A seat in the highest governing body in the land was strongly coveted for political, economic, or social advantage. It opened up opportunities to the greatest honors that one could possibly obtain. The House of Commons was at the center of all aspects of English life. There was nothing comparable to it anywhere, according to most Britishers. "To be out of Parliament is to be out of the world," wrote the renowned naval hero Admiral George Rodney in 1780, surely echoing the sentiments of many of his contemporaries.[46]

In America, on the other hand, a seat in one of the thirteen Assemblies did not hold the same attraction. Although various colonial political leaders in defending the rights of the lower houses referred to them as miniature Houses of Commons, places in them were not always highly sought after. Numerous gentlemen, such as Henry Beekman of New York, found Assembly service extremely burdensome. "If other good men Can be fixed on," said Beekman in 1745, "I had rather be out than in."[47] The journey to the legislative seat was frequently long and tedious and the sessions themselves, with their endless debates, even more so. In light of these conditions, many qualified individuals tried to avoid serving whenever possible. George Mason, author of the Virginia Bill of Rights (1776), rarely sat in the House of Burgesses. He much preferred the peaceful life at his estate, Gunston Hall, to the continuous haggling over bills and the seemingly pointless discussion that accompanied every action the House proposed to undertake. In his will Mason urged his descendants not to seek a public career.[48]

Men who did agree to serve received little in the way of remuneration for the time spent away from their estates or businesses. There were no regular salaries, just a small allotment for each day's attendance, barely covering a person's minimum expenses. Joseph Galloway claimed it cost even more to live in Philadelphia than the amount received in the daily stipend. Virginians obtained ten shillings per day plus a travel allowance, hardly adequate compensation for someone away from a productive plantation for any length of time. In most other colonies the rate was much lower. Legislators in Pennsylvania earned five shillings for each day's attendance, deputies in Massachusetts three to six, while those in South Carolina had to serve without any pay. When Edward Shippen of Lancaster, Pennsylvania, considered running for office in 1756, he wrote to his father, "For my part I am not anxious to be in the House. A seat there would give me much trouble, take up a great deal of my time and yield no advantage."[49]

Some men who were reluctant to give up their rural tranquillity for the rigors of Assembly duty had to be pushed and prodded into standing for office or attending a legislative session. John Stoddard of Northampton, Massachusetts, who disliked the long trip to Boston and the extended periods spent there, had to be warned of impending disasters that would occur if he did not attend before he would travel to the capital. In April, 1734, Governor Belcher told Stoddard: "as the circumstances of the public affairs are at present, I can accept no excuse for your not coming to the next General Court."[50] Philip Schuyler of Albany was another who found it difficult to leave the calm, rustic life behind. He had to be begged by his friend William Smith, the noted lawyer, not to decline a seat after being elected to the New York Assembly in 1768. "Let me persuade you not to refuse your services to your Country," said Smith. "After 7 Years we shall both abandon to Ease. I will promise to leave you in full & quiet Possession of your Wolves Foxes Snow Mills Fish & Lands at Saratoga & give no Disturbance while the remaining Lands run out."[51]

Besides the long periods of hard work for low pay, there were other drawbacks and few compensating factors. The place where the Assembly or general court met was, to be sure, at the center of social, economic, and political life in the particular colony, but it did not provide the prospective office seeker with the great advantages that Parliament did. The social life of a provincial capital such as New York or Williamsburg could in no way compare to that of London, with all its glittering attractions. Social gatherings of various kinds did indeed take place during the time that the legislature was in session, but none had any of the regal splendor of similar events at the Court of St. James. Politically, the possibilities were also circumscribed. A politician from the New World could never rise to be a chief minister of state and make major decisions affecting the course of empire. Imperial policy was primarily determined by the king's councillors in England with the aid of the royal governors in their respective colonies. While a few colonials did manage to become governors, their numbers were exceedingly small.

Other forms of advancement were just as difficult to come by. The colonial Assemblyman could never obtain a peerage, and even promotion to the upper houses in America was limited. These bodies were usually just twelve in number and generally reserved for the governor's favorites. Furthermore, the patronage available for the average House member was relatively restricted. There were few positions as judges or tax collectors in each colony—far fewer than in England—and most of them were dispensed to persons on the Council or to Englishmen who had difficulty obtaining a place at home. In addition, the number of government contracts was severely limited in most periods. The colonies did not, of course, have a standing army or navy, which eliminated the prime source of suppliers. (A few men may have made some gains at times outfitting various militia groups, however. Some provinces such as Massachusetts even had a commissary-general for that purpose.) But only during the brief intervals of the French and Indian wars was there any real opportunity for contractors to provide large amounts of goods and to reap large profits.[52]

Yet if a seat in one of the colonial legislatures was not as attractive as a seat in the House of Commons, there were still men in America who keenly sought election to these positions. Moreover, despite the more limited benefits obtainable in the New World, many individuals on this side of the Atlantic desired office for some of the very same reasons as persons in England. Just as there were "inevitable Parliament men" in the mother country, dutiful sons of the politically prominent, so in the colonies one found similar individuals, such as Daniel Dulany, Jr., of Maryland and James Otis, Jr., of Massachusetts, carrying on a long family tradition of service. The fathers of both men had long served in their respective legislatures and groomed their sons to follow in their footsteps. There were also country gentlemen, such as John Stoddard of Northampton, Massachusetts, and Henry Beekman of Dutchess County, New York, who looked upon membership in the legislature mainly as a symbol of their primacy in their particular region. Men like Stoddard and Beekman wanted to be recognized as the dominant local figure and to have some control over their county's civil and military appointments. In the colonies, too, were numerous politicians, men such as James DeLancey of New York and John Dickinson of Pennsylvania, fervently aspiring to positions of political power. When first elected to the Assembly in 1762, Dickinson said to a friend, "I hope I can make a great bustle in the world."[53] If a man like Dickinson could not become one of the king's ministers and determine imperial policy directly, he could from his post in the Assembly surely exhibit a great deal of influence toward blocking those British measures he disagreed with, such as the Parliamentary revenue acts of the 1760's. In addition, it was possible in a few cases for a colonial to become a governor or, as in the case of James DeLancey, a lieutenant-governor, from which position he could in effect run a colony and make many of its policies.[54]

Generally, fewer social climbers could be found in the colonial legislatures than in Parliament, that is, men using their election as a stepping stone to greater social recognition and advancement to the upper house. Nevertheless, certain individuals had this end clearly in view. In Virginia, according to Thomas Jefferson, "the only object for the wealthy was a seat in the king's council. All their court then was paid to the Crown and its creatures."[55] Furthermore, there were some civil and military officers attempting to improve their professional status, but probably the number was small since several colonies barred placemen from sitting altogether. Meanwhile, very few "robbers, muddlers, bastards, and bankrupts," sought refuge in a provincial Assembly as there were fewer men of these types in the New World to begin with. Finally, given the underdeveloped nature of the American economy, few contractors deemed it a desirable spot either.

Despite America's lack of development, some economic advantages were obtainable through the provincial legislature. While patronage was limited in the colonies, it was far from being nonexistent. A man who remained in the House for several years could easily become a county justice of the peace, obtain a commission in the militia, or even be appointed to a judgeship in many instances. The House Journal for Massachusetts from 1764 lists fourteen militia captains, fifteen judges, and over sixty justices of the peace among the 113 representatives. Some enterprising individuals such as Thomas Hutchinson were ultimately able to possess four or five profitable places at the same time. During the early 1760's, Hutchinson was Chief Justice of the Superior Court, Judge of Probate for Suffolk County, a member of the Council, Commander of the Castle (the fort on Castle Island), as well as Lieutenant-Governor of the province. These offices brought him more than £400 sterling per year.[56]

If generous contracts were uncommon in the colonies, there were some persons who hoped to profit from whatever lucrative deals could be arranged. Indeed, many prominent figures originally sought election to the lower house for economic motives. The first Robert Livingston ran for the New York Assembly in 1708 in order to prevent confiscation of his estates because certain laws had brought the ownership of his lands into question. Elisha Cooke, Jr., and Oliver Noyes, leaders of the country party in early eighteenth-century Massachusetts, first stood for office to promote their paper-money schemes. In every colony there were numerous individuals interested in land speculation who believed that by being close to the governor they would eventually receive a substantial grant of valuable acreage.[57] It is obvious, too, that some rural gentlemen desired a seat in the legislature so they could be present in the provincial capital to engage in their own financial pursuits. As the townspeople of Marlborough, Massachusetts, remarked to their deputies on one occasion: "while the General Court sits in the town of Boston, are not many of the Representatives of the several country towns often found attending to their own private business, when they ought to attend to the public's only."[58]

Nevertheless, while some colonists may have sought office for personal gain, this was not such a dominant motive as it was in England. Rarely did an American seek to spend a lifetime in the legislature. Only a small number looked upon politics as a full-time avocation, absorbing most of their energy and interest. Although many persons served as representatives during the provincial era, few served very long. In most of the colonies the typical Assemblyman held his seat for just a few terms. New York had about a 33 percent turnover at each election over the course of the period. New Jersey experienced more than a 50 percent change with every contest (see table 2). The degree of alteration in Massachusetts was almost as high. Not until 1729 was the rate of substitution less than 50 percent, and after that 40 percent was the usual norm. In Virginia, the average length of service was approximately three terms, but over half of the Burgesses selected were chosen just once, and only five men remained for more than twenty years. The greatest amount of turnover occurred in South Carolina where the overwhelming majority of men who sat in the Commons House in the eighteenth century stayed but one term. Indeed, more than half of those elected in the 1730's and 1740's had never served before and never served again.[59]

Yet the high turnover rate in the eighteenth century had different implications than it would have today. When these persons did not serve in the lower house again, it was not usually because they were voted out of office. The evidence shows that only a small fraction were ousted by opponents. In most cases they refused to stand on subsequent occasions because they no longer wished to serve. Perhaps some of these people simply wanted to try legislating and dealing with affairs of state. Some may have desired to rub shoulders with the leading men of the time and obtain the prestige of having held a seat in a colonial governing body. But probably the majority of them agreed to serve for a short time primarily out of a sense of duty or obligation they felt they owed to their commu-

TABLE 2
Turnover in New York and New Jersey Assemblies

Year	Number	Year	Number	Year	Number
NEW YORK[a]					
1692	3	1709	10	1739	9
1693	8	1710	9	1743	7
1694	7	1711	2	1745	5
1695	11	1713	7	1748	6
1698	12	1715	8	1750	7
1699	9	1716	10	1752	5
1701	7	1726	13	1759	17
1702	11	1727	4	1761	7
1705	5	1728	5	1768	13
1708	3	1737	13	1769	7
NEW JERSEY[b]					
1704	11	1727	15	1746	2
1707	12	1730	10	1749	8
1708	13	1738	12	1751	12
1709	13	1740	9	1754	13
1710	14	1743	11	1761	13
1716	20	1744	7	1769	13
1721	20	1745	10	1772	11

[a]There were 18 seats in 1692, 22 in 1698, 23 in 1713, 24 in 1715, 26 in 1716, and 27 in 1737 and thereafter through 1769.

[b]There were 24 seats from 1704 to 1769 and 30 seats beginning in 1772.

nity. At that time a man of wealth and training was expected to share the burden of public affairs.[60] Even among those who were not of the highest class and who were not inevitable Assemblymen a strong desire to perform public service could be found.

In the newly emerging society of provincial America where there was a lack of educated men and few individuals were equipped to deal with important administrative matters, it was necessary that those with the ability to serve should volunteer to do so. If it were merely for the few benefits that one could obtain, it is doubtful whether many persons would have been willing to sit through the long legislative sessions for any number of years. Colonel Landon Carter of Virginia, for example, felt very strongly about his "Duty" to serve in the House of Burgesses. To Carter, sitting in the House was an honor, and to do his job well was a major responsibility.[61] George Washington, upon being elected to a seat there in 1758, also felt deeply about his "Sense of Obligation to the People." He declared that he would make "their interests (as it really is) my own" and do "everything that lyes in my little Power for the Hon'r and welfare of the Country."[62]

Many other leading public figures in early America believed that their entrance into politics was inspired by a sense of civic obligation and a wish to improve the public welfare. Looking back upon his initial election to the Pennsylvania Assembly, Benjamin Franklin said, "I conceived my becoming a member would enlarge my power of doing good."[63] John Adams claimed that upon being chosen a representative for the first time in Massachusetts, his thoughts were of anything but personal gain:

> Many Congratulations were offered, which I received civilly, but they gave no Joy to me. I considered the Step as a devotion of my family to ruin and myself to death, for I could scarce perceive a possibility that I should ever go through the Thorns and leap all the Precipices before me, and escape with my life. At this time I had more Business at the Bar, than any Man in the Province: My health was feeble; I was throwing away as bright prospects [as] any Man ever had before him: and had devoted myself to endless labour and Anxiety if not to infamy and to death, and that for nothing, except, what indeed was and ought to be all in all, a sense of duty.[64]

Perhaps certain men such as Adams and Franklin overemphasized in their later autobiographies the noble purposes for which they sought office. Although they had a strong sense of duty, it was probably intertwined with other feelings, especially ambition and honor. As Dumas Malone has written about young Thomas Jefferson's motives and attitudes when he first took his seat in the House of Burgesses (which can easily be applied to many others at this time): "He was not personally aggressive, and did not crave power, but he always set high value on the esteem of his fellows and at this stage he craved honor. In that sense but probably in no other he had more than the 'little spice of ambition' which he acknowledged."[65] Even Benjamin Franklin, after being placed in office, admitted that he was "flattered by all these promotions. . . . For considering my low beginning they were great things to me. And they were still more pleasing as being so many, spontaneous testimonies of the public's good opinion [of me]."[66]

Overall, many factors influenced a colonist to seek office, a lot of them similar to those reasons causing an Englishman to covet a seat in Parliament. Yet because of the underdeveloped nature of early American society, there was probably a more selfless attitude and a greater desire to serve the community on this side of the Atlantic than on the other. But few elected officials in the colonies obtained total fulfillment from this service. If some satisfaction was derived from helping America govern itself, the tangible rewards and benefits were limited, leaving most persons with little inclination to remain in their post any appreciable length of time. It is probable, too, that many colonials saw the British government as the main source of their frustration in this respect. The manner in which the Crown catered to favorites at home in dispensing patronage was, they believed, the prime obstacle in their quest for more profit, power, and place. Nevertheless, while the English system hindered many individuals from securing advancement, there were always some Americans willing to serve, albeit for short intervals, which kept the government in the thirteen provinces functioning reasonably well.

4

Nominations

★★★★★★★★★★★★★★

The nomination process in provincial America remains obscure with few contemporary sources mentioning the manner in which persons were designated to stand for public office.[1] In a sense, the absence of abundant information on the subject suggests that there was no uniform system of selection, and the available records confirm this, revealing that nomination procedures evolved in a variety of ways. Each region, indeed, certain areas within a region, developed different modes for choosing candidates and often changed them over the course of time.

The earliest and most common style of nomination to emerge in colonial times was self-announcement. Throughout the period, many individuals seeking public office personally indicated to the populace their desire to run. As one of the inhabitants of Albany, New York, remarked prior to the Assembly election of 1761, "the old Candidates purpose to advertise themselves this day, without the advice of any of the Citysens."[2] A person could announce his intention in several fashions. Aspirants for the position of sheriff or coroner in Pennsylvania sometimes placed advertisements in one of the local newspapers. For example, in September, 1754, Thomas Bartholomew of Philadelphia stated in the *Pennsylvania Journal* that he "intends to stand a candidate for the coroners office."[3] Other methods included tacking a notice on a courthouse door, writing letters to inform friends, or making a declaration at either a religious meeting or some informal public gathering.[4] An ambitious man might use all of these approaches.

Although an open declaration of candidacy was customary in most places, it was frowned upon in the majority of New England towns. Perhaps the people in those communities felt that such a step was an infringement upon their

Puritan concept of a free election. In effect, no separate nomination occurred. On election day the male citizens went to the ballot box and, without any prior consultation, delivered a vote for the persons of their choice. A writer in the *Connecticut Courant* insisted:

> . . . here there is no such thing as setting up for Assembly-men: but the Freemen, when met together, unsolicited & uninfluenced, bring in their votes in Writing for whomever they choose to serve them as Representatives in General Assembly. And the Deputies so far from appearing as Candidates, or soliciting for the Suffrages of the Freemen, that I am personally persuaded their so doing and would be the most effectual Way to miss of them.[5]

An examination of numerous volumes of town meeting records validates this claim.[6] Moreover, the results of the balloting sometimes disclose a scattering of votes for many individuals, which would not have been consistent with announced candidacies. Furthermore, a sizable number of those elected declined to serve, a clear indication that they were not consulted beforehand. On one occasion, the people of Norton, Massachusetts, chose for their representative Samuel Brintnell, a man who was not even present at the election meeting. When the selectmen went to Brintnell's house to find out whether he would accept and were told that he was out of town, the inhabitants were forced to start balloting all over again. This incident, and others very much like it, plainly illustrate the unplanned nature of the nomination process for local New England elections.[7]

A similar result occurred in many parishes in rural South Carolina where candidacies were unannounced and no residence requirement existed. People often voted with no previous arrangements having been made and elected one of the leading gentlemen in the province as their representative. They would often discover later that this person had consented to serve in another parish and would be unable to serve them so they would have to hold one or more additional rounds of balloting to find an agreeable delegate. This type of situation occurred in thirteen instances in 1746 and seven in 1762.[8]

In parts of New York and Virginia and other rural areas where county politics was well organized, the more promising candidates were "set up,"

that is, placed in nomination through a private agreement among a limited number of prominent gentlemen.[9] For example, in 1768, Sir William
Johnson, the famous Indian agent, congratulated Philip Schuyler upon
being unanimously approved "by the Principal People of Albany."[10] The
"principal people" would generally include the sheriff, the justices of the
peace, and certain influential members of the landed gentry, perhaps five
to ten in all.[11] These men would consult each other about the availability
of various persons, taking into account each one's qualifications, especially
his potentiality as a vote getter if a close contest was expected. Colonial
politicians naturally sought to nominate individuals who would appeal to
the broadest range of the electorate.

Some counties had two competing factions, with each one containing
a few of the leading persons of the area. Both sides would organize separately, and as these groups were seldom permanent, it was not uncommon
to have men switching their support from one candidate to another at
the start of a new campaign. Before the New York Assembly elections of
1748, Cadwallader Colden told Governor George Clinton, "It is agreed
in Orange County to set up Col. Mathews in opposition to [Thomas]
Gale. Col. Dukey who was formerly much in Gale's interest is now much
to the contrary."[12]

The amount of political activity prior to the nomination was often
greater than during the election competition itself. Certain leaders would
use every available means to find a standard-bearer who was acceptable
to all interests rather than engage in an open campaign, which was expen-
sive, time-consuming, and divisive. In addition, it might place in front of
the voters issues that they believed should not be bared. Such feelings
were reflected in the words of Abraham Ten Broeck at the start of the
race in Albany County in 1768: "Every body," he said, "is averse to a
Poll."[13] Therefore, the political managers in Albany and many other locales attempted to do most of their maneuvering behind the scenes before settling upon a nominee instead of afterward in the public view.

A nominee decided upon by the leading men was not necessarily guaranteed election. Several instances can be found where self-announced candidates, running without the backing of the gentry, emerged victorious
over the representative of the great families. Colonel Landon Carter of
Richmond County, Virginia, the son of Robert "King" Carter, one of
the wealthiest men in the colony, lost to a series of relative unknowns
before obtaining a spot in the House of Burgesses in 1752.[14] Yet, in the

majority of cases, the persons who were most repeatedly successful at the polls were those who had received the blessings of the eminent figures in the community.[15]

Perhaps the best illustration of the gentry's power regarding nominees for office can be seen in the early political career of George Washington. In 1755, at the age of twenty-three, Washington for the first time contemplated running for a seat in the Virginia House. Yet he would not commit himself unless his candidacy was initially approved by Colonel William Fairfax and other influential persons in the vicinity. To his half-brother Augustine, he wrote:

> As I understand your County is to be divided, and that Mr. Alexander intends to decline serving it, I shou'd be glad if you cou'd fish at Colo. Fairfax's Intentions, and let me know whether he purposes to offer himself a Candidate; If he does not I shou'd be glad to stand a poll, if I thought my chance tolerably good. . . . I shou'd be glad if you cou'd discover Major Carlyles real sentim'ts also those of Mr. Dalton, Ramsay, Mason, & c. w'ch I hope and think you may with't disclosing much of mine . . . if they seem inclinable to promote my Interest, and things shou'd be drawing to a crisis you then may declare my Intentions and beg their assistance. If on the Contrary you find them more inclin'd to favour some other, I w'd have the Affair entirely dropped.[16]

As it turned out, Fairfax did run, and Washington, wishing to get into politics, was forced to enter the race in neighboring Frederick County without any real backing. He was resoundingly defeated, acquiring just 40 votes, while the victors, Hugh West and Thomas Swearingen, received 271 and 270, respectively. Washington, however, managed to obtain the gentry's assistance for the next election and won handily, beating the same opponents by more than 100 votes, which surely indicates the value of high-level support.[17] Moreover, when he was up for reelection three years later, a friend assured him that "the Leaders and all the Patrician Families remains firm in their resolution of continuing for You." Washington won this election by more than 200 votes.[18]

While small groups of gentlemen met to set up candidates in many rural counties, residents of some of the rapidly growing towns and cities began establishing a larger and more formalized nominating body, which was increasingly referred to as a caucus. By the eighteenth century, conflicting interests had begun to emerge in many urban areas.[19] As these divisions occurred, it became apparent that the existing government could no longer satisfy all segments of the community. Soon, men holding a particular set of beliefs and values felt it necessary to organize for the purpose of selecting individuals who would best promote the interests of their own group. Even where clashing interests did not appear to any great extent, the very size of a city with its thousands of inhabitants warranted the establishment of more regular nominating procedures in order to facilitate the choice of candidates.

When and where the first caucus was formed is difficult to determine; evidence on this subject is extremely fragmentary. Because the caucus was usually a secret gathering, the barest traces of such meetings are hard to find. The private diaries and personal papers of political leaders of the time leave few clues to the answer. Not only are the date and place of the initial caucus in doubt, but the size and composition of all the early groups are also open to question. Whether the number attending was five, ten, or twenty and whether artisans and tradesmen were active participants is impossible to state in any precise manner.[20]

Even the origin of the term *caucus* is in dispute. Some authorities have proposed that it came from the word *caucasus,* a mythological meeting place of the ancient gods. John Pickering, the compiler of the first volume of Americanisms, claimed that since the meetings were held in the shipping areas of the port towns, the word *caucus* might be a corruption of *caulkers,* who were the men who tarred the ships. On the other hand, later writers have asserted that it derives from the Greek word *kaukos,* a wine vessel, suggesting a relationship between drinking and politics. To be sure, there was a close connection between the two activities at that time, if not more so than today, as liquor flowed quite freely at many provincial political gatherings. [21]

The earliest published notices that meetings had taken place to select candidates in advance of the balloting appeared during the mid-1730's in the *South Carolina Gazette.* In the first one, printed prior to a by-election in Charleston in April, 1735, it was announced that merchant John Dart "had the Honour to be named by a great number of the Inhabitants" to stand for the vacated seat in the Commons House.[22] The following year, a report mentioned that with the date for the regular Assembly contest in the city close at hand,

> . . . it was unanimously agreed by a considerable Number of
> the principal Inhabitants and Electors to put in Nomination
> for their Members the following Gentlemen, *to wit,*
>   Mr. Othniel Beale
>   Major Robert Brewton
>   Mr. John Dart
>   Mr. Isaac Mazyck
>   and
>   Mr. Charles Pinckney.[23]

Unfortunately, these statements do not tell us as much as we would like
to know. It is not clear whether the meetings were secret or how many
attended, though the words "great number" in the first instance indicate
that the figure was fairly high. Meanwhile, the term "principal Inhabitants"
in the second announcement implies that the proceedings were in large
measure dominated by the elite.

Although the first printed record of a gathering to select candidates
comes from Charleston in the 1730's, certain indirect evidence shows that
a regular caucus arose in Boston some years earlier. The Reverend William
Gordon, writing shortly after the American Revolution, claimed that the
Boston caucus had been in existence since the late 1720's. "More than
fifty years ago," said Gordon,

> Mr. Samuel Adams's father and twenty others, one or two
> from the north end of the town, where all the ship business
> is carried on, used to meet, make a caucus, and lay their plan
> for introducing certain persons into places of trust and power.[24]

G. B. Warden, in his recent study of provincial Boston, put the date even
earlier, asserting that it began around 1719. In that year, the popular Elisha
Cooke, Jr., who had been previously rejected from the Council by Governor Samuel Shute, began mobilizing support in order to combat royal policies in the colony. Cooke and his cohorts, Oliver Noyes, Thomas Cushing,
John Clark, and William Clark, all members of the local establishment,
planned to oust those officers sympathetic to Shute from positions of
influence and to replace them with their own followers.[25] The results of
the ensuing elections in the capital indicate that certain steps toward
organization were undoubtedly taken. In March, five of the town's seven

selectmen, and in May, three of the four delegates to the Assembly, were voted out of office. Moreover, as Warden demonstrates, the pattern of officeholding after 1719 reveals a greater degree of continuity than in previous years. For example, between 1719 and 1775, incumbents won 82 percent of the elections for representatives compared to only 63 percent before that date.[26] This implies a greater amount of political management in the later decades.

However, even if a caucus did operate in Boston as far back as 1719, it is not known whether it continued without interruption or whether its influence upon the eventual choice of candidates was always significant. Especially after the death of Elisha Cooke, Jr., in 1737, there is little demonstration of the organization's existence, much less its power. Opponents of the earlier leaders, such as Thomas Hutchinson and Andrew Oliver, were frequently elected to the lower house over the course of the next decade. But by the early 1760's, the Boston caucus, under the leadership of James Otis, Royall Tyler, Samuel Adams, and a few other notables, was definitely in command of the selection process. In February, 1763, Sam's cousin John Adams vividly described the scene in the garret of tradesman Thomas Dawes:

> There they smoke tobacco till you cannot see from one End of the Garrett to the other. There they drink Phlip I suppose, and there they choose a Moderator, who puts Questions to the Vote regularly, and select Men, Assessors, Collectors, Wardens, Fire Wards, and Representatives are Regularly chosen before they are chosen in the Town. . . . They send Committees to wait on the Merchants Clubb and to propose, and join, in the Choice of Men and Measures.[27]

A few weeks later, a writer in the *Boston Evening-Post* complained of the strong influence being exerted by a "Junto" upon the impending election. The group's activities, he said, were "composed by Bluster [Otis], under the direction and correction of Captain Bluff, Justice Gripe, Adjutant Trowel [Dawes], Pug Sly Esq. [Tyler], Tom Shallow Esq., [and] Sam Gamut [Adams]."[28] The next year a notice in the same newspaper calling upon the inhabitants to choose certain candidates and reject others was openly signed by the "Boston Caucus."[29]

While a formal nominating body probably met in Boston at an earlier date than in Charleston, it was not necessarily the first of its kind. A political club in New York City may have been involved in ticket making and electioneering as early as 1699. A letter from the Governor, Lord Bellomont, to the Board of Trade mentions both a "club of the dissatisfied merchants," led by former councillor William Nicolls, and also the use of "tickets" by the two competing sides in that year's Assembly elections.[30] It is not certain, however, that the two items are directly related to each other or that meetings to draw up party slates did in truth take place. Even if such gatherings occurred, it is probable that this was only a temporary development, since no further evidence of this organization's existence can be found.

In the mid-1730's regular meetings for the purpose of nominating candidates in New York first became established. At that time, tensions began to develop over a number of issues, legal and financial, between the Governor, William Cosby, and two influential members of the Council, Rip Van Dam and Lewis Morris. The quarrels soon resulted in Morris's ouster as Chief Justice of the Supreme Court. By late 1733, according to contemporary historian William Smith, "all the province was already divided into parties." Defenders of the administration in the city formed the Hum-Drum-Club (or Governor's Club), while Morris and Van Dam began organizing their supporters against the Cosbyites. The Morris-Van Dam faction evidently held some type of caucus prior to the municipal elections in September, 1734, since a full slate of candidates was set up in opposition to the incumbent officeholders. These new men, with one exception, were swept into office a short time afterward.[31]

Cosby died in 1736, but factional strife continued into the reign of his successors, George Clarke (1737-1743) and George Clinton (1743-1753). During those years, the two sides began to hold meetings to nominate persons for the Assembly. A few weeks before the polling occurred in March, 1739, the *New York Gazette* noted that "a great number of the Freeholders and Free-men of the said City, have Agreed and Resolved to choose the following Persons to represent them in General Assembly, *to wit.* Mr. Adolph Philipse, Coll. John Moore, Mr. David Clarkson, and Alderman William Roome."[32] Prior to many subsequent elections, similar statements appeared in the local newspapers, indicating that these gatherings were becoming habitual. But it is probable that these early meetings were not as large as they were to grow in the decade before the

Revolution. In fact, it is possible that the "great number of freeholders" merely seconded an agreement already reached by a smaller group consisting of a few of the factional leaders. Items in the *Gazette* in the early 1750's hint at caucusing taking place among just a handful of men. One satirical piece published in February, 1752, purportedly describing a meeting of the DeLancey faction to consider candidates shows only Chief Justice James DeLancey, his merchant brother Oliver, and some city aldermen present.[33]

In Philadelphia, caucusing most likely began in the early 1700's when David Lloyd started to build an opposition to proprietary rule. Lloyd's group was extremely "industrious," admitted Isaac Norris of the Penn faction, throwing "all into confusion." Between 1704 and 1706, at least fifteen of the twenty-six members of the Assembly, including entire county delegations, were sent down to defeat in each contest. By the end of the decade, Lloyd and his followers had gained control of the legislature, which Norris blamed in part on the other side's use of party tickets and "the unhappy way that a man must have eight men crammed down his throat at once."[34]

By the mid-1720's, the caucus was developing on a larger scale and in a more formalized manner. A pamphlet written by the Penn family's agent, James Logan, mentions a man who had gone through the streets on election day, distributing "heaps of prepared Tickets." Logan warned that this practice was taking away the voter's initiative and independence of choice. Many persons, he said, "seem to think and act as if a Set of busy fellows were appointed by Law to make the Tickets, and the People had only the Right to choose which they liked best."[35] The ticket distributor was probably in the employment of Governor William Keith, who had become estranged from the proprietors and was attempting to make Pennsylvania a royal colony. A short time earlier, Keith had established the Gentlemen's Club and the Tiff or Leather Apron Club for the purpose of devising political strategy. From their inception, one of the foremost activities of these groups was to select nominees for office. As Norris, one of Keith's adversaries, asserted: "All state affairs were agreed, directed, canvassed [and the] choosing representatives for the Assembly was decided at one or other of [them]."[36]

Caucusing was not unknown on the Penn side. Despite their disdain toward the ticket-making efforts of Lloyd and Keith, Isaac Norris and James Logan themselves in 1710, if not earlier, concerted plans for ousting several opponents. Moreover, in 1724, Logan wrote that in regard to the impending election, " 'tis to be hoped that the [Assembly] Members & Sherifs Tickets being on different papers will be of Service if well managed."[37]

Although Philadelphia, New York, Boston, and Charleston were establishing more formalized nomination procedures, seldom did these practices filter beyond city borders. Meetings to decide upon candidates did occur from time to time in a few medium-sized Bay Colony towns such as Braintree and Watertown, but not on a regular basis.[38] Moreover, nothing resembling a colony-wide selection process ever did develop in Massachusetts, New York, or South Carolina. Only in Pennsylvania, and later in Rhode Island, did this kind of nomination machinery operate on a large scale. Yet even in these two provinces, the system of choosing prospective officers tended to revolve around urban centers such as Philadelphia, Providence, and Newport, which provided both the leadership and the organizational techniques.

The Quakers in Pennsylvania were the first political group to nominate candidates for the lower house on a provincial basis. As opposition to Quaker rule expanded rapidly in the middle decades of the eighteenth century, those in power realized the need for greater organization. Wishing to maintain their political preeminence, they began discussing at their annual meeting "who should be chosen members of the Assembly."[39] This activity disturbed Thomas Penn, son of the original proprietor, who complained that "instead of making use of those meetings for regulating Religious Affairs of the Society they are become Councils for the Government."[40] By the 1750's the political agreements reached by this body became so decisive, according to Edward Shippen of Lancaster, that no ticket could be settled "until the result of the yearly meeting at Burlington is known."[41]

Nevertheless, the Quaker meeting should not be equated with a modern political convention. A number of sources suggest that those persons in attendance at Burlington merely acted in an advisory capacity and that the actual lists of candidates were drawn up by the faction leaders on subsequent occasions. For example, John Smith of Philadelphia, a prominent Quaker, noted in his diary a week before the election of 1750 that he "spent the even [in]g at Uncle & Isr[ae]l Pembertons with John Evans and other friends in endeavoring to settle the ticket."[42] Yet if the Quaker annual gathering was not exactly a political convention, it was definitely a step in that direction.

As the Quakers began to prepare lists of nominees, the newly organized opposition, the Proprietary faction, led by the influential William Allen, made its own effort to arrange tickets. Although the Proprietary group neither held annual meetings in the Quaker style nor prepared complete colony-wide slates, several county leaders often submitted their local choices for high-level approval. This was especially true in Lancaster where individuals such as Edward Shippen and Colonel James Burd maintained close contact with the party hierarchy in the capital. After taking part in the selection of candidates for the first time, Shippen disclosed to a friend that the persons named "were agreeable to Cousin Allen and the other Gentlemen of Philadelphia."[43]

In their attempt to outdo the more popular Quakers, Proprietary spoke men on one occasion called for the nomination of Assembly candidates in open meetings. An advertisement in the *Pennsylvania Gazette* in mid-September, 1754, requested that the people gather at the Philadelphia Acade for this purpose. The Quakers, however, refused to cooperate and wound up in the strange position of being accused by their opponents of deprivin the freemen of their liberties. At the same time, the Proprietary side continued to press for an open nomination and renewed its invitation to the populace to meet at the academy to "consult together" about the choice of officers.[44] Whether such an event did indeed take place is unknown, but in any case it was not reinstituted thereafter.

From time to time, the Proprietary faction, fearing certain defeat at the hands of the more efficient Quakers, resorted to devious maneuvers and various compromises in order to obtain at least a few places in the lower house. In 1755, Allen, a resident of Philadelphia, ran for the Assembly in two outlying counties—Cumberland and Northampton—so he would have a double chance at a seat.[45] During the following year, when the pacifists who had refused to provide for the defense of the colony had dropped out of the "Old Party," leaving "war Quakers" such as Benjamin Franklin in command, the Proprietary camp's main issue was lost. The leaders, William Allen, James Hamilton, and Benjamin Chew, were forced to make humiliating concessions to their opponents. According to the secretary of the province, Richard Peters, "Mr. Hamilton, Mr. Allen, and Mr. Chew have had two Meetings with Mr. Franklin, in the last Meeting a Ticket was agreed on." Under the stipulations, the Proprietary group was to place only two men on the ballot in Philadelphia County. Then, immediately prior to the election, Franklin repudiated the arrangement, apparently believing that it was no longer necessary to give his adversaries any seats whatsoever. Following the vote, Peters recorded the unhappy outcome. "Mr. Allen and his Friends have taken a great deal of Pains but after all their Industry and the Exertion of their whole Interest they have lost the Election entirely."[46]

Always seeking a new advantage, it was the Proprietary faction in Pennsylvania that initially adopted the now widely used technique of placing certain persons on the ticket on the basis of their ethnic origin. In 1764, the Proprietary leaders suggested an alteration in the list for Lancaster County in order to carry part of the heavy German vote, which had traditionally gone to the Quaker side. Two men of German extraction, Isaac Saunders and Ernani Carpenter, were included on the slate for the first time. As Samuel Purviance of Philadelphia informed his associate, Colonel Burd, "The design is, by putting in two Germans, to draw such a party of them as will turn the scale in our favor."[47] This plan met with some success; one of the new designees, Saunders, was elected. In the following year, Purviance hoped to acquire a second seat and recommended to Burd "to run Dr. Kuhn, or some other popular Lutheran or Calvinist." Without a doubt, he added, "If you can run Doctor Kuhn or any other popular German and keep Mr. Saunders in you will do great things."[48]

The Proprietary group was also concerned about the vote of the Scotch-Irish Presbyterians, of whom there were considerable numbers in rural Pennsylvania. "It would be imprudent to offend them," said Purviance, "by rejecting one of their proposing." To show the emerging importance of the Presbyterians as a factor in formulating the ticket in this colony, one need only look at the letter of Jasper Yeates to Colonel Burd, the faction leader in Lancaster, in September, 1769:

> The Current Objections against the Ticket . . . are, that no
> leading Men among the Presbyterians are introduced therein,
> which might be a Lure to Others of the same Persuasion to
> join the Party; And that the intended Alteration stands not
> sufficiently on the broad bottom . . . if they do turn out,
> will do it in Favour of the other side, unless there is a speedy
> Change.[49]

Some of the practices used in Pennsylvania were also common in Rhode Island, where caucusing had become standard procedure by the mid-1740's, if not earlier. The oldest surviving printed ticket comes from the campaign

of 1744, and the existence of several later ones attest to their continued
use. By the time of the clash between the Ward and Hopkins factions in
the 1750's and 1760's, the development of colony-wide nominating machinery was more advanced than in any other province, involving factional affiliates in all districts. Hopkins's chief supporters, the Brown brothers
of Providence, would travel to various towns to consult with the local
party faithful on the designation of standard-bearers. In April, 1765, for
instance, Nicholas Brown mentions that he is preparing to leave for "a
meeting in Cranston this Evening to settle their Deputys."[50]

Competition between the two factions was extremely severe, and each
side after a while tried to reach a compromise in the choice of candidates
so as to prevent further heated campaigns. Since Rhode Island was one of
the two colonies permitted to choose its own governor, deputy governor,
and upper house, the discussions naturally centered around these offices
rather than the seats in the Assembly. It was customary in the early 1760's
to propose that these high posts be divided equally between the two camp
the governor to come from one side, the deputy governor from the other.
But the faction deprived of naming the governor would never agree to
this scheme, so the meetings here, as in Pennsylvania, were generally to
no avail. Failing to reach any accord, the two groups would then consult
separately, and each would decide upon a complete slate of nominees of
its own.[51]

Arranging the whole list of officers often involved a great deal of ne-
gotiation. In 1770, Moses Brown, organizing the ticket for Hopkins's suc-
cessor, Joseph Wanton, against the Ward faction, mentioned that "in settling the prox for this County we had divers consultations and [it] was
finally determined in a Considerably Larger Meeting to Continue the old
Members."[52] Some candidates requested that certain conditions be ful-
filled prior to allowing themselves to appear on either slate. Before all
the details were worked out that year, Thomas Greene of Bristol wrote
to Brown: "Mr. Ward has put my name in his Prox & if it is agreable that
it goes in Mr. Wantons on the same terms you may be free to make use
of it."[53]

In Rhode Island as in Pennsylvania, an attempt was made at times to
place members of various minority religious sects on the ticket. Of course,
this did not occur as frequently because of the greater homogeneity of
the population. Moreover, it was not always easy to find the proper candidate. Joseph Wanton told Moses Brown on one occasion that he "could

not get a man suitable of the Babtist Church for having Try'd James &
Peleg Barker with several others recommended [by] them," none worked
out.[54] Still, the Hopkins men strongly endeavored when possible to put
a Baptist on their slate to attract the considerable Baptist vote in certain
areas.

When the list of candidates was finally set in order, it was printed on
tickets (or "proxes") of which thousands were distributed to the voters
throughout the province for use on election day. These tickets, however,
were not always deposited in their original form. In some instances, voters crossed off or added names as they saw fit. Then, too, faction leaders
such as Elisha Brown of the Ward group were known to print up deceptive proxes containing the names of Ward's disciples on supposedly Hopkins tickets in order to confuse electors in the opposition's strongholds.[55]

In the early stages of the Ward-Hopkins clash, several names on the
final lists, especially among the assistants, were accepted by both factions.
The two tickets for the 1758 election serve as an illustration.[56]

HOPKINS TICKET–1758	WARD TICKET–1758
Hon. Stephen Hopkins, Esq; Gov.	Samuel Ward, Esq; Gov.
Hon. John Gardner, Esq; Dep. Gov.	Jabez Bowen, Esq; Dep. Gov.
1. James Honyman, Esq; Assist.	1. James Honyman, Esq; Assist.
2. Nicholas Easton, Esq; Assist.	2. Nicholas Easton, Esq; Assist.
3. Elisha Brown, Esq; Assist.	3. Elisha Brown, Esq; Assist.
4. Henry Harris, Esq; Assist.	4. Gideon Comstock, Esq; Assist.
5. William Richmond, Esq; Assist.	5. Robert Lawton, Esq; Assist.
6. Joseph Brownel, Esq; Assist.	6. David Anthony, Esq; Assist.
7. Joseph Edmonds, Esq; Assist.	7. Joseph Edmonds, Esq; Assist.
8. Jonathan Randal, Esq; Assist.	8. Nathaniel Searle, Esq; Assist.
9. Daniel Coggeshall, Esq; Assist.	9. Daniel Coggeshall, Esq; Assist.
10. Jeoffry Watson, Esq; Assist.	10. Jeoffry Watson, Esq; Assist.
John Grelea, jun. Esq; Secret.	Thomas Ward, Esq; Secret.
Augustus Johnston, Esq; Att. Gen.	Augustus Johnston, Esq; Att. Gen.
Thomas Richardson, Esq; Gen.	Thomas Richardson, Esq; Gen.
Treas.	Treas.

As we can see from comparing the two columns, six of the ten assistants,
(James Honyman, Nicholas Easton, Elisha Brown, Joseph Edmonds,
Daniel Coggeshall, and Jeoffry Watson) appeared on both cards, as did
Augustus Johnston for the Attorney-General's position and Thomas
Richardson for Treasurer. By the mid-1760's, however, partisan strife

had become so intense that it was difficult to agree upon joint support for any individual, and practically all the names on the opposing slates were different. In 1767, at the height of the conflict, only one assistant, Thomas Wickes, plus the Attorney-General and Treasurer, Oliver Arnold and Joseph Clarke, were backed by both sides.[57]

Connecticut also was allowed to choose its own high magistrates, though its system of nominations developed in a unique manner: popular nomination of high officials by the entire electorate. In September, each freeman had the right to choose twenty persons as candidates for the top positions in the government, including the Governor, Deputy Governor, and twelve assistants.[58] Although the people as a whole generally renominated most of the incumbents, it was not always accomplished with unanimity. In fact, quite a number of additional names appeared in the selections. Existing nomination lists show that anywhere from 39 to 62 individuals received more than 100 votes for assistants each year. There were 39 in 1754, 46 in 1760, 43 in 1763, 62 in 1769, 57 in 1770, and 60 in 1771. Moreover, these results imply that if so many persons amassed more than 100 votes, dozens more would have garnered at least a smattering of the ballots cast in the nominations.[59]

Even more significant than the wide range of candidates was the fact that the highest-standing officials in the colony, including the governor, were far from being overwhelming choices in every community. Records of nominations from a number of towns in 1737 and 1745 make this abundantly clear. For example, Governor Joseph Talcott in 1737 polled only eleven of the twenty-two votes in Windsor. Eight years later, Governor Jonathan Law acquired just twenty-two out of forty-seven in Coventry and nine out of fifty in Groton. The high-ranking assistants often met with the same lack of favor. Samuel Eells, at the top of the list in 1737, registered but three votes in Lebanon and two in Windsor. Joseph Whiting, third assistant in 1745, managed no more than five votes in New Milford, three in Coventry and Stratford, and none in Groton. It is probable that Connecticut's division into Old and New Lights in the 1740's had something to do with the latter result; New Light communities frequently refused to reelect Old Light magistrates like Whiting regardless of their high position. At the same time, towns that were staunchly Old Light (Kent, for example) acted in a similar manner toward such New Light sympathizers as Nathaniel Stanley, completely omitting him from its list of nominees. On the whole, however, most of the towns renominated the vast majority of the holdovers, giving each of them a substantial number of votes.

In fact, in some localities, such as Derby and Danbury, the lists show almost complete uniformity in the results, with each of the incumbents receiving practically the same total. The voters in these communities displayed little individuality, merely seconding the names of those already entered. This causes one to wonder if the average person really played an important role in the nomination process in Connecticut and whether its system of nominations was as democratic as it seems. Even though there was, in effect, a form of direct primary, public interest in nominations was less evident than in Pennsylvania and Rhode Island where prepared tickets were the rule.[60]

Probably more important as a precedent for the future than the regular system of nominations was another development in Connecticut—one of an extraordinary nature. In March, 1766, before news of the Stamp Act repeal was received, "a General meeting of the Delegates of the Sons of Liberty, from a great majority of the Towns," took place in Hartford. At first the gathering was a public one, which approved many resolves, including a declaration favoring initiation of correspondence with the Sons of Liberty in neighboring colonies. Upon conclusion of this general business, the spectators were asked to leave, and the delegates went into a secret session. The leaders explained that "as there was a Dissatisfaction in the Colony, it was proposed whether a Change in the Ministry [that is, Magistrates] . . . might not be necessary among us." They declared that they needed "to collect the Minds of the People, for Unity, and by that Means be able to give the Freemen a Lead in the ensuing election, since, should they run upon different Men, the Persons desired might not be elected, by the Freemen."[61]

Many of the delegates, however, were shocked by this turn of events, which was, in effect, transforming the meeting into a full-scale nominating convention. They claimed that no instructions had been given to proceed in this manner. Moreover, they felt that such a session would be unconstitutional because it was

> fraught with the worst of Mischiefs, as it would tend to produce infinite Disquietude among the People, and lay a Foundation for perpetual Feuds and Animosities, in every future Election; especially as a Step of this Kind would . . . be establishing a pernicious precedent, unknown to, and unpracticed by, the virtuous Founders and supporters of the Colony.[62]

The meeting, they added, "was but a very partial, or rather, no just Representation of the Freemen."

Notwithstanding this criticism, the supporters of the movement, forming a majority, proceeded on the following day to divide into groups on the basis of counties and began deliberations. Subsequently, despite some dissent from the Litchfield and Hartford delegations, the body agreed to endorse William Pitkin for Governor and Jonathan Trumbull for Deputy Governor. Then they moved on to take up nominations for assistants, but there was such opposition to this latest proposal that it was quickly defeated. Yet, even with this setback, the Sons of Liberty in Connecticut had managed to create the first wide-scale nominating convention in American history.

This type of gathering did not become standard procedure in Connecticut; no follow-up took place in the period immediately thereafter. However, events in the province several years later led to the calling of another extralegal meeting, this time by the more conservative elements rather than the Sons of Liberty. In 1773, a speculative group known as the Susquehanna Company, which had long sought to attach certain western lands to the colony, finally received the legislature's approval. Opponents of the company, already a minority, felt that this decision would lead to a further loss of their influence and determined to make one last effort to block it. Beginning in February, 1774, they requested that town meetings be called for the purpose of choosing delegates to a convention to be held in Middletown the last week in March. It was necessary, they said, to "consult measures proper to be pursued to evade evils which we apprehend will attend present measures."[63]

Despite the fact that the Susquehanna supporters defended the organization's activities and claimed that a convention was both illegal and unnecessary, several towns began selecting representatives for the occasion. Because it was difficult to have all the towns set up meetings at a moment's notice, the date for the convention was pushed back to April 1. Even with the additional time, many communities were either unable or unwilling to designate persons. Nevertheless, on the date appointed, forty-five delegates representing twenty-three towns met in Middletown in a secret session. No minutes of this meeting have been preserved, yet reports indicate that many disagreements soon arose over what procedures to follow. Unable to resolve these questions, the convention was forced to dissolve with very little having been accomplished. However, some of the delegates who were united in purpose reconvened at the local tavern where they conceived several plans. Most importantly, they prepared a number of different slates of candidates for the upcoming election. One had Matthew Griswold for Governor and William Samuel Johnson for Deputy Governor, a second had Griswold and James Hillhouse in the top two spots, while a third was headed by Thomas Fitch. Because the incumbent Governor, Jonathan Trumbull, a supporter of the Susquehanna plan, was certain to be reelected, the organizers of these diverse tickets hoped that they could create so much confusion at the polls that no individual could obtain a majority. In that case, the selection of the chief executive would fall into the hands of the Assembly, where the conservatives felt they might be able to force a compromise.[64]

Although the initiators of the Middletown convention eventually failed in their scheme, it seems clear that the convention idea was beginning to catch on as a means by which dissatisfied persons could mobilize support for or against certain policies or individuals. It is doubtful that either of the two assemblages in Connecticut served as a direct model for colonists elsewhere. Yet during this same period, the crisis with the mother country, as well as various domestic difficulties, led disaffected groups in other provinces to show greater concern over the choice of public officials and to hold open meetings for the nomination of candidates. Popular participation in political decision making was definitely on the rise.

In North Carolina, farmers in the frontier areas, seeking more responsible government for their section, formed groups known as Regulators to bring about needed changes. Among other things, they agreed to "choose more suitable men than we have heretofore done for Burgesses."[65] Toward this end, a band of a hundred Regulators in Anson County interrupted proceedings at the quarterly session of the court in April, 1768, driving all justices from the bench. Shortly before they dispersed, they chose one of their own members, Charles Robinson, as a nominee for a recently vacated seat in the Assembly. The Regulators had been so enthusiastic about elevating their own candidate, noted one observer, that they made their designation even before the Governor had time to issue a new writ of election.[66]

In South Carolina, the workingmen of Charleston, who had begun to play a greater role in politics following the Stamp Act, also held an impromptu meeting to nominate candidates. One week before the election in October, 1768, they met with some other inhabitants at Liberty Point "to consult each other upon the choice of proper persons to represent them, at this important conjuncture, in the ensuing Assembly."[67] At this meeting the artisans rejected Henry Laurens and Charles Pinckney, who were at this stage still not completely anti-British and instead designated men such as the more outspoken Christopher Gadsden.[68]

It is not clear how the New York City caucus became a larger and more popular body, but, as the late Carl Becker has shown, "by 1769 the public mass meeting for nominating purposes was an established fact."[69] In that year, the struggle between the Livingston and the DeLancey factions, who had come to dominate politics in the colony, had reached its highest point. Philip Livingston, head of his side in the city, tried to arrange a compromise whereby each group would choose two of the four candidates.[70] However, the DeLanceys were willing to accept only one member of the opposition on the ticket. When this offer was rejected, each group decided to nominate four men from its own side at a public meeting. By permitting wide-scale participation in the nomination process, the leaders believed that they would be encouraging greater support in the election campaign to follow. Accordingly, the Livingstons, along with "Several hundred Dissenters," gathered "in the Fields" and by a unanimous vote designated Philip and Peter Livingston, John Morin Scott and Theodore Van Wyck as their candidates. The DeLanceys and their backers then assembled at the Exchange and selected James DeLancey and his merchant associates, James Jauncey, Jacob Walton, and John Cruger.[71] For the first time, two full slates, both popularly chosen, competed against one another in New York City.

In Boston, designation of candidates still took place behind the scenes. But by this time, the nomination machinery had been considerably broadened, both in size and in the spectrum of the population involved. The small caucus that appeared in Boston beginning in 1719 had burgeoned into three separate groups by the late 1760's: one in the North End, one in the South End, and one in the "Middle part of town."[72] Each of these clubs had a membership many times the size of the original organization. The North End caucus, for example, consisted of sixty members and contained for the first time several tradesmen, including the silversmith Paul Revere. According to a contemporary, the Reverend John Eliot, "It answered a good purpose to get such a number of mechanicks together; and though a number of whigs of the first character in the town were present, they always had a mechanick for moderator, generally one who could carry many votes by his influence."[73]

Records from the meetings of this body indicate that the nomination process in Boston in the early 1770's consisted not only of selection by the North Enders but also of the concurrence of the other two caucus clubs in town. A week before the election of representatives in May, 1772, they adopted the following resolutions:

> Voted—That this body will use their influence that Thomas
>   Cushing, Samuel Adams, John Hancock and William
>   Phillips, be Representatives for the year ensuing.
> Voted—That Gibbons Sharp, N. Barber, and John Lowell, be
>   a Committee to write votes and distribute them, for these
>   gentlemen.
> Voted—That N. Barber, Dr. T. Young, and Thomas Hitchborn,
>   be a Committee to wait upon the South End Caucus, and
>   let them know what we have done, and that we shall be glad
>   of their concurrence with us in the same choice.
> Voted—That Messrs Campbell and J. Ballard be joined with the
>   Committee aforesaid, wait upon the Caucus in the Middle
>   part of town, for the same purpose, and with their Commit-
>   tee, to agree upon a Moderator for the meeting.[74]

The expansion of the nomination process did not, however, spread immediately to all areas. In Philadelphia, the caucus remained much the way it had been in previous years—run by a small group of faction leaders who controlled the selection of all officials. Possibly aware of the changes that had been taking place elsewhere, the mechanics and small tradesmen of the city started denouncing those in high places who blocked their participation in the choosing of candidates. "It had been customary," protested one artisan,

> for a certain Company of leading men to nominate Persons,
> and settle the Ticket, for Assembly-men, Commissioners, As-
> sessors, etc., without ever permitting the affirmative or negative
> Voice of a Mechanic to interfere, and when they have conclud-
> ed, expect the Tradesmen will give a sanction thereto by pass-
> ing the Ticket.[75]

He called upon his fellow tradesmen to unite in support of one or two workingmen candidates for the Assembly. This plan apparently met with some success as Joseph Parker, a tailor, was placed on the ticket by the faction led by John Dickinson.[76] Moreover, by the year of independence, artisans and shopkeepers had become a powerful force in nominating candidates for other offices, especially for the new committees created in the revolutionary crisis.[77]

By the pre-Revolutionary era, the democratization of society and politics and the greater interest in government stimulated by the new British measures had led to a broadening of the nomination process. Simple methods of selection involving a few individuals were being replaced by increasingly complex ones encompassing large groups. Mass meetings and expanded caucuses were beginning to provide wide-scale popular sanction to the choice of candidates.

5

Electioneering

★★★★★★★★★★★★★★

Once a man was nominated for office, he faced the challenge of getting elected. In some places this posed no great difficulty as competition was either limited or nonexistent. A candidate could often succeed merely on the basis of his family name and reputation or just by the fact that he was the only person running. But in areas in which elections were keenly contested, much effort was required to obtain victory. Ideally a provincial office seeker was not supposed to appeal actively for public support.[1] However, the realities of political life soon compelled many to forego this passive stance. Even the most prominent gentlemen found it necessary at times to engage in a fierce struggle with one or more opponents in his attempt to win over the majority of the people.

The candidates' quest for votes during the provincial era followed a different pattern from the one we are familiar with today. Political campaigns in early America were generally quite brief. Rarely did the whole race extend for more than a week or two, and sometimes it lasted no longer than the morning of election day itself. Thus, the principals had to devise plans to fit a relatively short time span. Moreover, the actual techniques utilized in that period were in many cases distinctive ones suited especially to the primitive forms of transportation and communication existing then. Yet the differences between the campaign practices of the two epochs should not be overemphasized. If technological advances have added new dimensions to the conduct of electioneering, the politician then, as now, had to secure the allegiance of the voters and inspire them to go to the polls. The methods used in accomplishing this feat two hundred years ago resembled present ones in many ways.[2]

In most cases, elections in provincial America took place on a more modest scale than contests in later times. There were no intercolonial parties, and within each colony political development had not reached the point where highly organized permanent groups had been created. As a result, the vast majority of campaigns tended to be local in nature, confined basically to a single voting district. Electioneering involved a small operation as candidates usually relied upon their own personal resources or those of trusted friends for support. Even in the provinces in which many of the representatives voted along the same lines inside the Assembly, the members from each constituency commonly carried out their own reelection bids and did not depend upon outside help.

But in a few colonies campaigns did develop beyond the local level. In New York, Pennsylvania, Maryland, and Rhode Island, as relatively stable factions emerged from time to time, widespread and complex electioneering activities did occur with some frequency. Here political leaders such as James DeLancey of New York, William Allen of Pennsylvania, Stephen Bordley of Maryland, and Stephen Hopkins of Rhode Island attempted on several occasions to organize operations on a broad basis. Although the exertions of these party managers did not always extend to all parts of their respective provinces and often focused upon only a few key areas, many aspects of their approach were surely in the direction of modern-style campaigning.[3]

When an election was announced, these men would, as part of their course of action, arrange entire tickets well in advance of the balloting, place candidates in those contests where they could bring the greatest advantage, provide backers with money to get out the vote, and send letters to friends and relatives to request their assistance. A good example of the last-mentioned tactic can be seen during the court-country struggle in Maryland in 1745. Stephen Bordley of Annapolis wrote to his brother Thomas in Kent County asking his help in promoting the candidacy of Matthias Harris, a country party stalwart:

> I am informed you have always a large share in the Elections
> for your County, and as particularly at this time, while the
> Court party are making so violent a push every where to Carry
> the Elections agreeable to themselves. . . . I wish you would
> make use of your best Interest to get Mat Harris into the
> House. . . . I am thoroughly satisfied of his hearty disposi-
> tion to Serve the Country to the utmost of his power, and
> of his ability to do more to that end, than any man from
> your County. . . .[4]

To his brother John Bordley of Kent, he repeated his pleas for the neces-
sity of aiding Harris and also urged him to do everything possible to thwart
the designs of court candidates in his vicinity, James Calder, John Gresham,
and Colonel Thomas Colville:

> I must now begg that you will not only give him your own
> but likewise promise him all the Interest in your power, &
> particularly recommend him to T.B.'s Interest. . . . And for
> Godsake and that of your Country, endeavor by all means
> not only to keep out J.C. for your County but likewise J.G.
> —and if possible T.C. for Cecil. . . .[5]

At times, emissaries or the factional leaders themselves traveled to
outlying areas to supervise local machinery, and occasionally, to make
direct appeals to the voters. During the New York campaign of 1750,
James DeLancey went into the country "personally to influence the
People in their elections," according to Governor Clinton. In Westchester,
moreover, "He had his two Bullies, [brothers] Peter and Oliver to fright-
en those, that his artful Condesention & dissimulation could not persuade
to vote against their Conscience."[6] Amid the great partisan battle in Pennsylvania in 1764, the proprietary agent, Samuel Purviance, an associate of
William Allen, journeyed first from Philadelphia to Chester, "and there
concerted some measures for dividing the Quaker interest in that county."
Then he went on to Bucks County, ostensibly for the same reason, holding a number of meetings with local supporters in order to encourage an
all-out effort for his side.[7] Throughout the Ward-Hopkins controversy in
Rhode Island, Moses Brown, a member of the famous Providence merchant
family, would usually visit several communities to coordinate plans for the
Hopkins group. He would travel initially to Newport to talk over strategy
with Deputy Governor candidate Joseph Wanton and then go on to politically divided towns such as Gloucester to distribute money to the party
faithful and discuss the most effective ways of capturing additional votes.[8]
Besides noted factional leaders, certain royal governors sometimes
played a major role in organizing campaigns. This occurred most frequently in New York, New Hampshire, and early eighteenth-century Virginia.
Crown-appointed executives such as Alexander Spotswood, Robert Hunter, Jonathan Belcher, and Benning Wentworth would engage in various
maneuvers, some plainly deceitful, in order to enlarge the number of
court members in the Assembly. One of the favorite mechanisms of these

officials was to distribute large amounts of patronage just before the balloting to secure the loyalty of those who were wavering. As Spotswood approached the Virginia contest in 1718, "Commissions flew about to every fellow that could make two or three votes," declared one observer. "He gave the power to his friends to make discreet use of [them]. And indeed never fouler play was used by men, than at most of our elections."[9]

Another device some governors used was to create new voting districts in distant areas where sympathy for their policies had been ascertained previously. Robert Hunter effectively resorted to such methods to obtain a majority in the New York Assembly in the year 1713. Yet perhaps the most successful practitioner of this art was Benning Wentworth of New Hampshire. During the 1740's, when Wentworth was having difficulty gaining the acceptance of his legislative proposals, he called for new elections and issued writs to several frontier townships that had not been represented before. Although the opposition leaders in the House refused to seat some of the new delegates, enough of his partisans were admitted to bring about approval of his program.[10]

Making personal appearances and capitalizing upon the dignity and grandeur of the office of governor was not yet common in the provincial period. Nonetheless, such actions were certainly not unknown. Jonathan Belcher, for instance, planned a tour around a number of New Hampshire communities just prior to polling time in 1734. "As I have not seen Kingston, Exeter, or Streatham, I will make my route that way," he told his secretary, Richard Waldron, "and your thought is well of having a grand appearance. Who knows but that & passing thro' those towns may give some turn to the elections? I wou'd to be sure, have a full troop to meet me."[11] Clearly, a shrewd governor could employ a wide variety of moves in his quest to maintain his regime's strength and influence.

As time passed, however, the central role of the chief executive in provincial elections tended to diminish. Assemblies became larger and larger, making them more difficult to control, especially as patronage and the possibility of establishing new districts had their limitations. Moreover, the lower houses, as they expanded in power, increasingly looked upon electioneering by Crown officials as outside interference in local matters. Fearing reprisals, George Clinton of New York, who had openly intervened in earlier campaigns, tried to disguise his participation in the election of 1748 since "twould look as if the Governour interested himself too much in the Choice of Members."[12] When Arthur Dobbs of North

Carolina injected himself into the fray in 1760 he was sharply criticized
by House leaders for attempting to "modell the Assembly for his own
particular Purposes."[13] Consequently, the royal governors, although undoubtedly concerned about the outcome of a provincial contest—perhaps
to a greater extent than anyone in their domain—found it more and more
expedient to remain on the sidelines during the event. To be sure, these
men still operated behind the scenes to some degree, yet for the most
part they gradually left the matter of getting elected to the candidates
themselves.[14]

Individuals who were closely identified with a particular faction might
campaign on the basis of an issue or on their group's past performance,
but the great majority of office seekers who had no such connections did
not run on a platform or make major promises. Most men simply stood
upon their family name or their own position and achievements within
the community. Because competition in most areas was seldom based on
issues, it would have been quite unusual to hear a provincial politician
committed to any program. Silence on public matters also reflected the
attitude of certain legislative bodies such as the House of Burgesses in
Virginia, which strongly frowned upon campaign commitments because
it did not wish to be bound to the views of any individual member.[15]
Of course, a few persons ignored this tradition and made solemn pledges
to their constituents about what they proposed to accomplish. Some of
these statements were honest and pragmatic; others were exaggerated and
totally unrealistic. Adam Stephens, who opposed George Washington in
1761, attempted to win votes by "Introducing various Commercial Schemes,
which," said one bystander, "are to diffuse Gold and opulency thro' Frederick and prove a sovereign remedy against poverty."[16] On the more practical side, James Littlepage of Hanover County insisted that he would work
for the repeal of the tobacco inspection law, which he regarded as unfair.
"My plan," he stated, "is to serve the people that's now injured by the
damn inspecting law. . . . You may depend I have interest enough to have
that taken off, and I want to have the inspectors chosen every year by
the freeholders of the county."[17] In their respective races, Littlepage won
and Stephens lost, though it is by no means certain that their public pro-
nouncements had any meaningful effect upon the outcome.

The most fundamental method of campaigning during the provincial
period was direct canvassing and handshaking. At that time, probably
more so than today, many people felt it extremely important to be per-

sonally acquainted with the men for whom they were voting. With election districts far less populous, representation had a much more personal meaning then. Therefore, persons running for office, especially if they were not well known, strived to meet individually with members of the electorate. When a close contest was expected, they often traveled far and wide to greet the prospective voters. William Parsons of Northampton County, Pennsylvania, for example, noted that his opponent in 1752, James Burnside, was "going from place to place, beating his breast," in order to be chosen.[18]

Failure to meet the electorate could sometimes place the political career of even the most prominent persons in jeopardy. Colonel Landon Carter, a member of one of Virginia's wealthiest families, explained that he had in one instance been "turned out" of the House of Burgesses because "I did not familiarize myself among the People." On the other hand, Carter recalled a subsequent occasion of his "son's going amongst them and Carrying his Election." To be sure, fraternizing with the voters was not always a guarantee of victory. Young Robert Wormley Carter was defeated in Richmond County in 1776, even though he had "kissed the arses of the people, and very servilely accommodated himself to others."[19] Yet notwithstanding the younger Carter's temporary downfall, visiting with the electors would almost always prove beneficial to the candidate.

There were usually several occasions where an enterprising office seeker could meet with larger numbers of prospective voters at a single time. A militia training was one of the best because it traditionally brought out most men in the district. At the conclusion, refreshments would often be served by the candidate and some pleasantries exchanged. The monthly meeting of the county court also provided an opportunity to see a great many freeholders. On court day, people would gather from throughout the county to watch the proceedings, catch up on the latest news, and have a few drinks with friends. They would, in this setting, generally be available for a handshake or personal chat. Another excellent chance for greeting the electorate was at Sunday church services. In Virginia, some would-be burgesses planned to visit as many churches within their county, both Anglican and Dissenting, as circumstances would allow. To those houses of worship they were unable to reach, they would sometimes send a letter espousing their candidacy to be read and passed around to the individuals in attendance.[20]

One of the most important places for campaigning, particularly in northern towns and cities, was the inn or tavern, which served as a central spot for men to gather for business and leisure purposes. Factional leaders in Boston, New York, and Philadelphia often got together in their favorite tavern for strategy sessions, and in every town the public house offered the candidate a ready-made audience for his views. Oliver DeLancey of New York, seeking support for his brother's cause in the Ulster County community of Esopus, "brought up all the songs & faction papers with him [and] read them in the tavern."[21] John Adams believed that "an artful man has little else to do but secure the favor of taverners, in order to secure the suffrages of the rabble that attend these houses, which in many towns . . . makes a large, perhaps the biggest number of voters."[22]

Urban candidates and their supporters canvassed from door to door to procure votes during crucial contests. In Philadelphia, John Smith, a member of the Quaker faction, spent election day in 1750 walking about the city "spreading ticketts" for Isaac Griffitts, who was seeking the post of sheriff.[23] On the other hand, Andrew Belcher of Milton, Massachusetts, son of the former governor, found going to each man's home less effective than simply stopping to talk with people in the street. Thanking his friend, Edmund Quincy, for recommending this mode of campaigning to him, he said, "I much approve your method of accidently *(on purpose)* speaking to the good Miltonics as they come within your reach, which I am now convinced would have a better effect than a labored, designed application to them at their houses."[24]

Speeches, rallies, and other types of open-air meetings were not very common in the provincial period. Such events, however, did happen on occasion prior to an important election. Broadsides from the late 1760's in New York City called for large gatherings to take place in the "Fields," while a writer in Annapolis in 1773 mentions "public orations" having occurred, as well as "parading with drums." In one notable instance during the 1764 campaign in the Maryland capital, Samuel Chase, who became a famous Revolutionary figure, organized a procession of artisans to march around the town in his behalf. As described by the young artist, Charles Willson Peale, "banners were displayed to designate the freedom of tradesmen, and parades of this nature were made through all the streets with the friends of Chase at the head of them."[25]

Canvassing, even when supplemented by outdoor gatherings, was not always sufficient for victory. For additional support, some candidates eagerly sought the backing of the most prominent citizens in their district, who could influence many votes. In fact, in certain areas such as Albany, New York, the favor of someone like Sir William Johnson, the celebrated Indian agent, could spell the difference between success and failure. In 1761, Jacob Ten Eyck and Volkert Douw, running for reelection in Albany, pleaded with Sir William to aid their cause. "If it's agreeable to you," they wrote, "we beg your Interest in wch you'l very much oblige us."[26] At a subsequent juncture, another Albany resident, John Duncan, informed Johnson that he would be willing to stand for election, "provided you approve and will favor me with your Interest . . . otherwise I will think no more of it."[27]

Besides prominent gentlemen, members of the local clergy could often exert enormous power over the choices made at election time. As people in the eighteenth century placed a great deal of trust in the advice of their ministers, the latter could change the outcome of an apparently one-sided contest. In Edgecombe County, North Carolina, during the administration of Governor Dobbs, Francis Corbin, a friend of Dobbs, seemed assured of winning a seat in the lower house. At the outset, Corbin had obtained all "the influence of the Governors Faction in these parts and had got the Huzzah on his side." But before the balloting took place, Reverend James Moir intervened, publicly denouncing Corbin as a corrupt official, turning his almost certain victory into crushing defeat. Afterwards Moir exclaimed, "I painted the scoundrel in his proper colors and overset his election."[28]

Ministerial influence upon voters was probably most effective in Connecticut, where clerical authority was strongest in all aspects of life. In addition to the usual forms of persuasion, clergymen would sometimes use their talents in a subtle manner at the election meeting itself. They would quote a passage in the Bible glorifying an individual who just happened to have the same name as the candidate that they favored. According to Reverend Samuel Peters of Hebron:

> All the voters in a township convene in the town meeting house. One of the ministers, after prayers, preaches from some such text as, "Jabez was more honourable than his brethren" . . . So Jabez is elected; and the meeting is concluded with a prayer of thanks to the Lord God of Israel for turning the hearts of his people against the enemies of Zion, and for uniting them in Jabez, the man after his own heart.[29]

Once in a while, candidates who had entered an electoral race were too busy to canvass for themselves, and would have to rely primarily on personal friends and relatives to carry on the campaign for them. For instance, George Washington was so completely absorbed in fighting the Indians on the Virginia frontier during the summer of 1758 that he could not even put in an appearance at the election in Frederick County where he had agreed to stand. The young colonel was forced to depend almost entirely upon his associates, James Wood, Gabriel Jones, and John Kirkpatrick, who managed to gather a majority of the voters for him. Again in 1761, much of the work for Washington's reelection was undertaken by others. Captain Robert Stewart kept close watch on George's chief opponent, Adam Stephens, while two other friends, Craik Woodrow and Jacob Hight, solicited votes on excursions to the "lower part of the County."[30]

Some of the most enthusiastic campaigners in early America were women. Although they could not vote or hold office, they sometimes took an active part in getting out the vote for others. In Georgia, prior to the balloting in 1768, two women, Mrs. Heriot Cooke and Elizabeth Mossman, drove around in a carriage soliciting votes for their favorite, Sir Patrick Houstoun. They insisted that if the people did not come out for Houstoun, they would be compelled to accept a higher tax for the importation of Negroes and would be liable to pay the Governor's salary plus additional money for defense against the Indians.[31] Women were especially influential in Lancaster County, Pennsylvania, judging by their efforts on at least two occasions. During the fall of 1732, when Andrew Galbraith of Donegal was vying for a seat in the Assembly, his wife "mounted her favorite mare, Nelly; a spur, she fastened to her ancle, and away she went, her red cloak flowing in the wind, to scour the country for Andrew." Ten years afterward, Susannah Wright, who later became famous as the first woman in Pennsylvania to make a pair of silk stockings, played an even bigger role in the county's election. As a member of the opposition sadly noted:

> Could any one believe that Susy cou'd act so unbecoming and
> unfemale a part as to be employ'd in copying such infamous
> stuff [campaign literature, which was circulated among the
> Presbyterian congregations of the county] and to take her
> stand as she did at Lancasr in an Upper Room in a publick
> House and to have a Ladder erected to the window and there
> distribute Lies and Tickets all day of the eleccion?[32]

While some individuals approached campaigning with great zest, others, especially within the various court or proprietary factions, found it rather distasteful. In 1756, Edward Shippen of Pennsylvania, when asked by his supporters to participate personally, replied: "It is a very disagreeable task to appear to solicit for one's self," but added, "if it is necessary I must submit."[33] Governor Horatio Sharpe of Maryland complained that the experience of going out among the people and asking for votes proved so unpleasant to his friends that it was almost impossible to find any loyal Assemblymen. "Few Gentlemen," he said, "will submit so frequently to the inconveniences that such a canvass for Seats in that House must necessarily subject themselves to."[34] Of course, if a man was overwhelmingly popular as was Isaac Norris, the long-time leader of the Quaker party in Pennsylvania, he did not have to go through the ordeal of active campaigning. Norris always was proud of the fact that he "had never to ask a Vote" to get into the House. Most office seekers were not so fortunate, however, and not only had to ask but sometimes beg for votes.[35]

In addition to meeting, shaking hands, and talking with the people, one of the most commonly accepted forms of campaigning was treating the electorate to food and drink. Contemporaries often referred to this practice as "swilling the planters with bumbo." In the southern and middle colonies, especially Virginia, Maryland, Pennsylvania, and New York, it was customary for the candidates to provide refreshments for the voters either before or after the balloting. Although laws in several provinces prohibited the offering of "Meat, Drink, Monies, or otherwise" to influence persons at the polls, these statutes were sometimes interpreted loosely or else not strictly enforced. Invariably those seeking office managed to distribute large quantities of liquor and other items to the electors. George Washington was not unusual in spending thirty-nine pounds for "treats" on the occasion of his first election in 1758. This included payment for 160 gallons of various beverages, an average of a quart and a half per person.[36]

The types of offerings varied according to geographic section. Rum punch and wine were the most popular in the South; cider and beer were the favorites farther north. A writer in one Pennsylvania newspaper claimed that during the Assembly contest in 1728, some 4,500 gallons of common Beer" were consumed in the city of Philadelphia alone. Along with the brew, southern gentlemen often set up picnic tables for the prospective voters, where cakes and cookies would be laid out. Some planters also provided slices of barbecued beef or roast pig. After a major victory, a prominent Virginian might even have a supper and ball with music and dancing on the night of his election. Nicholas Cresswell, a visiting Englishman, attending one such event in 1774, noted that coffee and chocolate were served but no tea. "This Herb is in disgrace among them at present," he concluded, evidently referring to the situation following the Boston Tea Party.[37]

By southern standards, treating in the middle colonies might have seemed less lavish. However, candidates in this area could be just as expansive and generous. Prior to an election in Dutchess County, New York, the wealthy Henry Beekman stocked his tables with beef, pork, and bacon, along with a hundred loaves of bread and six barrels of cider. One of the most extravagant displays ever recorded took place in South Amboy, New Jersey. After the House contest in 1772, the two successful candidates went to the local tavern with their supporters and ran up a bill for 37 mugs of beer, 38 jills of rum, 47 bowls of punch, 141 bowls of sangarie, 37 bottles of wine, 35 bowls of toddy, 89 dinners, plus 33 quarts of oats for the people's horses.[38]

Treating, like other forms of electioneering, was far less prevalent in New England. A writer in the *Connecticut Courant* denied that any tavern or alehouse had ever been open on election day in his colony. Providing liquor for the voters, he stated, was completely unknown. In some instances, admittedly, the newly elected deputies had called for a bowl of punch to drink with the constables after the ballots had been counted, but even this, he said, had not been countenanced for long since it had the "Air of Bribery." Another Connecticut inhabitant agreed that giving a "dinner" or a "glass of cider" to a voter was a form of bribery. And in this province, he mused, "bribery is the next greatest crime to a breach of the Sabbath."[39]

Treating in Massachusetts may have occurred a bit more frequently than in Connecticut, especially toward the end of the provincial period. But there, too, it was generally frowned upon. The prevailing attitude in the Bay Colony may be seen in the advice of one commentator who warned: "he that will *bid high*, and *give the most Drink to-day*, may chance to be a person that will sell their *Religion*, and *Liberties*, and *Fortunes* to-Morrow."[40] The always outspoken John Adams seconded this position. In an essay entitled "A Dissertation Upon Seekers," he condemned those would-be Assemblymen who were "very liberal with their drams of Brandy, and lumps of Sugar, and of their Punch, &c. on May meeting days." "These," he said, "are commonly Persons, who have some further Views and Designs. These Largesses aim at something further than your Votes." Once elected, he added, "they will be hired and sell their Votes, as you sold yours to them."[41] Only in neighboring Rhode Island were there few qualms about treating; and the Ward and Hopkins factions each gave generous amounts of brandy, sugar, punch, and many more items to prospective voters.

Although treating could influence the outcome of a contest, it was not the same as outright bribery. Because people frequently traveled a great distance to reach the polls, they thought it only proper that they be rewarded for their efforts. "The Camps will not move to an Election without being payed for their time," Robert Livingston told Abraham Yates, Jr., when the latter sought a seat in the New York Assembly.[42] In an era of personal politics, many persons probably felt that a treat or a handshake created a bond between them and the prospective officeholder. If a candidate attempted to ignore this custom, he often found himself in great difficulty. At the time of the American Revolution, James Madison, believing "the corrupting influence of spiritous liquors, and other treats," "inconsistent with the purity of moral and republican principles," tried to introduce "a more chaste mode of conducting elections in Virginia." He found, however, that the old habits were too deeply rooted to be suddenly reformed" and was defeated by an opponent who continued to use "all the means of influence familiar to the people."[43]

The distinction between treating as a token of regard and treating as an open bribe was, of course, a difficult one to make. Sometimes the verdict depended upon the whims or political preferences of the officials judging a particular dispute. In order not to bring any charges of bribery against them and to prevent the creation of any animosity, some candidates made it a point to treat all the electors present, not only those who promised them their support. As George Washington wrote to his campaign organizers in Frederick County: "I hope no Exception were taken to any that voted against me but that all were alike treated and all had enough."[44] In many places treating customarily came after, rather than before, the balloting, which reduced the possibility of claims of undue influence. Often it was agreed that the victors should pay the entire bill for the postelection refreshments. Following the contest in Queens County, New York, in June, 1737, it was reported that the two winners, Colonel Isaac Hicks and David Jones, Esquire, "treated the Electors very handsomely."[45]

Inevitably the fine line between friendly treating and outright bribery was sometimes overstepped. Several instances occurred in which the various legislatures took action to curb notorious offenders. This happened most frequently in Maryland where fierce election struggles led to many abuses and eventually caused the colony to take stern measures against them. Following a flagrant incident of bribery in St. Mary's County during 1749, the Committee of Privileges and Elections reported that it had been the practice in several counties of late

> to give uncommon Entertainments, and great Quantities of strong and spirituous Liquors, to the Electors of such counties thereby engaging the Promises of the weaker Sort of the said Electors to vote for them at such Elections. . . . This practice, if not prevented for the future, your Committee humbly conceive, must tend to the destruction of the Health, Strength, Peace and Quiet, and highly contribute to the Corruption of the Morals of his majesty's Loyal Subjects. . . .[46]

Although the proprietor, Lord Baltimore, rejected a subsequent act making treating illegal, the lower house continued to void elections where excessive use of liquor marred the proceedings. Finally, after several years filled with numerous violations, the Assembly decided to crack down. In June, 1768, following an especially controversial episode in Baltimore County, the House unanimously resolved

> that on any petition for treating, this house will not take into consideration, or regard the greatness or smallness of any treat, but will, in all cases, in which any person or persons, . . . directly or indirectly give, present, or allow to any person having a voice or vote in such election, any money, meat, drink, entertainment, or provision, or make any present, gift, reward, or entertainment, . . . whatsoever, in order to be elected, or for being elected, will declare the election of such person void.[47]

When a new election was held in Baltimore the next month, the *Maryland Gazette* reported: "We are informed the . . . Gentlemen carefully avoided treating both before and after the Election to prevent the least colour for a second complaint on that account."[48] During a contest the subsequent year, two of the men chosen from Charles County, Captain Francis Ware and Josias Hawkins, were brought before the House and charged with excessive treating. After a hearing at which several witnesses were heard, the Speaker signified that "their attendance was no longer required," though they were reinstated after another poll was held.[49]

At this time, the practice of treating was coming under widespread criticism, even in Virginia. In 1774, the citizens of Williamsburg presented an address to Peyton Randolph, who was standing for reelection to the House of Burgesses, in which they declared themselves to be

> greatly scandalized at the Practice which has too much prevailed throughout the Country of entertaining the Electors, a Practice which even its Antiquity cannot sanctify; and being desirous of setting a worthy Example to our Fellow Subjects, in general, for abolishing every Appearance of Venality (that only Poison which can infect our happy Constitution) and give the fullest Proof that it is your singular Merit alone you are indebted for the unbought Suffrages of a free People; moved, Sir, by these important Considerations, we earnestly request that you will not think of incurring any Expense or Trouble at the approaching Election of a Citizen, but that you will do us the Honour to partake of an Entertainment which we shall direct to be provided for the Occasion.[50]

Yet regardless of this opposition, treating continued to play a large role in Virginia elections for many years to come. As late as 1795 Thomas Jefferson wrote to James Madison that such "low practices" were still successful in Albemarle County "with the unthinking who merchandize their votes for grog."[51]

Treating costs and other campaign expenses are difficult to determine because of the lack of financial statements. A Virginia planter like George Washington, judging from his account book, spent anywhere from £25 to £40 when a serious contest was expected. About £50 seems to have been the amount estimated by the Livingston faction for the effort in Albany County in 1761, while James DeLancey alone was charged £62 for "victuals" and "drinks" on just one evening prior to the New York City election in 1768. The large-scale, colony-wide campaigns in Rhode Island cost a great deal more. Over £5,000 was provided by Stephen Hopkins's supporters in 1763, and even larger sums were collected in 1765 and 1767. An interesting document from the Brown family papers permits us to observe the manner in which some £2,200 in party contributions were divided for use among the various towns. The greatest shares were allotted to important swing areas such as Coventry and Gloucester, each of which was given £130 or more, whereas Providence, safely in the Hopkins camp, received only £20 (table 3).[52]

Over the course of the eighteenth century, competition for votes in some areas, especially the larger towns and cities, became increasingly severe and, in many eyes, disturbing to internal peace and tranquility. On one occasion, the leaders of the Quaker meeting in Chester, Pennsylvania, complained that "at the last election where moderation should have appeared . . . other fruits were brought forth, and seditious words and practices, insinuations and turbulent behavior." Other commentators frequently described political campaigns as filled with "contention & wrangling" or "animosities & divisions."[53] Inflamed rhetoric, name calling, and even violence became part of the scene at times. As this trend continued, a number of observers began to see such occurrences as endangering the welfare

TABLE 3

Hopkins Faction Campaign Fund Distribution, 1765
(in Rhode Island Currency)

Newport	30	Charlestown	80
Providence	20	West Greenwich	120
Portsmouth	50	Coventry	130
Warwick	50	Exeter	100
Westerly	90	Middletown	80
New Shoreham	50	Tiverton	140
North Kingstown	100	Little Compton	40
South Kingstown	100	Warren	30
East Greenwich	100	Cumberland	50
Jamestown	40	Richmond	80
Smithfield	50	Cranston	60
Scituate	100	Hopkinton	80
Gloucester	150	Johnston	120

of provincial society. By exciting the passions of the entire populace and turning the political arena into a full-fledged battlefield, the whole social order was being threatened with destruction.

Several persons strongly condemned the unrestrained nature of electioneering as deeply divisive and openly questioned the ultimate value of such efforts. One critic, Archibald Kennedy of New York, declared that "elections are carried on with great animosity and at a vast expense, as if our alls were at stake." "What," he asked, "is all this for? Is the public good really the point in view?"[54] John Adams, upon analyzing the impact of fierce election struggles in neighboring Bay Colony towns, concluded that the tempest aroused by campaign controversies could destroy the harmony of a community and undermine the respect for its rulers. After watching several subsequent legal battles develop between competing candidates, he exclaimed: "Such rivals have no friendship for each other. From such rivalries originate contentions, quarrels and suits. What affection can there be between two rival candidates for the confidence of a town?"[55] Expanding upon the theme of disunity, Daniel Dulany of Maryland stated that he had "often lamented that *Electioneering* . . . should be so ruinous to private attachments and good fellowship and should generate such black blood in society as it does." "We frequently see the bonds of nature rudely torn asunder," he added, placing the blame on "bands of Politicians" for having "divided a house against itself, and kindled the inextinguishable flames of hatred and animosity, even in the hearts of brothers."[56]

In part, these statements represented a conservative reaction to the increasing democratization of politics as the vigorous appeal for votes was bringing a wider range of the populace into the political process. But in spite of the criticism, it is doubtful that many candidates were discouraged from continuing in the same manner. Even in New England, where overt competition was generally more limited than in other regions, sharp encounters were on the upswing. In Watertown, Massachusetts, the inhabitants readily admitted to the burning rivalry in their midst. Following the disputed election of 1757, they told the General Court:

> As the town is and for some years past has been divided into
> two parties nearly equal in number and as their contentions
> have been so sharp, we have reason to think but that some
> of each party have done everything in their power to procure

one of their party to represent the town, and it is not so easy
to determine which of the parties have carried these measures
to the greatest lengths. . . .[57]

One outgrowth of the increasing competitiveness of provincial elections was the emergence of the press, particularly newspapers, as a significant electioneering tool. The weekly publications, plus frequent supple-
ments at election time, enabled candidates to reach added numbers of
people who might not otherwise have been touched by a campaign. This
medium achieved its greatest importance in the northern cities of Boston,
Philadelphia, and New York, whose delegations to the legislature were
usually larger and more influential than those of other localities. The urban populations were generally more literate, sophisticated, and attentive
to the printed word than persons elsewhere, providing a ready-made audience for campaign literature. In the southern colonies, since the population was primarily rural and less literate, few papers were published.
Therefore, the press had little impact upon political events below Pennsylvania, with the possible exception of a few spots, such as Charleston,
South Carolina, and Annapolis, Maryland.[58]
Candidates used newspapers chiefly in two ways. First they solicited
votes through direct advertisements. Although not operating on as grand
a scale as present-day office seekers, colonial aspirants would place at
least a few lines in the local weeklies in order to promote their candidacy.
As far as can be determined, the first such instance occurred in March,
1733, in Charleston, when the following item appeared in the *South Carolina Gazette:*

To the several WORTHY ELECTORS of Members of Assembly for the Parish of St. Philip's, Charlestown

GENTLEMEN
Your Votes and Interest are humbly desired for Gabriel Manigault, of *Charlestown,* Merchant, to be your Representative
in Assembly in the Room of Robert Hume, Esq: who is gone
off this Province.

Gabriel Manigault[59]

In February, 1739, a similar statement appeared in a New York City news paper.[60] Five years later, more elaborate notices began to be printed. Whe Mordecai Lloyd and his brother Thomas sought reelection as sheriffs of Philadelphia County in 1744, the former inserted this announcement in the *Pennsylvania Journal:*

> To the Freeholders &c. of the City and County of Philadelphia
>
> Gentlemen,
> Having for several Years been favour'd with your Votes and
> Interest for the Sheriff's Office, I take this publick Method of
> returning you my most hearty Thanks for your past Favours:
> And as I intend again to stand a Candidate with my Brother
> *Thomas* Lloyd for said Office, I request the Continuation of
> your Interest the ensuing Election.[61]

The next week, the Lloyds's chief opponent, Nicholas Scull, adopted the same method of appealing to the voters. The subsequent issue of the *Journal* carried this message:

> To the Freeholders of the City and County of Philadelphia
>
> Gentlemen,
> THO' it has not till this Time been customary to request
> your Votes in Print; yet that Method being now intro-
> duced, I think my self obliged in this publick Manner to
> return to you my hearty Thanks for the Favour I have al-
> ready receiv'd. And to acquaint you that I intend to stand
> a Candidate for the Sheriffs Office, and request your Votes
> and Interest at the next Election. . . .
>
> > Your real Friend,
> > Nicholas Scull[62]

Actually Scull went one step further than the Lloyds by having his letter published not only in English but in German because of the large German-speaking population in the area.

Four years afterward, in 1748, the candidates for the Assembly from New York City voiced in the public prints a more impassioned appeal. Desiring reelection, David Clarkson, Cornelius Van Horne, Henry Cruger, and Paul Richards, country opponents of Governor George Clinton, placed the following in the *New York Evening-Post*:

> If securing your Rights and Privileges from Arbitrary Power be of any Concern to you; if you are satisfied your late Representatives have done their best to secure them against the Greatest Opposition with the utmost hardships, Fatigues and Ill-Treatment, your chusing them again is a reasonable Return.[63]

Hereafter announcements requesting public support appeared before all elections for the lower house in New York City and all contests for sheriff in Philadelphia; during the 1760's the practice started to spread elsewhere.[64] By that time it was becoming evident to individual candidates and factional organizers that the newspaper could play a vital role in a campaign, helping to inform the public about the persons running for office.

A second way in which candidates used newspapers, and perhaps a more effective one, was to submit anonymous articles or essays on important questions. These would generally be published in partisan organs one or two weeks before the polling date, under such titles as "A Letter to the Freeholders," "To the Freemen and Freeholders," or "A Letter from a Gentleman in the City to his Friend in the Country." Sometimes they would be signed with a classical name like "Publius" or a patriotic phrase such as "A Friend of Liberty." Partly because of strict libel laws, many colonial writers refrained from personal attack and simply requested that voters choose an ideal man. Some of them, however, did speak out on crucial issues, such as taxation, Indian policy, or the rights of religious dissenters. Others warned against the selection of certain types of individuals or demanded the ouster of inept incumbent officials. In the latter vain, an opponent of the Quaker faction stated in the *Pennsylvania Gazette*:

> I am of Opinion that the Majority of the Members of the last Assembly, are entirely unworthy [of] your Notice in the next Election. And I believe when you have read their Minutes, and considered their Behavior as I have done, you will be of the same Sentiment. . . .[65]

Perhaps the most unique and effective use of the newspaper in provincial America occurred in the Massachusetts election of May, 1766. Although the Stamp Act had become null and void by this time, many alleged supporters of the measure were still in office. In order to effect a full-scale purge in the House, the leaders of the "popular party" inserted in the *Boston Gazette* and other local papers a list of thirty-two friends of the act, calling for their ouster as enemies of the people. The voters were asked to reject "the old leaven" and "look out for good and honest and free men—men that are unshackled with posts and preferments; men who will not warp, nor be cajoled into any measures that will tend to impoverish and enslave their country."[66] Largely as a result of this maneuver, nineteen of the thirty-two men named were defeated at the polls in the ensuing contest.

In conjunction with newspapers, election broadsides were another weapon employed by urban candidates and their supporters. Hundreds of copies of a single sheet would be printed and distributed to the voters on or shortly before election day. These broadsides were generally reprints of significant articles or shortened versions of them. Sometimes the material they contained was entirely original, at least in style. The statements made in them were usually to the point, though they could be rather demagogic. During the New York election of 1768, several broadsides were issued sharply attacking certain members of the legal profession seeking office. One of the most devastating exclaimed:

> [It] would be more gross and dangerous to choose Lawyers
> than other Men, in Proportion as they have more Cunning,
> Ability and Temptation to injure us, than other Men have.
> The more eminent their Abilities are, the more ought we to
> dread and avoid them, for we may be assured, that all those
> Abilities will be exerted against us, if our Folly should give
> them an Opportunity.[67]

Another was even more direct. "The freeholders and freemen," it said, "will find: 1st, that the good people are supported by trade and merchant 2nd, that the lawyers are supported by the people."[68] How effective these broadsides were is difficult to estimate, though it should be mentioned that John Morin Scott, the man against whom the above items were primarily aimed, was soundly defeated. The same result, however, was not achieved in Hartford, Connecticut, in 1766, where, despite the use of broadsides against him, Governor Thomas Fitch obtained a majority of the votes in that town. As one observer reported to Fitch backer, Jared Ingersoll: "Your New Haven plain facts [a reprint of an article in the *Connecticut Gazette*] was handed about yesterday, but did not prevent our freemen from giving Governour F——h Three Hundred Votes."[69]

Before major elections there sometimes appeared more elaborate discourses on political subjects in the form of pamphlets. In a few instances these tracts were expanded versions of newspaper articles and carried the same title, but in most cases they were purely original works. Pamphlets were frequently general in nature, covering a wide range of matters relevant to the election; sometimes they were narrowly specific and dealt solely with one issue. Like newspapers, pamphlets were primarily utilized in northern urban areas, although a considerable number originated in the southern colonies, especially in North Carolina, where the Regulator controversy gave rise to a large outpouring of these items in the late 1760's.[70]

Many of the political pamphlets were written by lawyers or clergymen and displayed a profound knowledge of history, philosophy, and other branches of learning. They often included references and analogies to past world events or extensive quotes from the Bible and various classical writings. Striking allusions to cataclysmic episodes in biblical times were used to warn voters of future dangers to the society if no steps were taken to mend its ways. Reverend John Barnard of Boston, in his election sermon printed in 1734, inserted the following, "O remember the awful commination of God to his people of old: How is the faithful city become an harlot! it was full of judgment; righteousness lodged in it; but now . . . " (Isa. 1.21).[71]

One of the biggest series of election pamphlets came during the various controversies in Massachusetts regarding the use of paper money. For more than half a century, pamphleteers engaged in intermittent warfare on this issue. The leading advocate of paper currency, the merchant John Colman, continuously argued that only by rejecting hard-money supporters at the polls would the inhabitants be able to extricate themselves from their financial difficulties. In one of his most famous works, *The Distressed State of the Town of Boston* (1720), Colman declared:

> I hope our good Friends in the Country will consider our
> miserable circumstances, & send such Men to Represent

> them next *May*, as may be Spirited for our Relief, not
> Sheriffs and Lawyers, who are the only Men who are bene-
> fited by the straights of their Neighbors, else I fear Ruin
> and Destruction will come upon us. . . .[72]

The number of political pamphlets showed a marked increase in the
middle decades of the eighteenth century. Whereas only a handful of
such items appeared in earlier years, more than a hundred different works
were printed in Boston, New York, and Philadelphia alone in the period
from 1725 to 1734. Though this figure tapered off for a time, it eventually rose again in the 1760's to a point where New York and Philadelphia
were each publishing as many as forty pamphlets in a single year. The
greatest outpouring came in the Philadelphia election of 1764 amid the
controversy over making Pennsylvania into a royal province and in the
New York City elections of 1768 and 1769 as a product of the struggle
between the Livingstons and the DeLanceys.[73]

Besides the expanding use of the printed word, some office seekers,
especially during crucial campaigns, would stoop to rather unsavory methods to gain additional backing. One of the most common of these was to
make temporary freeholds, thus creating qualified voters out of unqualified ones. A candidate needing a few extra votes would convey land to
a number of landless males just in time for the balloting and then regain
title shortly afterward. An inhabitant of Windham, New Hampshire, declared after a disputed local contest in 1768 that some of the voters "had
Got Deeds of Small Bitts of Land the night before the Election."[74] This
practice of making instant freeholds or so-called fagot votes had been
fairly typical in England and was utilized in several colonies from Virginia northward. It was most frequently employed in borough elections
where only the household requirement was necessary for enfranchise-
ment. A house deed could be more readily transferred about without
question than one involving a large parcel of land.

In rural areas, some cunning politicians tried to take advantage of the
people's isolation and their lack of familiarity with the latest news of public events. They would travel through the countryside, circulating tales
of their alleged accomplishments or creating fears of impending disasters.
One of the foremost practitioners of this technique was James DeLancey
of New York, of whom it was said: "he has in every County his Emissaries . . . sounding out his praise by his pretended Endeavors, for the Liberti

and Properties of the People; which he says, must be in danger of being swallowed up by *Hungry* Dogs."[75] In Pennsylvania, the country Quakers sometimes operated in a similar fashion among the German population. As Proprietary leader William Allen told Thomas Penn: "they had the address, or I might say the Craft, to delude the Dutch by false storys, so that they . . . were induced to oppose our friends, and carried the elections against them. They were made to believe that, if they changed the Assembly, the [form of] Government would be changed."[76]

Another trick some candidates used was to spread a rumor that their opponent was withdrawing from the race. The lack of rapid communication made it difficult to overcome such a charge. For example, James Littlepage of Hanover County, Virginia, wrote to several freeholders in 1763 informing them that his rival, Nathaniel Dandridge, had "declined serving" and asking that they support him instead. As a result of this, Dandridge lost the election. Although he formally protested against such a maneuver, his petition was rejected by the House of Burgesses.[77] Even in New York City rumors of withdrawal were difficult to extinguish. In 1761, the DeLancey faction used this ploy against the lawyer, John Morin Scott. Scott acted immediately to discredit the story by publishing a sharp denial in the local newspapers, a means less readily available to Dandridge in Virginia. "A Report," Scott stated,

> having been industriously propagated, That I had altered my
> Resolution proposing myself as a Candidate at the ensuing
> Election of REPRESENTATIVES, I thought it best, in this
> Manner, to inform the Publick, That I am still determined
> to serve the City in that Office, in Case they shall think
> proper to elect me to it.[78]

Despite the affirmation of his candidacy, Scott was defeated in his bid for an Assembly seat. To be sure, further factors may have been responsible for the losses by both men, but these rumors undoubtedly contributed to the outcome.

Other devious tactics were employed at times by crafty candidates. In certain colonies, especially where the community supported its representatives out of local funds, some men tried to get elected by declaring that, if chosen, they would gladly serve without pay. To poor, heavily taxed farmers not overly concerned with who their deputies were, these seemingly generous offers were readily welcomed. A number of provinces outlawed this practice as unfair and deceptive, but in Massachusetts and New York no such steps were taken, and men regularly volunteered to serve for no pay. It became fashionable in several Bay Colony towns for an office seeker to announce that he would donate his stipend to some charitable cause or give the money toward rebuilding a tottering bridge. Some individuals warned against such displays of benevolence, claiming that persons making these gestures probably had ulterior motives for their actions. As a writer in the *Boston Evening-Post* declared:

> Let us remember, that according to a vulgar proverb, *Every man who puts water into the pump to fetch it, intends to pump it out with advantage.* Such men are therefore to be *Shrewdly suspected* that they have some *lucrative post* in view; or, that they are concern'd in jockeying our unimprov'd and unappropriated lands.[79]

Candidates in major urban areas used several additional schemes in order to obtain popular support. Royall Tyler, for example, head of the Boston delegation to the Massachusetts Assembly around 1760, fraternized with various craftsmen and called upon them to do house repairs just prior to the balloting. He hoped that the increased business and friendship would be returned in the form of votes. As he told young James Otis, who was about to embark upon his career in politics:

> Two or three weeks before an election comes on, I send to the cooper and get all my casks put in order: I say nothing about the number of hoops. I send to the mason and I have some job done to the hearths or the chimneys: I have the carpenter to make some repairs in the roof or the wood house: I often go down to the ship yards about eleven o'clock, when they break off to take their drink, and enter into conversation with them. They all vote for me.[80]

An example of vote-getting procedures much less upright in nature occurred in the famous New York City election of 1768. John Morin Scott charged that his opponent, merchant James Jauncey, had given loans to several individuals, had donated large amounts of money to various chari-

ties, and had also promised to pay freeholders for their time lost in traveling to the polls in order to win their support. Jauncey denied most of the
allegations against him and countered with a number of his own. He claimed
that Scott had advanced money to certain persons in order that they
could become freemen, hence eligible to vote for him. Moreover, he insisted that Scott had contributed heavily to the carpenters' relief fund and
had even offered one man a canoe in return for his vote.[81]

Only in Rhode Island, however, did outright bribery seem to be fully
countenanced and commonly practiced. Supporters of both the Ward
and Hopkins factions in the 1760's openly provided money to purchase
votes. In 1765, one of Ward's agents was dispatched northward from Newport with a bundle of cash which was considered "very handy" for "friends
in Gloucester, Scituate &c."[82] Two years later, Hopkins' chief backers
in Providence delivered a hundred pounds to Sheriff Beriah Brown of
North Kingstown, which was to be used to "obtain both Deputies and a
Considerable Majority in the Proxies in Favr of Mr Hopkins."[83] They also
sent an emissary to West Greenwich "with the mony allotted for that
Town who is to Stay their till [the] town meeting is over, and to take a
Room to him self in order for pay[in]g off all those who may be agreed
with by our Friends."[84] At times some Rhode Islanders were paid by
one of the factions not to vote, especially if the individuals were known
to be aligned with the opposition. The Reverend Ezra Stiles claimed that
on one occasion only two-thirds of the eligible voters cast their ballots
in Newport—"one third lie still, silenced by Connexions."[85] The reputation of Rhode Island's style of electioneering was such that the famous
military hero of the French and Indian War, Robert Rogers, wrote of
the colony's politics in his *Concise Account of North America:*

> Generally he that distributes the most cash, and gives the
> best entertainments, let him be merchant, farmer, tradesman,
> or what he will, is the man who obtains a majority of votes,
> which fixes him in the chair (death excepted) for that year.
> These election expenses run high, as each candidate endeavors
> to excel his competitor.[86]

There were various artful ways in which persons could influence the
final results by means of the balloting process itself. One technique several campaigners used was to make certain that their supporters voted early.

By proceeding in this manner, a large lead could be created, perhaps producing a landslide effect and swaying a number of fence-sitters. When he ran together with George Mercer for seats in the House of Burgesses in 1761, George Washington told an associate: "could Mercer's Friends and mine be hurried in at the first of the Poll it might be an advantage."[87] Evidently, this advice was followed, for on election day fifteen of the first twenty voters were Washington's and Mercer's men, building up a margin that was difficult for the opposition to overcome. It was also beneficial to have the eminent gentlemen in one's county polling at the outset in order to given an impetus to later electors. In 1758, Washington was able to have Thomas, Lord Fairfax, and other leading figures cast the initial votes, which helped establish a pattern for the remainder of the contest.[88]

Another related stratagem was sometimes pursued where more than one seat was being contested. Promoters interested in ensuring the choice of their favorites attempted to convince electors to vote for fewer than the requisite number of places. This practice, though illegal in Pennsylvania, was frequently employed in Virginia and New York. Many voters in New York City consistently named just two or three men instead of the usual four.[89] This design reached its highest development in Connecticut in the late 1760's when New Light elements east of the Connecticut River were invariably able to elect their sympathizers as assistants. The process was fully spelled out by a gentleman in New London to his friend in New Haven, which was west of the river:

> You all think yourselves bound in Duty to vote for twelve
> Persons, out of the Twenty in the Nomination; whereas we
> vote only for those Persons we fully approve, let the Number
> be 6, 8, or 10; but more especially, at a Time of any general
> Strife; and indeed, this alone gives us the Advantage, and Pro-
> duces so many more Votes for the Assistants on this Side of
> the River; and until you come into this Plan, your Endeavors
> will be Fruitless besure, in this present Case; for if One of our
> Assistants has not a Majority of Votes on the East Side of
> the River, when your Votes come to be thrown into the Scale,
> it raises them above yours, who are the fullest voted for with
> you.[90]

Because the polls remained open in some colonies for several days, supporters of certain candidates would sometimes engage in the practice of "vote hunting," combing the town and countryside for those who had not yet cast their ballots. Often these extra few votes would make the difference between victory and defeat. During the Albany County election of February, 1752, Henrick Frey, an emissary of Sir William Johnson, wrote to his chief:

> This is to inform you that I Left Albany Last Night And had not an Oppertunity to Speak to you or Any body Else intending to go to the falls this morning in hopes to gett Some Votes there I therefore Desire you'll Keep the pole opened Till Monday in the Afternoon.[91]

During the hard-fought election in Philadelphia County in 1764, when the Quaker faction began trotting out more and more voters including its "reserve of the aged and lame," the Proprietary party responded with a ploy of its own. An alarm was given to the backers of the "New ticket":

> Horsemen and footmen were immediately dispatched to German town, etc., and by nine or ten o'clock they began to pour in, so that after the move for a close, seven or eight hundred votes were procured; about five hundred, or near it, of which were for the new ticket and they did not close till three in the afternoon, and it took them till one next day to count them off.[92]

By the end of the provincial period, some office seekers seemed willing to do almost anything to obtain victory, though few perceived the consequences of their actions. The new and intensive methods of gaining votes inevitably brought added numbers of people into the political process. Although the candidates from the upper classes had little interest in advancing greater participation, the need to outdo their opponents invariably caused them to court popular support, with the result that the electoral system started to include a wider spectrum of the citizenry and eventually began to reflect a broader range of individuals' concerns.[93]

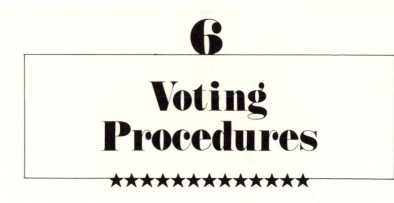

6

Voting Procedures

★★★★★★★★★★★★★★★

Election day in provincial America was "a movable feast," that is, there was no single standard date for balloting throughout the thirteen colonies.[1] The few corporate and proprietary provinces—Rhode Island, Connecticut, Pennsylvania, and Delaware—in which several high officials were chosen annually did set up specific dates for themselves, but the others did not. In the eight royal colonies plus proprietary Maryland, where only the lower house was elective, the English system, in which elections occurred at the discretion of the Crown, was followed. Whenever the governor decided to dissolve the Assembly and create a new one, the contest would take place. This sometimes happened early in the session if the House seemed unruly to him, but more frequently it came about later on when the existing body was about to expire. Most assemblies were scheduled to last a certain number of years, and the laws merely stipulated that the chief executive set in motion the choice of new members by the end of this fixed period of time.[2]

The maximum length of time between Assembly elections varied considerably from colony to colony. North Carolina established a two-year limit for much of the era; others such as Maryland and New Hampshire resolved upon three years; while New Jersey and New York, adhering to English precedent, eventually set theirs at seven years.[3] To be sure, the seven-year time span was thought rather excessive by many people in the latter province. Indeed, the leaders of the country party in New York prior to the passage of this measure had demanded the introduction of annual or triennial contests. They insisted that frequent elections were "requisite to preserve a due Regard and Faithfulness in the Deputy, to the Interests of the Person, who deputed him."[4] Men not subject to short-term renewal of authority, they believed, would be much less trust-worthy and more liable to corruption. However, this movement to insti-tute brief intervals proved unsuccessful as the Privy Council in Great Britain ultimately rejected a proposed triennial bill. Yet, in practice the gap between elections in the former Dutch settlement was really no great-er than in provinces with shorter legal time spans. Political quarrels sprang up so often in New York that new assemblies had to be initiated on thirty-one occasions in eighty-five years, an average of less than once every two and three-quarter years. New Jersey was not far behind with twenty-two assemblies in seventy-four years as a royal colony (1702-1776), or once in three and a third years.[5]

The number of separate contests within each province usually varied according to its size and its type of election districts, whether county, town, parish, or combination of the first two. The biggest amount—gen-erally about one hundred—occurred in Massachusetts, where the town was synonymous with the district. Other similarly based New England colonies also had fairly high totals; Connecticut had sixty-nine, New Hampshire and Rhode Island both twenty-eight by the latter part of the era. Among those designated by counties, plus a few towns, Virginia, the largest colony, had by far the greatest number, sixty-one. It was followed by North Carolina with thirty-five, Maryland with sixteen, New York with fourteen, New Jersey with twelve, Pennsylvania with eleven, and Delaware with three. South Carolina and Georgia, which were divided into parishes, had eighteen and twelve, respectively. Of course, the number of individuals elected for each unit differed considerably, ranging from one or two in Massachusetts to eight for the original counties of Pennsylvania.

Election districts in most colonies were not usually based on popula-tion, so that the apportionment of seats in the legislature was often in-equitable. Warwick County in Virginia with 1,224 people had the same number of burgesses as Amelia County with 7,962. In Pennsylvania around the year 1760, the five newer counties of Lancaster, York, Cumberland, Berks, and Northampton had but ten representatives compared to twenty-six for the three older counties of Philadelphia, Bucks, and Chester, de-spite a roughly equivalent proportion of taxpayers. Not until just prior to independence were any steps taken to rectify such cases of malapportion-ment.[6]

The first step in calling for a new election was the governor's issuance of a writ addressed to the county sheriff or commensurate official in charge of election proceedings. It directed him to summon all the eligible voters under his jurisdiction to meet at a particular spot and time for the purpose of choosing certain men for public office. The types of individuals qualified to vote and the number of seats to be filled were in most cases carefully defined in order to prevent misunderstandings. At times, however, disputes arose; in North Carolina in 1729 the writs sent out by Governor Burrington stated that only freeholders could vote though the provincial laws had always allowed taxpaying freemen to participate as well.[7] While writs may have varied to some degree, the following one prepared by Governor William Phips of Massachusetts in 1692 is in many ways typical of those issued in every colony.

> William and Mary, by the grace of God, of England, Scotland, France and Ireland, king and queen, defenders of the faith, &c.
> To our sheriff or marshall of our county of —— Greeting: WEE command that upon receipt hereof you forthwith make out your precepts, directed into the selectmen of each respective town within your precinct requiring them to cause the freeholders and other inhabitants of their several towns, duly qualified as in and by our royal charter is direct, to assemble at such time and place as they shall appoint, to elect or depute one or more persons . . . according to the number set and limited by an act of our general assembly within the same, to serve for and represent them respectively, in a great and general court or assembly. . . .[8]

The date of election in each separate town was left to be established by the local selectmen. Outside of New England, the dates were decided by the county sheriff or provost marshal. Except in the colonies with standard annual contests, the governor's writ did not mention a specific date of election but only the one upon which the new Assembly was to convene.[9] Within a single colony, the dates for each county were sometimes the same, though usually they were set a few days apart. Proper spacing was considered very important by some individuals in provinces like New York, where no residence requirement for voting existed and men could exercise the franchise in more than one place. Whenever the sheriffs of that colony appointed by the court faction scheduled a number of contests on the same date it aroused bitter criticism. Country faction opponents claimed that it unjustly deprived persons with property in several counties from casting a like number of votes. During the election of 1752, one man sharply condemned such actions as "flagrant Instances of unfair Dealing."[10]

As a rule, each province required that the elections take place and the writs be returned within forty days of the original announcement. The writs in Massachusetts, however, were issued only thirty days in advance of the new Assembly, and in New Hampshire just fifteen days before. When setting the date for a contest, the officials were usually compelled by law to give prior warning. Virginia ordered its sheriffs to set the event at least twenty days after the deliverance of the writ, though Maryland permitted them to give as little as ten days' notice.[11] Once in a while this provision was deliberately circumvented, as the men in charge hoped to give an advantage to the candidates they favored. Such deception was most commonly employed in Maryland where on several occasions sheriffs were called to account by the legislature for failing to allow proper notice.[12] Yet even when the rules were fully adhered to, the relatively short time between the initial announcement and the election itself limited the possibilities for organizing a campaign. On the other hand, in Pennsylvania, Delaware, Rhode Island, and Connecticut, which had fixed dates of election, men had the opportunity to concert plans over a longer period.

The news of a forthcoming election was announced in several ways. Some provincial statutes decreed that a statement be read out loud and then posted on buildings in the village square. Others required the local minister to mention the subject at the conclusion of his Sunday service or requested that a broadside containing the particulars be tacked onto the church or meetinghouse door.[13] Many New England towns established their own ways of informing the public. The selectmen of Litchfield, Connecticut, ordered that the details be "posted on all grist-mill doors, and on the school-house door in South Farms."[14] Pennsylvania probably had the most thorough system. Besides using many of the sites already mentioned, the Quaker colony called for placing notices on trees and houses along the roads leading to the principal towns in each county.[15]

In a few colonies, such as Maryland and Georgia, the voting dates for each district were sometimes listed in the newspapers several weeks prior to the event.[16] The newspaper was also one of the chief sources of notification in the large cities of New York and Boston.[17] The following announcement, prepared by the sheriff and published in the *New York Gazette* in February, 1761, resembles those that appeared in other papers, as well as the notices placed on public buildings. The statement contained much of the information included in the writ, plus the details for the specific contest in question.

> Pursuant to His Majesty's Writ to me directed and delivered, for the Electing Four Representatives to serve in a General Assembly of this Province, Notice is hereby given to the Freemen and Freeholders of the City and County of New York, in my Bailiwick, to assemble and meet together on Tuesday the Seventeenth Day of *February* next, at Ten o'Clock in the Forenoon of the same Day, on the Green near the Work-House, in the City of *New-York*, and then and there to nominate and chuse, . . . four able and sufficient Freeholders of the City and County of *New-York* aforesaid, to be Representatives of the said City and County, to assist the Captain General, or Commander-in-Chief of the Province of *New-York*, in a General Assembly.
>
> John Roberts, Sheriff[18]

Now and then, especially where there were no newspapers to list the dates, partisan officials purposely withheld the election announcement from some areas in order to help certain candidates and hinder others. William Moore of Chester, Pennsylvania, after being defeated for an Assembly seat in October, 1756, protested that "very few townships of the County had regular notice to attend."[19] On one occasion, petitioners from Derryfield, New Hampshire, complained to the General Court that although a "copy of [the] Warrant was to be left in three different spots, "neither of the places had any notification set up." Some of the townspeople "knew not the time of Day the meeting was to be held."[20] Another type of deception occurred in Brunswick, Massachusetts, where the selectmen were accused of misleading the public by putting the facts about the impending contest on the inside door rather than the outside door of the meetinghouse.[21] However, despite a few such instances, most provincial Americans were adequately informed of the time and place of election.

The kinds of places at which the polling occurred differed from region to region and even within the same province because they were not ordinarily designated by statute. Pennsylvania, for example, had no reference whatsoever to voting sites in its regulations, and the New York law merely stated that the proceedings should be scheduled "at the most publick & usuall place of election where the same has most usually been made." Whether legally established or not, each colony eventually developed its own particular sites and surroundings for the event and held it perennially in the same locations. In New England, the town meetinghouse was commonly used; in South Carolina, the parish church; in Pennsylvania, Delaware, Maryland, Virginia, and North Carolina, the county courthouse or, in good weather, the courthouse green.[22] The voting in New York and Georgia was conducted in a number of these settings, and in the latter it was sometimes transacted at a private residence. During the Georgia election of 1768, the poll for the district of Little-Ogeechee was taken at "Mr. Cherry's house," while the one for Abercorn and Goshen was recorded "at the house of Mathias West."[23]

Normally only one voting site was designated in each election unit, though in a few instances others were added. In Orange County, New York, because of the difficulty of crossing the mountains that intersected it, two places were provided.[24] Large and populous Baltimore County in Maryland also had two spots for a time.[25] Beginning in 1725, New Jersey officials tried to alleviate travel problems by permitting county sheriffs, with the candidates' consent, to carry a ballot box from village to village to collect the votes. This experiment did not find many adherents, however.[26] At a somewhat later date, a similar proposal was made in Suffolk County, New York, to accommodate the voters better, but it, too, gained little support. One writer in the *New York Gazette* argued that moving the polls about would serve just to magnify disputes and animosities. Moreover, this practice, he said, would increase the "great Evil and Inconvenience of Labourers, Servants, and Apprentices," who, instead of tending to their work, would gather more frequently for purposes of amusement. If the freeholders refused to travel, he concluded, they had only themselves to blame.[27]

Almost everywhere in early America voters had to travel great distances to cast their ballots. Outside of New England, a five- or ten-mile trip to the polls on horseback or wagon was not uncommon. In fact, people in the spacious frontier counties of the middle and southern colonies sometimes had to ride twenty-five miles or more to reach the place of election.[28] Traveling that far would necessitate leaving home at dawn or spending the previous night at a friend's house along the way. On occasion, Virginia voters were put up at the residence of one of the candidates on election eve. In 1764, when James Littlepage of Hanover County heard that several men did not wish to ride the twenty-five miles to the county seat in cold weather, he offered to let them stay overnight at his house, which was en route, thereby easing their travel burden. At the Littlepage estate they were cordially entertained with cider and other beverages before finishing their journey the next morning.[29]

The weather was not usually a significant factor in keeping voters away from the polls. In the southern colonies, the climate was generally favorable much of the year, and even low seasonal temperatures did not deter too many of the electors. For most of the northern colonies, province-wide elections were regularly held in the mid-spring or early fall so that the natural elements did not pose too many problems. Connecticut and Rhode Island made their choice of officers in mid-April, while Massachusetts did so at the end of May. Both Pennsylvania and Delaware scheduled their event for the first day of October.[30] Only in New York, which had no established date, did weather conditions sometimes play a decisive role, especially in the midst of an icy winter. As Sir William Johnson sadly noted after the contest in Albany County in January, 1769: "the roads are so bad and the Rivers impassable," which made it "impracticable to Assemble the Freeholders from so many remote places under these Circumstances." Some New York officials were known to delay an election purposely so that a flood or thaw would cut off part of a county, thus preventing men in that area from casting their vote.[31]

The number of voting days for a particular contest varied to some degree. Throughout New England, since the township was synonymous with the voting district, the entire process was usually confined to a single day. This was considered time enough for all the townspeople to cast their ballots. In many other colonies where traveling distances were much greater, the balloting continued for two or more days. New York's and New Jersey's proceeded at least that long. Under Pennsylvania law, elections were to "continue from day to day till the freeholders and electors then and there present shall be polled." In Philadelphia County, especially, it often became necessary to keep the machinery going for at least two days to implement this statute.[32] Maryland allowed the polls to stay open as long as the candidates could show cause that additional voters were en route, even if it took a number of days. Heated contests in Baltimore, Dorchester, and Frederick counties thus frequently lasted three or four days.[33] The Chesapeake province probably set the record for the longest time spans: one election in Frederick ran for six days, while another in Anne Arundel County, perhaps delayed by inclement weather, was not terminated until after thirteen days.[34]

In those places where the polls were open several days, it would seem that more electors appeared on the second and subsequent days than on the first. During the New York City Assembly contest in 1761, 36 percent of the votes were delivered on the first day and 42 percent on the second. In 1769, when the voting continued for five days, the totals for the second, third, and fourth all exceeded the first. Only 14 percent of the overall tally took place the initial day, while more than 25 percent was recorded on each of the next three. The election results for Burlington, New Jersey, in 1738 show 29 percent ventured out on opening day, 31 percent the day after. Perhaps many voters as well as political organizers wanted to see who was ahead in the early stages before casting their ballots or mobilizing others to do so. Of course, this pattern was not always followed. The Philadelphia County turnout in 1765, the only other for which there is a daily breakdown, indicates that about 47 percent came out the first day, with just 30 percent the next day and 23 percent on the third and final one.[35]

Just as the number of voting days differed in some colonies, so did the extent of voting hours. English law had provided that Parliamentary elections take place "betwixt the hour of 8 and the hour of 11 before noon." Yet not all the American provinces required that the voting occur within a specific period of time. Moreover, those that did usually allowed a longer span than just three hours. Massachusetts, for example, did not set any particular time limits for the event. The statutes in Connecticut stated simply that the proceedings should begin at nine o'clock in the morning. Pennsylvania and Delaware began elections between ten and two in the afternoon. The laws of many of the other colonies stipulated that the polls be open throughout most of the daylight hours. Ballots were accepted in South Carolina from nine in the morning until four in the afternoon. In Georgia, the hours extended from nine to six, although the polls might be closed two hours after the last voter appeared, or even earlier if all the candidates consented. North Carolina generally held two sessions, one from ten in the morning to one in the afternoon and the other from half past two until sunset.[36]

Usually when the moment came for the polls to open, a small but enthusiastic crowd had already gathered. Some people obviously chose to arrive early so they could promptly cast their vote and return to their homes or their work. Others hoped to see the initial appearance of the candidate who might ride up on horseback or in a fancy coach together with his family. Once in a while the candidate's supporters accompanied him in a grand parade on the way to the polling place. Perhaps the greatest procession to appear at the beginning of an election was the one organized by Lewis Morris in Westchester County, New York, in October, 1733. Morris had previously been ousted by Governor Cosby as Chief Justice of the province and sought vindication by attempting to gain a seat in the Assembly where he could lead the opposition to the chief executive. A correspondent for the *New York Weekly Journal* described the event as follows:

> First rode two Trumpeters and 3 Violines; next 4 of the principal Freeholders, one of which carried a Banner, on one Side of which was affixed in gold Capitals, KING GEORGE, and on the Other, in like golden Capitals LIBERTY & LAW; next followed the Candidate, *Lewis Morris* Esq., late Chief Justice of this Province; then two Colours; and at Sun rising they entered upon the Green of *Eastchester* the place of election, follow'd by above 300 Horse of the principal Freeholders of the County, (a greater Number than had ever appear'd for one Man since the Settlement of that County:)....[37]

Shortly afterward, his adversary, William Foster, also came to the courthouse green with a large group of backers. He was "attended by about 170 Horse of the Freeholders and Friends" of his. But in this contest, Foster, who had been prompted to run by the Governor, proved no match for Morris, who won by a wide margin.[38]

Election day was a time of great excitement for many people. Not only did they have a chance to see the candidates and deliver a vote, they could find many alternatives to the daily routine of farm or town life. Going to the polling place offered a good excuse for visiting with friends, enjoying some convivial drinking, or engaging in various sports and games.

In the southern colonies, one might also attend a session of the county court or watch the militia training, as these events often coincided with the choice of Assemblymen. Such diversions could at times so consume the populace that they would forget the prime reason for coming to the election site. On one occasion, John Adams reported that a group of men, after arriving in Braintree, were so busy carousing at the local tavern that they failed to cast their ballots during an important contest.[39]

The large congregation of persons in the vicinity of the polls on this day sometimes presented problems of crowd control. Before a crucial election in Salem, Massachusetts, in 1728, the town selectmen hired six extra men to stand watch "to prevent & Suppress all disorders & Tumults that may arise from so great A Concourse of people, as usually-there are on Such publick Occasions."[40] But even the presence of special guards meant no guarantee that order would be maintained. Especially in the southern and middle colonies it was not uncommon for some young by-standers to get carried away by their own exuberance and become in-volved in a quarrel of their own, which the officials would be helpless to restrain. At the Fairfax County, Virginia, poll in 1755, George Washington, who was supporting Lord Fairfax, was knocked down by William Payne, a member of the opposing camp. The possibility of a duel between the two arose, but on the next day they were able to resolve their differ-ences amicably.[41] A year earlier, at a contest in Calvert County, Maryland, two onlookers suddenly started to fight, and one of them during the en-gagement "bit Part of the other's Nose off." Subsequently it was discovered that in a previous encounter this same individual had "bit off a Man's Ear; and at another Time, almost bit off a Man's Finger." This prompted the printer of the *Maryland Gazette* to ask "Whether this Fellow ought not to have all his teeth drawn?"[42] In some instances, the fighting resulted in full-scale tumult or riot, which disrupted the entire voting process. At the Orange County, Virginia, election in 1742, such an upheaval took place when the polls opened that the sheriff had to station deputies with drawn swords at the courthouse doors to preserve order. The deputies, however, were unable to keep the peace for long, as the people began swarming into the building in a "drunken riotous manner," causing considerable delay in the taking of votes.[43]

Although such outbursts were usually spontaneous and without real purpose, some election violence was the result of prior planning. Various individuals and factions obviously felt that the only way of ensuring victory would be to disrupt the proceedings and frighten away the other side's supporters or close down the polls before they could vote. In Regulator-controlled Anson County, North Carolina, during the balloting in 1773, "sundry evil-disposed persons" stationed themselves several feet in front of the courthouse and stopped "the freeholders on their way to the Table," asking "who they intended to vote for." Those who opposed the Regulator candidates were "obstructed and hindered . . . some of them being violently pushed back, others of them pulled back by the hair of their heads; and others so rudely and violently treated that great numbers . . . were detered from voting."[44]

Pennsylvania was not immune from turbulent incidents, especially York County, which was distinguished by its heavy concentrations of competing Scotch-Irish and German settlers. The Scotch-Irish on one occasion even tried to prevent their rivals from voting altogether. On October 1, 1750, they arrived early, cast their ballots, and then sealed off the entrance to the polling place. When the Germans realized what had happened, they became angry and retaliated with sticks and clubs eventually driving their opponents off. By this time, however, the polls were closed by the pro-Irish sheriff and the contest declared over. But the Germans refused to accept the verdict and began beating down the courthouse doors. Meanwhile, the sheriff and his assistants had disappeared through the back window, taking the ballot box with them. The Germans, undaunted, got another ballot box and made the coroner continue the affair until all their partisans had put in their votes.[45]

Perhaps the biggest election riot happened in Philadelphia in October, 1742, when the struggle between the Quaker and Proprietary parties was beginning to reach fever pitch. Previously the Quakers, with their German allies, had always been able to secure a majority of voters. They achieved this in part by stationing several men at the foot of the stairs leading to the courthouse who would intimidate those persons approaching the polls carrying opposition tickets. Frustrated by this tactic, the Proprietary leaders decided to hire a group of hefty sailors to chase their adversaries away from this spot. These men were "armed with clubbs and other weapons, which they flourished over their heads with loud huzzas, . . . in a furious and tumultuous manner approached the place of election." When they were asked to leave by the presiding officials, they refused to do so and began striking the magistrates and other citizens with great ferocity. At first, the rioters were held back, but their charge was "so furious as to

break the constables' staves, who were then obliged to give ground."
Many inhabitants were struck down by the attackers, among them an
alderman, who might have been "barbarously murthered" had the alter-
cation not been stopped. The sailors then marched off, but when the
balloting began, they returned and unexpectedly made a second attack
upon the freemen, "throwing down all they were able, without regard
to age or station." However, the townspeople quickly recovered and,
finally banding together, began turning on their assailants, forcing the
latter to flee in all directions. Subsequently, fifty of the sailors were
rounded up and put in jail, bringing an end to this turbulent and chaotic episode.[46]

To be sure, the vast majority of provincial elections were not accompanied by any violence or bloodshed. On the contrary, they usually took
place amid a scene of quiet and serenity. In fact, many commentators
expressly mentioned the tranquil and dignified atmosphere at the contest
they were observing. A reporter at the courthouse in Burlington, New
Jersey, in October, 1738, noted that the event was carried on in "a can-
did and peaceable Manner."[47] The English traveler, Nicholas Cresswell,
remarked that the one he attended at Alexandria, Virginia, in the summer of 1774 "was conducted with great order and regularity."[48] Furthermore, no evidence of any disorderly activity has ever come to light regarding elections in New England beyond a bit of name calling. Even in
New York City, where factionalism was rampant, the only casualties ever
recorded were a few bloody noses during the Van Horne-Philipse scuffle
in 1737.[49] Nonetheless, violence in the New York capital was never too
far from the surface. As Peter R. Livingston warned prior to the clash
with the DeLanceys in 1769, if the opposition broke any rules, hostilities would surely erupt, "as we have by far the best part of the Brusers
on our side who are determined to use force if they use any foul play."[50]

At the polling place, the election process was generally overseen by a
staff of several officials. In most cases it was headed by the county sheriff, though in New England it was run by the town selectmen and in South
Carolina by the church wardens in each parish. The sole exception to this
practice of local control occurred in Georgia where the governor's agent,
the provost marshal, appointed deputies to supervise the event in each
district. The presiding election officer had a great deal of influence over
the outcome. Not only did he in most instances set the exact date of election, but he also chose the clerks who recorded the votes and counted

them. Moreover, he opened and closed the polls at his own volition, sometimes closing it despite the pleas of one of the candidates to keep it open
until more freeholders arrived. The sheriff in a few provinces even had the
right to cast the deciding vote in case of a tie. Perhaps his most important
power was to determine whether individual electors were properly qualified. As director of the proceedings, he could either throw out questionable votes or accept them as he saw fit.[51] Many petitions to the legislature
throughout this period were protests against an official who permitted
ineligible voters to cast ballots for the men he favored or who rejected
eligible voters known to oppose his choices. For example, the sheriff in
Bladen County, North Carolina, in 1740, was accused of allowing "several unnaturalized Foreigners and others not qualified" to be polled without any interference on his part.[52]

Nevertheless, the men in command of elections were not nearly as
powerful as they might at first seem. Although some of them may have
violated the rules, they were usually disciplined severely for such actions
by the colonial legislature. Following a disputed contest in York County,
Virginia, Sheriff Francis Heyward was charged with fraud, then strongly
reprimanded by the House of Burgesses, and compelled to pay the costs
of presenting the petition against him.[53] The sheriff of Baltimore County
in Maryland was condemned by the Assembly in 1769 for engaging in illegal maneuvers

> in closing the Polls on the Second day of the Election, against
> the consent of one of the Candidates, and when [he] had rea-
> son to believe that a Number of Persons were on their Way,
> and that many others might be expected the next Day, to vote
> at the said Election; whereby the People were prevented from
> having a full and free Election.

He too was forced to pay the costs, which amounted to more than ten
pounds, and was "admonished to be more circumspect for the future in
[his] conduct as Sheriff."[54] From these and many other such accounts,
it appears that high election officials, though possessing considerable
power and influence, had to remain within certain bounds; their authority was not unlimited.

The officer in charge would customarily start the election by reading
out loud the governor's writ. In some place the church bells would be

rung or a town crier sent around to signal the opening of the polls. Then the voting itself would begin. The actual process of casting votes in provincial America occurred in several distinct fashions. It differed not only from one colony to the next but sometimes from one election to the next within the same colony. North Carolina, for instance, changed its methods four times over the course of the eighteenth century. Moreover, procedures in certain provinces varied according to the offices under consideration. In New York, local magistrates were chosen in one manner, Assemblymen in another.[55]

The forms of voting adopted in the provincial period were based partly upon English precedent and partly upon the colonists' previous experience in America. The earliest settlers had experimented with all sorts of objects thought suitable for counting, including "hands," "crys," "papers," and even a few items of food. A Massachusetts Bay statute in 1648 had ordered "that for the yearly choosing of Assistants for the time to come . . . the freemen shall use Indian Corn & Beanes, the Indian Corn to manifest Election, the Beanes contrary."[56] Beans had also been utilized in early Pennsylvania. After a dispute at the polls in 1689, a member of the Council indicated that balloting had been accomplished "by black and white beanes put into a hatt." The authors of the West Jersey constitution of 1676, perhaps influenced by James Harrington's *Oceana,* had called for the use of balls rather than beans. In order to prevent partiality they stipulated that elections should be determined by "putting Balls into Balloting Boxes."[57]

By the early eighteenth century, however, each of the colonies had settled upon a system of voice voting or paper balloting or a combination of the two. Oral or viva-voce voting was the most widely used form. It had long been the prevailing style in the mother country and eventually proved to be the most popular one in America too. At least six of the thirteen provinces—New York, New Jersey, Maryland, Virginia, North Carolina, and Georgia—used a form of open voting for much of the provincial period. In fact, voice voting continued to be the standard procedure in many areas of the South until the end of the Civil War.[58]

The process of oral voting, wherever it was adopted, had many common characteristics. When it appeared at the beginning of the proceedings that the number of candidates was no greater than the number of available places, no poll was necessary. The official in charge might simply ask for a show of hands to confirm the verdict. Similarly, when it seemed that one individual would be an obvious choice, the election might

also be decided "by view." The people would be divided according to
which man they supported, and the one with the largest group behind him
would be declared the winner. But in those cases where none of the contestants had a large advantage and the outcome was somewhat in doubt,
a poll had to be taken. If a poll was used, the voters would come up one
at a time to a long table situated inside or in front of the courthouse.
Standing there within the hearing of the election officials and all interested spectators, each man would state his name and then in a loud voice
announce his preferences. In Virginia and possibly elsewhere, the candidates themselves were often present and publicly thanked those who
had just voted for them. One of the clerks at the table would then record the voter's name in the appropriate column on a large paper or poll
sheet. Because no formal registration existed at that time, the candidates
or the presiding officers could request that an elector swear as to his being properly qualified. An oath, of course, was not always foolproof. On
many occasions, the county tax list for the current year was kept at
hand for the purpose of checking upon someone of dubious credentials.
Seldom, however, were people's qualifications seriously challenged except during a very tight contest. There seemed little point in haggling
over a vote or two when the race was heavily one-sided.[59]

The polls ordinarily stayed open a considerable period of time, at
least long enough to give everyone present a chance to vote. Yet this
was not true in every case. Some candidates, seeing themselves soundly
beaten, conceded the election rather early. When this happened the voting would immediately stop, even if only a small part of the electors on
hand had actually cast their ballots. At the Westchester County election
of 1750, when Frederick Philipse and John Thomas completely overwhelmed Lewis Morris, Jr., from the very beginning, the latter quickly
bowed out, leaving the majority of men with no opportunity to vote.
Just 289 persons had been processed, while it was estimated that "there
were, by a moderate Computation, upwards of 300 more Freeholders
attending, to vote for the two First named, if Col. Morris had not given
up."[60] Nevertheless, as long as the slightest chance of victory remained,
the trailing candidate would invariably allow the polling to continue until the end.

At times certain candidates who had little hope of winning were known
to withdraw even before the polling began for the purpose of improving
the chances of one adversary over a number of others. This occurred especially in those colonies with a strong court-country division, such as

New York. During the Queens County election of 1739, Thomas Alsop had originally planned to oppose Thomas Cornell, who was running for one of the two seats in the district against the court nominees, Isaac and Benjamin Hicks. But "when he perceived that the People were generally inclined for Mr. Cornel," he dropped out of the race, "in order to strengthen the Party against the Hicks's."[61]

The excitement of a close contest was magnified by oral voting. Anyone present could usually hear how the totals were accumulating or could obtain the latest count by asking a clerk at the table. Sometimes loud cheers could be heard as one candidate pulled ahead of another. The polling would continue in this manner until it appeared that all the votes were in or until it became time to shut down the polls for the day. At that point, a crier might be sent around to warn prospective voters of the intention to terminate the proceedings. Finally, the sheriff would call out: "Gentlemen Freeholders, come into court, and give your votes, or the poll will be closed." Following this announcement, the last few entries would be tallied.[62]

To a modern observer, oral voting may appear to place the elector in a pressure-filled situation and present an open invitation to undue influence and corruption. Yet many people living in the eighteenth century thought this style respectable and insisted that it encouraged rather than discouraged honesty. Irregularities were held to a minimum, it was believed, because such occurrences could be readily discovered. Open voting, contemporaries argued, kept everything above board so that nothing could be concealed. Secret balloting, on the other hand, would soon lead to disreputable activity, including outright bribery. Hidden by secrecy, artful and designing politicians could easily buy the necessary votes to control an election. According to Governor James Glen of South Carolina, this method would have "a tendency to destroy that noble generous openess that is characteristick of an Englishman, and to introduce a Vile Venetian Juggle and Cunning." Putting in extra ballots was impossible with voice voting but easy to accomplish with pieces of paper. Under the latter system, Glen declared, "any Person who attends the balloting Box may, with a very little slight of Hand, give the election to whom he pleases." Unsigned paper ballots, moreover, made it difficult to track down unqualified voters in case of a dispute.[63]

On another level, philosophers like Montesquieu reasoned that "public" voting was necessary to maintain order and stability in society. Only with open voting, he insisted, would the common man designate a respectable

member of the community. "This," he wrote, "should be considered as
a fundamental law of democracy." "The lower classes," he added, "ought
to be directed by those of higher rank, and restrained within bounds by
the gravity of eminent personages." Both Montesquieu and Sir William
Blackstone cited the failure of secret balloting when it had been tried in
ancient times and warned against its resurrection in the future. "By rendering the suffrages secret in the Roman republic," Montesquieu concluded, "all was lost; it was no longer possible to direct a populace that sought
its own destruction."[64] To be sure, certain commentators in early America recognized some of the dangers inherent in a system of open voting,
yet most of them believed that any change toward secrecy would have
little positive value. A person using a secret ballot who was under an obligation to one of the candidates would be "as much compelled to vote
against his Inclination, as if he had voted *viva voce*," asserted one gentleman.[65]

In spite of this widespread opposition, paper balloting was practiced
for a considerable period of time in several colonies, including North and
South Carolina, Pennsylvania, Delaware, and all of New England.[66] The
legislatures in these provinces rejected English parliamentary tradition
and ignored critics of closed voting, establishing secrecy as the norm. New
Englanders, for example, strongly sought consensus in political as well as
social affairs and believed secret voting a better method of achieving this
end than open voting. As Michael Zuckerman has written, "Elections were
a potentially divisive force in a society which could not afford division.
Secrecy was essential for the prevention of town dissension and the pre-
servation of group solidarity."[67]

In Massachusetts, Connecticut, New Hampshire, and Rhode Island, although a few Assembly elections were decided by a show of hands or
voice votes, the vast majority of the voting was done by ballot, customarily a secret ballot. At the town meeting, the freeholders were generally
asked to place a written ticket or paper into a hat or ballot box. One of
these depositories would be set down at the front of the meetinghouse
near a table where the constable and the selectmen sat. These officials
would then request that the citizens fill out their ballots. Once this was
accomplished, each individual would come forward to deliver his vote.
Since secrecy prevailed and Assembly candidacies were not announced
beforehand, no one would be present to thank the voters as was the case
in Virginia.[68]

While the balloting continued, the selectmen would watch the entire proceedings very carefully. Each elector's name would usually be checked against a tax or valuation list to ensure that only qualified persons handed in tickets. Moreover, the officials had to make certain that no man dropped more than one paper in the box. In order to prevent such a possibility, the colony of Rhode Island enacted a statute requiring each individual to sign his name on the other side of the sheet. But the law proved so unpopular that it had to be repealed the following year. The members of the legislature found that it had led to "great dissatisfaction and uneasiness" in the province. The people had felt it "a very great hardship to have their names exposed upon such occasions, to the creating of animosity and heartburning of their particular friends."[69]

Originally the electors of Rhode Island and Connecticut chose their governor and upper house by bringing their ballots directly to the General Court in the capital of each province. As time passed, however, it became too burdensome to assemble all the freemen in Newport or Hartford. Thus, it was decided to permit a person to vote by proxy, that is, "putting in a proxy vote, in the town meeting to which he belongs." Although these were the only two colonies ever to allow proxies, in each it was soon the commonest practice. By 1750 in Connecticut and 1760 in Rhode Island, proxy voting for the high magistrates became mandatory as men were forbidden to present their tickets in person at the statehouse. Rhode Island officials declared that the massive gatherings at Newport were "very injurious to the interest and public weal of the colony." Besides the problems of dealing with the large crowd, they argued that traveling to the city "occasions a very great loss of people's time at a season of the year when their labor is abundantly necessary for preparing the ground and planting the seed: on which the produce of the whole season must depend."[70]

The early proxy ballots were most likely blank pieces of paper that the voter filled in. But toward the middle of the eighteenth century, as the factional struggles in Rhode Island grew more heated, the competing sides began printing and distributing tickets in advance. Some Connecticut leaders introduced prepared tickets in the early 1770's, but only those from Rhode Island survive. The "proxes" used in the latter province were generally seven or eight inches high and four or five inches wide. They listed the nominees for Governor, Deputy Governor, Secretary, Attorney-General, Treasurer, and ten assistants. Usually the gubernatorial candidate's name appeared in large capital letters, the others in somewhat smaller letters. At times, especially during the 1760's, the tickets contained a party slogan such as "Seekers of Peace" or "Supporters of the Colony's Rights." The electors were not compelled to accept all the names on the slate. They could, if they wished, cross out certain ones and add others before depositing the sheet.[71]

In Pennsylvania various methods were used in the earliest years of settlement, including the deposit of beans. But after the passage of the election law of 1706, paper balloting became the primary means of voting. When Pennsylvanians came to the polling place, they were supposed to present tickets listing the names of the candidates they wished to elect. Many of these ballots were not fully secret; they had been prepared in advance by the various factional leaders and passed out to the voters on election day. Others were plain pieces of paper containing a man's personal selections. On a few occasions, men arriving at the polls without a ticket were allowed to cast a voice vote. In the case of an illiterate person, the sheriff or inspector would read aloud the names on a ticket and ask the individual if those were his choices. If they were, the ticket would be marked and deposited; if not, the man would deliver his vote orally.[72]

Men in neighboring Delaware as well usually voted by paper ballot. Elections in the lower counties were conducted by inspectors in each district, or hundred, each of whom was provided with a ballot box by the sheriff. After taking an oath asserting that he was qualified, the elector handed in his ballot. Then the inspector called out the voter's name and inserted the paper into the proper box. However, as in Pennsylvania, if a man brought no paper or ticket, he was permitted to give his vote verbally, and the names were entered by the clerk. Illiterates, too, were allowed to present oral votes.[73]

Although secret ballots were commonly employed in New England, Pennsylvania, and Delaware, their use was merely customary and not legally required. As we have seen, alternative open methods were often available. Only in the Carolinas was secrecy fully established by law. Beginning in 1716, South Carolina, which had long used paper ballots, stipulated in its election statutes that "the elector shall not be obliged to subscribe his name." Each man was requested to indicate his preferences on a piece of paper, roll it up, and bring it to the church wardens who conducted the proceedings. When the polls closed, these "scrolls" were deposited in "some box, glass or paper [and] sealed up with the seals of any two or more" of the voters present. At the same time, each individual's name was placed in a book in an attempt to prevent duplicate voting.[74]

North Carolina, which started with oral voting in the late seventeenth century, established paper balloting in 1715 but asked that the voter "subscribe his name" to the bottom of the sheet. The clause was omitted in the election law of 1743, implying that secrecy should prevail. Under the new law, the voter was supposed to deliver to the sheriff "a scroll of Paper rolled up with the Name or Names of the Person or Persons he votes for written therein." The sheriff was then to place these papers into a "small Box with a Lid or Cover having a hole in it not exceeding Half an Inch in diameter."[75] This method continued until 1760 when a return was made to the viva voce style. Why this reversal occurred is unclear. Perhaps a few instances of fraud stirred up so much pressure against the use of paper ballots that the system had to be abandoned.

If closed balloting proved adequate in some colonies, those without it rarely demanded its adoption. No formal movement to abolish open voting appeared anywhere except in faction-ridden New York. From time to time, the country faction, partly out of idealism and partly out of desire to reduce the court opposition, would advocate the introduction of a secret ballot, pointing out the advantages that would result from it. As early as 1732, one country enthusiast declared that after such a change, "People would then vote for the deserving Man they Love, and not for the haughty Tyrant they fear, and consequently hate. They would elect the generous Patron of Liberty, and reject the subservient Tool of Slavery."[76] Some years later, another opponent of the court faction complained of the existing system whereby rich men using "Threats of Hardship" prevented persons from voting as their conscience told them.[77] However, not until the end of the 1760's did agitation for secrecy at the polls become so widespread as to be considered a major issue. The Livingston faction, after losing the election of 1769, saw the new mode as a means of regaining power and began drumming up support for it. During late 1769 and early 1770 they distributed countless tracts calling for the passage of a secret ballot law. One broadside claimed that such a law would halt "Tumults, Riots, and Disorders at Elections," stop the "Dangerous and Detestable Practice of Bribery and Corruption," and curb "Men of Property and Power, and Tyranical Dispositions from prostituting their Wealth and Influence."[78] Yet when the measure was brought before the legislature, it was rejected by the DeLancey majority in the House by a vote of thirteen to twelve.[79] Despite the narrow margin of defeat, no further attempt to replace the viva voce method occurred until after 1776, when open voting was beginning to be questioned in many places.

Once the ballots were cast and the polls closed, the votes had to be tabulated. The records indicate that some colonies set up rather elaborate procedures to do so. In North Carolina, while the secret ballot was in effect, the sheriff would open the ballot box in the presence of the inspectors and the candidates. Then, the scrolls of paper were removed, the names upon them called aloud, and the results tallied by the inspectors. Pennsylvania followed a similar method. After the ballot box was opened, the tickets were handed over to the clerks, who would enter the votes on a tally sheet with "him whose name is oftenest mentioned in said Papers to be the first elected," and so on. The tally sheet was then compared with an earlier list marked with those persons who had voted. Delaware had perhaps the most complicated system of all. First, the sheriff added up the votes for each hundred separately and checked them against the list of voters for that particular district. When this phase was completed, the ballots from all parts of the county were placed in one big box, mixed together, and finally counted up by the sheriff's clerks.[80]

Several provinces took measures to protect against the counting of fraudulent or defective ballots. Pennsylvania, Delaware, North Carolina, and South Carolina each enacted laws voiding those tickets with more than the required number of names on them. Delaware also rejected those having fewer names than the proper total. Certain other underhanded tactics were specifically outlawed in colonies where paper ballots were used. In the Carolinas, when two or more scrolls were rolled together and deposited as one, they were to be "cast away as useless and void." Pennsylvania and Delaware officials discarded all ballots that were "deceitfully folded together" for the purpose of giving the elector more votes than he was entitled to.[81]

Regardless of these strict laws against election fraud, "stuffing the ballot box" and related infractions did occur at times. Judging from the records, the most flagrant violations took place in Massachusetts and Pennsylvania, paper users who had the greatest frequency of contests. Following the election in Lancaster, Pennsylvania, in 1749, a number of inhabitants protested against various abuses in the balloting. The crowd at the courthouse had become so huge, they said, that

> it was impossible the Names of the Voters should be known
> and entered . . . by which Means great Frauds were committed,
> Tickets put in by Boys, and repeated several Times unnoticed
> by the Inspectors, so that the Number of Votes in casting up,
> amounted to above double Number of Voters in Town. . . .[82]

In Haverhill, Massachusetts, during a dispute between the east and west parish in the election of 1748, a selectman from the east parish was said to have taken all of the opposition's "votes out of his hatt and cast them away."[83] Six years later in the community of Swansea, which was divided by religious differences, it was reported that when the polling took place in the meetinghouse,

> sundry persons in the said town when they put in their votes
> put them in folded and twisted up together and others would
> hold their votes in the hands shutup and so keep them until
> they put them into the hat so that it was impossible to see
> how many votes they put in.[84]

Irregularities at the ballot box actually comprised only a small part of the total quantity of disputed elections. In the majority of cases, conflict stemmed from disagreement over the qualifications of the voters or the qualifications of the candidates in regard to religion, citizenship, residence, and, especially, property holding.[85] After a close race it was by no means unusual for the losing candidate to question the eligibility of several electors as to whether they were legitimate property holders in the community they resided in. The largest number of protests occurred in those colonies where elections were extremely competitive, such as Virginia and Maryland. In Maryland, between 1728 and 1771, there were at least twenty-nine separate incidents.[86] The smallest number of disputes took place in provinces such as South Carolina and Connecticut, which had relatively few severe contests. Here the alleged violations amounted to no more than a handful.

In the event of any questionable activities at the polls, a defeated candidate might formally protest the result by petitioning the Assembly for a hearing. By the middle of the eighteenth century, practically all of the lower houses had acquired the privilege of judging their own membership, which gave them the right to resolve disputed elections. When such an incident occurred, sometimes the entire body would hear the case. However, most colonies south of New England had a standing committee on elections that would conduct an inquiry into the proceedings. This committee would review all the details of the controversy. It would summon various officials, interrogate witnesses, and listen to legal advice before rendering a verdict. If a dispute centered upon the eligibility of certain electors, a scrutiny of the poll list was sometimes made and the challenged votes closely examined as to their legitimacy.[87]

The elections committee would go about its work most diligently, sometimes spending more than a week considering a single incident. Following one contest at Annapolis between Dr. Alexander Hamilton and George Stuart, the Maryland committee heard testimony from thirty witnesses before reaching its decision. In some instances the Assembly would sustain the plaintiff's appeal and reverse the original result or else call for a new election. But the majority of these disputes ended with the petition being dismissed and the previous outcome confirmed. For the most part, the lower houses tended to overlook small infractions of the rules and were generally unwilling to bother with listening to a counterappeal or the problems of holding a new poll. This was quite frequently the case if the candidate himself was not responsible for the alleged misdeeds.[88]

The proportion of votes necessary for a candidate to be elected— majority or plurality—was not always clearly defined in the statutes. In fact, one New Jersey law used the two words synonymously. Most of the colonies probably required that the victor achieve just a simple plurality. For example, a measure passed by the Rhode Island legislature stated that since there might "happen a division in the votes soe as the greater half may not pitch directly on one ceratine person, yett the person which hath the most votes shall be declared elected." However, in six of the colonies—Connecticut, Massachusetts, New York, New Jersey, South Carolina, and Georgia—a full majority was needed. When a majority was not obtained in the first balloting, usually another round or two had to be held. But in Connecticut, if no gubernatorial candidate received a major part of the votes, the election would be decided by the members of the Assembly. This latter formula perhaps provided the precedent for the founding fathers at the Constitutional Convention to have indecisive presidential elections determined by the House of Representatives. It was Connecticut delegate Roger Sherman who was responsible for introducing that motion and championing its adoption.[89]

When the ballots were counted, the names of the victorious candidates would be announced. Usually this was followed by loud cheers from the waiting crowd, especially from the backers of the winning side. At the election in New York City in 1750, "the People expressed the most ardent Affection for their . . . Representatives, by three of those popular and triumphant *Huzzas.*"[90] The successful gentlemen then would thank their supporters individually or else give thanks publicly to the entire group. After his victory in the Somerset, New Jersey election of 1772, Hendrick Fisher addressed the audience:

> *Dear Friends, and Gentlemen Voters.*
> Press'd with a due sense of gratitude, for the repeated and distinguishing marks of your sincere respect for my person; the honours you have conferred on me are very obliging; trusting your delicate and most tender concerns again into my hands, is really affecting; by this you not only approve of my former, but pledge your honour to my future conduct. I am at a loss for words on this renewed occasion, to express the grateful sentiments of my enlarged mind; I must therefore content myself, returning you my humble, my most hearty thanks, and refer the proof of my sincerity and this assertion, to my future actions. . . .[91]

Subsequently the winners might parade through the town or village on horseback, on foot, or on the shoulders of their followers. Then they would adjourn to one of the gentlemen's homes or to the neighborhood tavern for further celebration of the victory.[92]

Overall, the election process in provincial America was characterized by a lack of uniformity. In each region, and in some cases in each individual colony, the proceedings were conducted in a distinct fashion. Moreover, much change took place during the era, as the colonists experimented with various new forms. Out of this wide range of experience the styles and procedures for the later American voting system gradually developed.

7

Turnout

★★★★★★★★★★★★★★★★

The question of how many people actually voted in provincial America has often been pondered but never satisfactorily answered. The only published statements on the subject have been a few unreliable speculations based on rather little concrete evidence. The primary reason for the failure to deal with this problem in a proper fashion has always been the absence of sufficient data. Until a short time ago, not many election returns from this era had ever appeared in print. Summing up the material he compiled three-quarters of a century ago on voting in the colonies, the late Albert E. McKinley concluded: "These figures are entirely too few, and too scattered in time and territory, to justify any accurate generalization from them."[1] In the past few decades, however, studies of political developments in particular colonies have furnished a good deal of additional information. Scholars looking at politics in general have uncovered numerous poll lists, diary notations, and other source material containing voting results. Although hardly complete, these statistics, together with totals obtained from recently cataloged archival and newspaper collections, now enable us to draw at least some tentative conclusions as to how many persons voted during the provincial period.

Even with the added information, of course, we can never arrive at anywhere near a definite figure. A great many of the returns, especially from before 1730, have been lost or destroyed over the past two centuries. Moreover, in numerous contests held in the provincial era the overall number of voters was not even recorded. Elections were frequently uncontested or were so one-sided that a polling of the people present was not deemed necessary. On these occasions balloting was often accomplished by a show of hands, with no precise count being made. Another problem is that some polls remained incomplete, most notably when one of the competitors forfeited the race in its early stages. Even when a full and accurate poll was taken, it was customary in many towns and counties to register just the name of the winning candidate in the completed writ or summary statement. Rarely did it include his total vote or the name of the opposing candidates, much less his opponents' totals. In Massachusetts, for example, an examination of the records of more than fifty towns yielded but a small quantity of scattered results. Similar searches in Connecticut and New Hampshire were no more fruitful. The only communities to list the returns in a regular fashion over any length of time were a few of the large cities, such as Boston and Portsmouth. Except when the tally was extremely close and the outcome in dispute, most colonists were concerned solely about who won an election, not how many ballots were cast. As Daniel Boorstin has pointed out, past generations of Americans were much less statistically oriented than their counterparts today.[2]

The absence of abundant returns is only the first obstacle in trying to discover the number of colonists who voted. Even when the results are known, one is frequently faced with the difficult problem of figuring out what proportion of the adult males these totals represent. In some colonies, such as South Carolina, there was almost a complete lack of accurate census data for the entire period. And in those provinces where this information does exist, it is often incomplete or unavailable for the years in which the voting figures are recorded. At times the male population was expressed in terms of taxables (Pennsylvania) or rateable polls (New England), which are not always synonymous with the number of men over twenty-one. This forces rather questionable estimates of the equivalent to be made and raises many doubts about the ultimate value of the conclusions reached.[3]

The use of adult males rather than eligible voters as the means of comparison can be questioned, too. This method does not always give an accurate picture since each province established a distinct set of qualifications. Certainly the proportion of eligible voters varied from colony to colony. If the figures were determined solely on the basis of qualified electors— that is, those who met the religious, residence, property, and, in some instances, the freemen's requirement—the results would come out somewhat differently. Anywhere from 10 to 25 percent would have to be added to the totals. The gap would be most readily observable in Connecticut, many of whose male inhabitants did not become freemen, or in several counties in New York and Maryland, where it proved difficult to meet the minimum landholding standard. Given the absence of complete data, however, it is impossible to provide a formula by which all these factors can be taken into account. Therefore, in the interest of setting up the most workable criterion for an overall comparison, adult white males were used regardless of shortcomings.[4]

Despite all the handicaps involved in the process, it is still possible to make a number of important judgments about how many colonists voted. A good many figures exist for several of the settlements, mainly covering the years after 1730, and from these, certain calculations and rough projections can be attempted. The results of the computations show, most significantly, that the average turnout was really quite high considering the circumstances of the era, higher surely than the 2 to 10 percent estimated by some scholars. Among the colonies where a fairly sizable sample has been located, Virginia had the largest percentage, well above 40 percent of the adult males. New York and Pennsylvania came next with a range of approximately 20 to 40 percent. Further down are Rhode Island, Connecticut, and Massachusetts, whose average was commonly between 10 and 25 percent. The statistics for the remaining colonies are too few to generalize from, though it would seem from the available returns that the totals in Maryland, New Jersey, New Hampshire, and Delaware were rather substantial at times. On the other hand, attendance at the polls in the Carolinas and Georgia was usually quite small except in rare moments of political crisis.

Even with limited figures it is often possible to ascertain where the turnouts were relatively stable and where heavy fluctuations occurred. We can find out which towns and counties had the highest percentages and which had the lowest and also take note of significant deviations from the regular pattern. In a few provinces we are able to judge the degree of competitiveness and tell when elections were normally one-sided and when they were extremely close. Finally, we can look at the overall trend of the vote over the course of time and attempt to draw some general conclusions about it.

In Virginia, few voting returns have been preserved prior to 1740, but after that date almost one hundred of them have survived (see table 4). From these many samples, it appears that more than 43 percent of the

TABLE 4

Virginia Assembly Voting Totals, 1740-1776[a]

County	1741	1748	1752	1755	1758	1761	1765	1768	1769	1771
Accomac	482	555	486	540	561			508		
Amelia					465			591		
Brunswick		345								
Elizabeth City					106					
Essex	325	377	318	356	356	374	376	352	329	245
Fairfax		292		349			272			
Fauquier									399	
Frederick				291	398	601				
Halifax							758	445	314	
Henrico										
King George			255							
Lancaster	202	201	183	243	218	202	172	191	167	166
Norfolk			182	143		357	227	588	576	
Northumberland					329			339	336	291
Prince Edward				83	140					
Prince George					270	194				
Prince William	414									
Richmond			255	215	229	250				
Spotsylvania		193	175	209			248		228	259
Surry										286
Westmoreland	322	363	407	338		306				240

[a]The results for the by-elections are: 1740: Accomac 448; 1744: Accomac 386, Fairfax 239; 1750: Lancaster 214; 1753: Spotsylvania 109; 1754: Prince Edward 195, Westmoreland 331, Lancaster 154; 1755: Lancaster 114; 1756: Spotsylvania 156; 1757: Westmoreland 179; 1758: Lancaster 146; 1761: Northumberland 313; 1764: Halifax 500; 1770: Essex 89; 1771: Northumberland 296; 1772: Lunenburg 331; 1773: Frederick 354; 1774: Lancaster 212.

adult men were taking an active part in electing their burgesses. Statistics available for several counties in five different elections over the period of a quarter century clearly attest to this. The results from seven in 1748 (Accomac, Brunswick, Essex, Fairfax, Lancaster, Spotsylvania, and Westmoreland), indicate that 48.8 percent of the adult white male tithables voted in that year's Assembly contest. Four years later, in 1752, approximately 45.4 percent of the individuals in a similar list of eight counties participated in the choice of delegates. This represented a decline of nearly 3.5 percent, a small one, however, compared to the drop at the next election. Figures for ten counties in 1755 show that about 37.4 percent of the tithables went to the polls that year, 8 percent less than in 1752. Applying this same list of tithables to the returns of 1758 (for which six of the ten counties are the same as in the 1755 grouping) shows about 43.4 percent voting, a rise of 6 percent. Finally, taking the known totals for 1771 in conjunction with a subsequent list of tithables illustrates a 3 percent reduction to 40.4 percent (see table 5).

As we can observe, the turnouts fluctuated at times, with eleven points separating the high of 48.8 in 1748 from the low of 37.8 in 1755. Why th

TABLE 5

Percentage Turnout for Virginia Assembly Elections, 1748, 1752, 1755, 1758, and 1771

	Adult White Males	Number of Voters	Percentage
1748			
Accomac	1140	555	48.7
Brunswick	755	345	45.7
Essex	717	377	52.6
Fairfax	700	292	41.7
Lancaster	348	201	57.8
Spotsylvania	416	193	46.4
Westmoreland	692	363	52.5
Average			48.8
1752			
Accomac	1140	486	42.6
Essex	717	318	44.4
Henrico	438	255	58.2

TABLE 5 (continued)

	Adult White Males	Number of Voters	Percentage
King George	540	183	33.9
Lancaster	365	182	49.9
Richmond	571	255	44.7
Spotsylvania	499	175	35.1
Westmoreland	708	407	_57.5_
Average			45.4
1755			
Accomac	1130	540	47.8
Essex	666	356	53.4
Fairfax	984	349	35.7
Frederick	1630	291	18.9
King George	540	243	45.0
Lancaster	365	143	39.2
Prince Edward	312	83	26.6
Richmond	571	215	36.6
Spotsylvania	499	209	41.8
Westmoreland	708	338	_47.7_
Average			37.4
1758			
Accomac	1130	561	49.6
Amelia	937	465	49.6
Elizabeth City	237	106	44.7
Essex	666	356	53.5
Frederick	1630	398	24.4
Lancaster	365	218	59.7
Northumberland	735	329	44.8
Prince Edward	312	140	44.9
Prince George	488	270	55.3
Richmond	571	229	_40.1_
Average			43.4
1771			
Essex	731	245	33.5
Lancaster	365	166	45.5
Northumberland	755	291	38.5
Richmond	701	259	36.9
Spotsylvania	587	286	48.7
Surry	540	240	_44.4_
Average			40.4

figure in 1748 was the largest one recorded is impossible to discern, though it possibly could have related to conditions in the tobacco market. Not only did the turnout vary from election to election; it also differed from county to county. Essex, in the Tidewater region, had particularly high levels of involvement; over 50 percent appeared on a number of occasions. Meanwhile, Frederick, located farther west, registered much lower totals. Only 18.9 percent came out in 1755 and 24.4 percent attended the famous election of 1758 when George Washington first obtained a spot in the legislature.[5]

The abundance of polls preserved from certain counties (such as Richmond, Essex, Accomac, Lancaster, and Northumberland) listing both winners and losers enables us to analyze their results in greater depth than is normally possible elsewhere. We can gauge not only the percentages of those who voted but also the closeness of the contests and the number of candidates participating. In Richmond, which was fairly typical of the old Tidewater plantation counties, approximately 40 percent turned out on the average. Competitors for the two House seats were few; it was generally a three-man race with perhaps a fourth person receiving a scattering of votes. Some Richmond contests were rather one-sided, with the winners having a margin of 70 to 100 votes out of a total of 250; others proved to be quite evenly matched. In 1758, Landon Carter defeated Colonel Tarpley by only nine votes, and in 1761, he beat Colonel John Smith by just eight votes. Neighboring Essex had rather extensive turnouts, perhaps the largest in the colony. The number of candidates was large too; frequently five or six men competed at each election. Yet it appears from the results that no more than three or four were serious contenders. Many of the Essex encounters were relatively close. The winning contestants in 1755, for example, William Daingerfield and Francis Smith, polled 188 and 173, respectively, while the losers, Captain James Garnett and John Upshaw, obtained 158 and 137. Six years later, three men tallied more than 200: John Upshaw received 276, John Lee 243, and Francis Waring 211, the latter in a losing effort. Accomac, located on the Eastern Shore, frequently had turnouts of more than 45 percent. Moreover, it traditionally had the largest number of candidates entered. Some ten individuals ran in the elections of 1752 and 1758, with nine doing so in 1755. In the latter contest, which was especially tight, six of the nine persons surpassed 100 votes, as Ralph Justice edged Charles West for the second spot, 190 to 188. In Lancaster, in the northern part of the colony, the poll ranged from 40 to almost 60 percent. Yet despite the rather heavy turnouts, most of the contests were not very close. Usually the two winners, generally members of the Carter, Mitchell, or Ball family, had little competition, the third man in the field obtaining less than half the total of those above him. The two exceptions to this took place in 1752 and 1761 when serious challenges were apparently made. In the first instance, only twenty-one votes separated the four main candidates, while in the second, George Heale lost out to Richard Mitchell by eighteen votes, 126 to 108, in a three-man struggle. Northumberland's contests were, on the whole, much tighter ones. Most of them involved major clashes among three, if not four, members of the gentry. In 1768, the two losing contenders, Newton Keene and Samuel Eskridge, were defeated by just three and seventeen votes, respectively, in a race where 677 ballots were cast.[6]

The voting results preserved from the colony of New York are somewhat fewer in number. Adequate figures are available for only three counties, New York, Queens, and Westchester, with merely a scattering of returns listed for a few others. In just one instance, the election of 1761, are there totals from as many as four counties. Yet the limited data give a fairly good impression of the turnouts in the province since the places for which statistics are known comprised a considerable segment of the whole population. The average for three counties in 1739, containing half the populace, was 41.4 percent, while similar compilations for 1761 and 1768 were about 33 percent and 36 percent, respectively. These amounts denote the approximate range of voter involvement for the major counties, and after adjusting for the minor counties, where few turned out, it would seem to show the overall span to be 20 to 40 percent (see table 8).[7]

In the lower counties the percentages were generally higher than in those farther up the Hudson River. New York City and County, the main center of political activity, frequently saw 40 to 55 percent of the adult males casting ballots, and sometimes even more. In 1699, some 632 men voted in the Assembly contest, which comprised at least 80 percent, and in 1701, 224 took part in the municipal election in the three wards tabulated, or almost 60 percent. The local struggle in 1734 between the Morris and Cosby factions brought out 440 persons, while the disputed Assembly election of 1737 between Adolph Philipse and Cornelius Van Horne saw 812 (55.4 percent) come to the polls, the largest single total as of that time. By the end of the latter event, according to Cadwallader Colden, "The sick, the lame, and the blind were all carried out to vote."[8]

Approximately 633 voters (41.8 percent) participated in 1739 as the party battle continued, but only 177 were in attendance in 1745 (10.7 percent), the smallest number on record. Apparently by this time, the court faction, which had suffered several defeats in the city, did not think it worth the effort to campaign. The elections of 1748, 1750, 1752, and 1759 were so one-sided as to be determined without a poll, though in one instance the turnout must have been extremely large. The *New York Weekly Post-Boy,* surveying the contest held in September, 1750, stated that the four members were unanimously reelected "by a much greater Number of Persons than ever appeared . . . on the like Occasion."[9]

During the 1760's, as competition became increasingly severe, high totals were again the rule. In 1761, 1,447 men (56.1 percent) voted, and 1,924 or 53.6 percent were present in 1768. Interestingly enough, when factional strife between the Livingstons and the DeLanceys reached its peak in 1769, a significant drop occurred; just 1,515 individuals (40.6 percent) came out. Why a larger percentage showed up in 1761 and 1768 than in 1769 is difficult to explain. Perhaps the reason lay in the fact that the two earlier elections involved six and seven candidates who did not appear in any clear-cut alignment. Factional lines had not yet hardened, and people felt freer to vote than they did in the final encounter when the choice was between two fully competing four-men slates with sharply contrasting viewpoints. Because of viva voce voting, many men who had friends on both tickets did not want to offend either side and thus remained silent (see table 6).[10]

The average turnout in neighboring Queens County, where partisan battles rarely subsided, was probably just as high. About 47 percent participated in the eight elections for which figures are available between 1698 and 1768. Some 389 men appeared in 1698 (54.5 percent), and approximately 700 to 800 (48 to 50 percent) were on hand for the court-country encounters in 1737, 1739, and 1748. After that, the returns were slightly lower, with 35 to 45 percent delivering votes in 1750, 1761, and 1768. The highest total ever recorded took place during the latter period in a special election held in April, 1761. In a rematch of a disputed contest pitting former Speaker of the House David Jones, along with Thomas Cornell, against court candidates Thomas Hicks and Zebulon Seaman, around 1,100 males (56.2 percent) went to the polls. On

TABLE 6

New York County Elections, 1761, 1768, and 1769

1761		1768		1769	
Candidate	Number of Votes	Candidate	Number of Votes	Candidate	Number of Votes
J. Cruger	1,069	P. Livingston	1,320	J. DeLancey	936
P. Livingston	916	J. DeLancey	1,204	J. Walton	931
L. Lispenard	838	J. Walton	1,175	J. Cruger	882
W. Bayard	795	J. Jauncey	1,052	J. Jauncey	877
J. Scott	722	J. Scott	870	P. Livingston	666
J. DeLancey	700	W. Bayard	584	J. Scott	646
		A. Dodge	257	P. V. Livingston	535
				T. Van Wyck	518
Total Number of Voters	1,447		1,924		1,515

the whole, the outcome in most of the Queens races was rather one-sided as the Jones-Cornell duo generally won by a margin of more than 200, capturing at least 60 percent of the ballots cast. The major exceptions occurred in 1761, when in the regular event Cornell and Jones won by only 21 and 40 votes, respectively, while in the second clash Cornell had 546, Seaman 538, and Jones 537, the latter being defeated by just a single tally (see table 7).[11]

Elsewhere in the province, where division was less pronounced, the figures were somewhat smaller, in some cases much smaller. In Westchester County, although 420 (32.9 percent) of the adult male population voted in the famous election of Lewis Morris in 1733, fewer than 30 percent appeared in 1750, followed by 14.0 percent in 1761 and 18.3 percent in 1768. Of the 826 adult males in Ulster County, 117 voted in the contest in 1748 (only 14.2 percent). The turnout in Kings and Suffolk counties and on the three manors—Livingston, Rensselaer, and Van Cortlandt—where practically every election was uncontested was probably

TABLE 7

Queens County, New York, Elections, 1739, 1750, and 1761

1739		1750	
Candidate	Number of Votes	Candidate	Number of Votes
D. Jones	518	D. Jones	452
T. Cornell	460	T. Cornell	477
I. Hicks	272	I. Hicks	293
B. Hicks	206	D. Simmons	288

1761		1761a	
Candidate	Number of Votes	Candidate	Number of Votes
D. Jones	382	T. Cornell	546
T. Cornell	363	Z. Seaman	538
T. Hicks	342	D. Jones	537
Z. Seaman	227	T. Hicks	479
W. Talman	42		

[a]Special election.

smaller still. The only known figure for any manor was the 143 votes recorded at Van Cortlandt's estate in 1769. However, individual results from Albany, Richmond, and Dutchess counties indicate that the participation in these places was considerable at times. Some 636 went to the polls in Albany in 1739 (35.3 percent), 151 voted in Richmond in 1761 (38.5 percent), and 1,296 in Dutchess in 1769 (37 percent) (see table 8).[12]

The voting analysis for Pennsylvania is based upon more than sixty examples from the five largest counties—Philadelphia, Bucks, Chester, Lancaster, and York—plus the city of Philadelphia, which had separate elections. (Residents of Philadelphia could legally vote twice—first in the county, the next day in the city.) Actually, the precise number of participants is almost never mentioned in the Pennsylvania returns; just the totals for the winning candidates are listed. Nevertheless, the fact that certain individuals like Isaac Norris of Philadelphia captured virtually every ballot in each contest helps give us a fairly accurate picture of the results in the colony.[13]

The overall Pennsylvania vote seems to have ranged from slightly below 20 percent to slightly above 40 percent judging by six samples, which included at least three of the four most populous counties. In 1737, approximately 25.9 percent came to the polls, followed by 30.1 percent in 1738, 19.2 percent in 1739, 33.3 percent in 1740, and 36.6 percent in 1742. The higher turnouts in the early 1740's surely reflected the increasing amount of strife between the Quaker and Proprietary factions. The *Pennsylvania Gazette* noted at the time that "there was a greater Number of Votes in all the Counties of this Province, than have appear'd for several Years past."[14] The biggest total of all occurred in 1765 when 41.4 percent showed up amid the struggle between the two sides over the continuance of proprietary government.

On a local basis, the highest percentages came from ethnically divided York and Lancaster counties, where most results fell between 35 and 45 percent. The city of Philadelphia averaged 32.7 percent, while more homogeneous Chester and Bucks counties came up with less than 30 and 25 percent, respectively. Philadelphia County, for which we have the greatest number of returns (twenty-eight), averaged only 24.4 percent. Nevertheless, in Philadelphia, the percentage in years of crucial elections was often higher than in any other county. In 1765, for example, 46.4 percent of the adult males voted, five points above the average for the four

TABLE 8
New York Assembly Voting, 1698-1769

Year	New York Number of Votes	New York Percentage	Queens Number of Votes	Queens Percentage	Westchester Number of Votes	Westchester Percentage	Other Number of Votes	Other Percentage
1698			389	54.5				
1699	632	80.0						
1701	224[a]	55.-60.						
1733					420	32.9		
1734	442							
1737	812	55.4	726	48.6				
1739	633	41.8	728	48.4				
1745	177	10.7						
1748			800	50.1			Albany 636	35.3
1750			755	45.8	289-500	14.-30.	Ulster 117	14.2
1761	1,447	56.1	678	34.6	476	14.0	Richmond 151	38.5
			1,100	56.2				
1768	1,924	53.6	871	40.0	739	18.3	Dutchess 1296	37.0
1769	1,515	40.6						

[a]Total for three wards recorded.

counties surveyed. In fact, the lower overall figure for Philadelphia County may merely reflect the larger quantity of returns when competition was light than can be located elsewhere (see table 9).

The abundant statistics available for Philadelphia County from 1725 to 1775 allow us to examine the size of the turnouts over a long period and see how it relates to the factional conflict there. Considerable numbers of voters appeared at the ballot box during the late 1720's as former Governor William Keith and his followers sought to outduel the Penn interest. After Keith's departure, the totals tended to drop off a bit, but they started to rise once more at the end the next decade as the newly created Proprietary faction began organizing against the entrenched Quakers. In 1740, almost twice the usual complement came out (1,822), as the Proprietary group made its first serious attempt to take over the Assembly. Notwithstanding a valiant effort, its standard-bearers were defeated by approximately 250 to 300 votes. Two years later, they made another fierce bid, capped by use of force at the polls, but this time they were beaten by an even wider margin as faction leader William Allen's tally of 336 was 1,150 beneath the lowest Quaker figure.[15]

For the next eleven years opposition to the Quakers was minimal with the turnout rarely approaching earlier levels except when there was a close race for sheriff. Indeed, in this time span the sheriff's race was the only one that excited any attention. No Assembly contest of any magnitude took place until 1754 and the outbreak of the French and Indian War. On that occasion, the Proprietary candidates were again soundly subdued as they managed little more than 600 votes apiece while the Quaker stalwarts had upwards of 1,500. The Allen faction offered no formal competition the following year, but in 1756 they tried once more to oust the Quakers who were bothered by internal divisions stemming from their ambivalence on the war issue. Yet, despite a shake-up in personnel (the pacifists dropping out), the Quaker party was still able to top their opponents by at least 500 ballots (see table 10).[16]

Again for several years, no real contest occurred. Not once in the next seven elections did as many as 20 percent of the adult males take part. But in 1764, when controversy developed over retaining proprietary government, the ensuing clash brought out the greatest number of voters ever. Almost 3,900 persons went to the polls as the Proprietary party or New Ticket was finally able to edge out a number of Quakers from their Assembly seats. A breakdown of the returns demonstrates just how close

TABLE 9

Pennsylvania Assembly Voting, 1725-1775

Year	Philadelphia County		Philadelphia City		Bucks		Chester		Lancaster		York	
	No.	%	No.	%	No.	%	No.	%	No.	%	No.	%
1725					323							
1727	787	27.7										
1728	971	32.8										
1730	622	19.4			304							
1732	904	26.2										
1734	821	22.2			339							
1735	1,097	28.3										
1736	719	17.6										
1737	904	21.2	238	14.7	522	26.0	724	28.6	753	31.5		
1738	1,306	29.3			382	19.1	963	36.7	1,019	39.8		
1739	555	11.9			450	22.5	866	31.8				
1740	1,822	37.6							988	33.7		
1741	1,151	22.8							1,150	36.9		
1742	1,793	34.2					961	32.0	1,480	44.8		
1743	1,028	18.8										
1749									1,000	31.9		

TABLE 9 (continued)

Year	Philadelphia County No.	%	Philadelphia City No.	%	Bucks No.	%	Chester No.	%	Lancaster No.	%	York No.	%
1750	2,004	29.1										
1751	1,473	20.7	831	36.5								
1752	948	13.1										
1754	2,181	29.2										
1755	1,236	16.3										
1756	1,770	23.0									1,248	45.5
1757	785	10.0	603	22.7					709	13.8	1,106	38.4
1758	1,567	19.7	183	06.8								
1761	950	11.1										
1764	3,874	42.2	1,300	42.2	1,450	45.8	1,150	22.4				
1765	4,332	46.1	1,973	61.8					2,919	47.7		
1766	3,019	31.4	1,512	45.8								
1771	1,300	12.4										
1774			1,336	35.6								
1775	3,122	29.9	775	26.6								

TABLE 10

Philadelphia County Elections, 1740, 1742, 1754, and 1756

1740		1742		1754		1756	
Candidate	Number of Votes	Candidate	Number of Votes	Candidate	Number of Votes	Candidate	Number of Votes
T. Leech	1,822	T. Leech	1,793	E. Morgan	2,181	I. Norris	1,758
J. Kinsey	1,097	J. Kinsey	1,786	I. Norris	2,169	J. Fox	1,754
R. Jones	1,105	R. Jones	1,786	H. Evans	2,169	T. Leech	1,723
I. Norris	1,088	I. Norris	1,775	J. Stretch	2,167	D. Robedeau	1,218
E. Warner	1,087	E. Warner	1,773	E. Warner	1,583	J. Hughes	1,189
J. Trotter	1,070	O. Evans	1,767	J. Fox	1,576	J. Baynton	1,152
J. Morris	1,073	J. Morris	1,494	J. Morris	1,567	J. Galloway	1,147
O. Evans	1,070	J. Trotter	1,488	J. Trotter	1,555	R. Pearn	1,140
W. Allen	807	W. Allen	336	A. James	600	W. Coleman	616
W. Branson	756	J. Robson	334	J. Duche	593	J. Dresler	612
W. Momington	751			J. Hall	590	H. Pawling	599
W. Rowle	747			T. Leech	621	P. Bond	579
G. Boon	740					J. Lakers	525
S. Lane	731					J. Hall	61
J. Maddox	731					W. Allen	14

the struggle was. Merely twenty-six votes separated Henry Keppele, sixth on the list, and a winner, from Benjamin Franklin, thirteen on the list and a loser. Isaac Norris and Joseph Richardson, running on both tickets, were the only men to win handily. The complete totals for 1764 were:

Isaac Norris	3,874	Henry Harrison	1,921
Joseph Richardson	3,848	Joseph Galloway	1,918
John Dickinson	2,030	Frederick Antis	1,914
Joseph Fox	1,963	Rowland Evans	1,911
Henry Pawling	1,955	Benjamin Franklin	1,906
Henry Keppele	1,932	Plunkett Fleeson	1,884
Amos Strettle	1,930		
John Hughes	1,925		

The following year, 1765, when the Stamp Act became an added issue, the turnout was even larger as the Quaker group managed to coax hundreds of additional voters to the polling place to win back a number of the lost seats. Some 4,332 people, the biggest single county total anywhere in the provincial period, cast ballots, as Proprietary men John Dickinson, Amos Strettle, and Henry Keppele, winners the previous year, were sent down to defeat. The individual results for 1765 were:

Isaac Norris	4,332	John Dickinson	1,920
Joseph Richardson	2,451	Amos Strettle	1,951
Joseph Fox	2,466	Isaac Jones	1,936
Henry Pawling	2,432	Redmond Conyngham	1,934
Rowland Evans	2,427	Henry Keppele	1,927
Thomas Lewiszy	2,423	Frederick Antis	1,917
Michael Hillegas	2,415	Jacob Winey	1,912
Joseph Galloway	2,400		

Thereafter, the returns grew appreciably smaller as the factional struggle began to subside. No more than 3,019 voted in 1766 (31.4 percent), and just 1,300 (12.4 percent) showed up in 1771. Not until the crisis of independence did the figure rise to any degree (3,122 participated in 1775) and then not to the 1764-1765 level.[17]

In Rhode Island, few results have been uncovered for the first half of the eighteenth century, and it is probable that overall turnouts were rather small. Only 888 persons came to the polls in 1749, and, according to the Reverend Ezra Stiles, voting totals before 1750 never exceeded 1,300 in any single contest.[18] This would have been the equivalent of no more than 25 percent of the adult males in the province. Yet in the decade extending from 1758 to 1767, when the rivalry between the Ward and Hopkins factions was in full bloom, the final count usually climbed above 4,000, and participation remained above 40 percent every year (see table 11). The percentages, based on census data from 1755 and 1770, ranged from 41.7 to 47.3 percent of the male population, averaging approximately 45 percent for the eight available samples. The largest percentage occurred in 1763, although the highest turnout in terms of numbers took place in 1767 when 4,497 Rhode Islanders cast ballots as the factional struggle was reaching its climax. The following year, 1768, as both Hopkins and Ward agreed to step aside in the interest of unity, only 3,238 (32.2 percent) bothered to vote in the race between Josias Lyndon, former clerk of the Assembly, and Joseph Wanton, the previous Deputy Governor. However, the figures increased once more in 1770 as 3,662 persons, almost 35 percent, handed in proxes when Ward reentered the fray against Wanton.[19] After 1770, the long encounter finally ended, and turnouts diminished rapidly. Probably not many more than 15 to 17 percent voted in 1771, 1772, and 1773, judging by the figures available for a handful of towns. The Newport figures, for example, declined

TABLE 11

Rhode Island Gubernatorial Voting, 1758-1770

Year	Number of Adult Males (Estimated)	Number of Voters	Percentage
1758	7,612	3,390	44.5
1760	8,099	3,600	44.4
1762	8,585	4,016	46.8
1763	8,829	4,177	47.3
1764	9,072	3,987	43.9
1765	9,315	4,401	47.2
1766	9,558	3,983	41.7
1767	9,802	4,497	45.9
1768	10,045	3,238	32.2
1770	10,532	3,662	34.8

from 387 in 1770 to 177 in 1771, and 188 in 1773; North Kingstown dropped from 153 in 1770 to 69 in 1771, 61 in 1772, and 53 in 1773.[20]

On the local level it is more difficult to determine the percentages during the Ward-Hopkins controversy since a few of the towns were not yet incorporated at the time of the census of 1755.[21] Nevertheless, by making some derivations from the census of 1770 together with the voting results for 1767, we can make a rough estimate of the turnout in each individual town for that particular election. In general, most of the communities fell between 35 and 60 percent, with four above that range and three below. The greatest outpouring of voters took place in North Providence where 82.8 percent of the adult males proxed. Other locales showing heavy involvement included Warren, Jamestown, and Middletown. The smallest proportions occurred in Providence and Newport, where fewer than 30 percent went to the polls. On a county basis, those located in the central part of the province, Bristol and Kent had the highest percentages, 52.9 and 48.9, respectively. Perhaps this was due to the vigorous electioneering efforts made there as the opposing sides strongly competed for the allegiance of this middle area. Bristol and Kent were followed by Kings County in the southwest with 45.4 percent, Providence County in the north with 43.1 percent, and Newport County in the south with 37.0 percent (see table 12).

The contests between Ward and Hopkins were almost always close. Neither man ever received more than 54.5 percent of the committed votes, and on four occasions the winner had 51 percent or less. In 1758, Hopkins took the election by just 66 votes, beating Ward by 1,728 to 1,662. Actually Ward received a higher total among the proxy ballots, but Hopkins collected a huge surplus among the hand ballots, giving him the victory.[22] Hopkins won by the sum of 351 in 1759 but only by 66 in 1761 as the struggle was becoming more heated. Ward finally secured the governorship in the following year, 1762, though by an even smaller number. No overall figures have been found for that gubernatorial race, but the assistants running on the Ward ticket defeated the men named on the Hopkins slate by an average of ten votes in a total of about 4,000. The next year, 1763, Hopkins succeeded by a margin of 271, but the gap dwindled to 24 in 1764 as he barely edged out Ward by 1,992 to 1,968. Ward took over the governor's chair in 1765 and 1766, winning by the substantial amounts of 255 and 235, respectively. However, the pendulum swung back again to Hopkins in 1767 as he achieved the biggest spread in

TABLE 12

Rhode Island County Voting, 1767

		Number of Adult Males (Estimated)	Number of Voters	Percentage (Including Average)
Bristol	Warren	178	118	66.3
	Bristol	204	84	41.2
		382	202	52.9
Kent	Coventry	356	189	53.1
	West Greenwich	322	163	50.6
	Warwick	427	203	47.5
	East Greenwich	312	138	44.2
		1,417	693	48.9
Kings	Exeter	329	160	48.6
	Westerly	316	152	48.1
	North Kingstown	404	208	51.5
	Richmond	215	102	47.4
	Hopkinton	320	140	43.8
	South Kingstown	413	173	41.9
	Charlestown	234	78	33.3
		2,231	1,013	45.4

TABLE 12 (continued)

		Number of Adult Males (Estimated)	Number of Voters	Percentage (Including Average)
Providence	North Providence	145	120	82.8
	Cumberland	300	175	58.3
	Johnston	182	96	52.7
	Scituate	682	325	47.7
	Gloucester	557	263	47.2
	Smithfield	557	253	45.4
	Cranston	357	156	43.7
	Providence	914	205	22.4
		3,694	1,593	43.1
Newport	Jamestown	76	47	61.8
	Middletown	158	96	60.8
	Little Compton	228	132	57.9
	New Shoreham	82	46	56.1
	Tiverton	314	120	38.2
	Portsmouth	257	91	35.4
	Newport	1,575	463	29.4
		2,690	995	37.0

any of the ten contests, topping Ward by 405, with a tally of 2,433 to Ward's 2,028 (see table 13).[23]

The reasons why the vote fluctuated and why the governorship shifted back and forth from one faction to the other reflected changes on the local level. Some writers in the past have intimated that the voting patterns in the colony were fairly stable and that they completely mirrored the sectional split between the Providence and Newport regions. While true for the most part, this explanation does not convey the total picture. An examination of the available figures for the five years from 1763 to 1767 shows that the idea of the Ward-Hopkins controversy embodying a sharp and consistent north-south division is somewhat exaggerated. Only in 1767 did the results indicate a clear-cut geographical split between the sections, with all the towns above the Bristol Ferry line supporting Hopkins and all the towns below it backing Ward. In earlier years, seven of the twenty-eight towns—Bristol, Charlestown, Coventry, East Greenwich, Gloucester, Jamestown, and Johnston—switched allegiance on at least one occasion and sometimes more often. These shifts included not only border areas in the middle of the province but communities close to the major centers of influence. Both Johnston and Gloucester, near Providence, and Jamestown, across the bay from Newport, changed sides several times over the five-year span. Johnston went from a Hopkins majority of 23 in 1763 to a Ward majority of 2, 19, and 17 in 1764, 1765, and 1766, respectively, and then returned to the Hopkins camp by 27 in 1767. Gloucester favored Hopkins by 23 in 1763, Ward by 17 in 1764, gave the nod to Hopkins by 2 in 1765, then supported Ward by 41 in 1766, and finally jumped back to Hopkins in 1767 by 35. Jamestown gave its vote by narrow margins to Hopkins in 1763, 1764, and 1766 and did so in a similar fashion to Ward in 1765 and 1767.[24]

In addition to the switching, the degree of commitment by certain towns that remained with the same candidate throughout was not always very solid. For example, Middletown, outside of Newport, gave a majority to Ward in each of the five years but only by an average of four and a half votes. To be sure, each man had a few local bastions of overwhelming popularity where he often received more than 70 percent of the total vote. Cumberland, Scituate, and Smithfield usually came out for Hopkins in very large numbers, while Ward's home ground Westerly and neighboring Hopkinton, along with Tiverton and Little Compton, always gave their hero heavy backing. The citizens of Newport, the faction's central

TABLE 13

Rhode Island Gubernatorial Elections, 1758-1767

| Year | Hopkins | | Ward | | Margin |
	Number of Votes	Percentage	Number of Votes	Percentage	
1758	1,728	51.0	1,662	49.0	H+ 66
1759					H+351
1761					H+ 66
1762[a]	1,995	49.9	2,005	50.1	W+ 10
1763	2,210	53.3	1,939	46.7	H+271
1764	1,992	50.3	1,968	49.7	H+ 24
1765	2,047	47.1	2,302	52.9	W+255
1766[a]	1,863	47.1	2,098	52.9	W+235
1767	2,433	54.5	2,028	45.5	H+405

[a]The figures for these years are approximate because of the absence of any totals for the governor's race in 1762 and the lack of any return for Bristol in 1766.

headquarters, naturally gave Ward a big numerical advantage too, though they were not as united around their man as the inhabitants of Providence were behind theirs. Ward usually obtained about 75 percent of the proxes in the capital, but in some instances Hopkins received practically 100 percent of the Providence ballots. In 1766, for example, Hopkins defeated his adversary there by 194 to 1 and in 1767 did so by 204 to 0. Table 14 gives a town-by-town breakdown of the available Rhode Island vote from 1758 to 1770. [25]

In Massachusetts, the turnout was probably somewhat lower than in the middle colonies or Rhode Island. From the three towns in which a substantial number of returns can be located, Boston, Salem, and Lynn, the average for each fell below 30 percent. Lynn averaged 28.8 percent in six contests, Salem 25.2 percent in seven contests, and Boston less than 25 percent in more than fifty contests.[26] In these coastal locales the number of eligible voters was somewhat fewer than in the outlying agricultural areas. This might convey the impression that the Boston, Salem, and Lynn results are not typical of the province as a whole. Yet the smaller percentage of electors was more than offset by the fact that these seaports were sometimes the scene of fierce competition at election time. The inland communities, on the other hand, rarely found themselves in such a situation because Assembly candidates usually ran unopposed. Many of these settlements would not even agree to hold an election, and in several that did, the biggest vote recorded was one against sending any representative. To be sure, heated contests did take place from time to time in such eastern towns as Cambridge, Woburn, and Dorchester, where 30 or 40 percent cast ballots on occasion. In Cambridge, approximately 45 percent voted in the disputed election involving John Vassal mentioned earlier. About 38 percent participated in the choice of Roland Cotton in Woburn in 1742, and 32 and 37 percent voted in Dorchester in 1750 and 1751, respectively. Even larger turnouts appeared in politically divided Watertown and Weston, if a couple of samples are any indication. Some 82 percent of the freeholders came to the polls in Weston in 1773, and an amazing 97 percent (131 of 135) did so in Watertown in 1757.[27]

Although the degree of participation in Boston was comparatively low, almost all the returns from 1696 to 1774 have survived. This enables us to trace its voting patterns accurately from the beginning of the period to the end, something that cannot be done for any other com-

TABLE 14

Rhode Island Town Voting, 1758-1770

	Ward	1758 Hopkins	Margin	1759 Margin	1761 Margin	Ward	1762 Hopkins	Margin
Bristol	31	30	W +1	H +5	H +2	42	39	W +3
Charlestown	26	24	W +2	H +5	0	46	40	W +6
Coventry	65	39	W +26	H +24	W +15	78	72	W +6
Cranston	31	72	W +41	H +46	H +17	71	80	H +9
Cumberland	0	98	H +98	H +83	H +119	13	138	H +125
E. Greenwich	57	42	W +15	W +5	W +19	76	65	W +11
Exeter	61	29	W +32	W +8	W +55	90	55	W +35
Gloucester	68	74	H +6	H +7	H +20	106	128	H +22
Hopkinton	56	10	W +46	W +42	W +80	105	23	W +82
Jamestown	15	13	W +2	H +5	W +1	18	15	W +3
Johnston	—	—		W +13	W +5	46	33	W +13
Little Compton	65	15	W +50	W +42	W +53	74	26	W +48
Middletown	36	16	W +20	W +10	W +19	41	26	W +15
Newport	173	68	W +105	W +106	W +158	281	126	W +155
New Shoreham	14	14	0	W +6	W +26	35	8	W +27
N. Kingstown	66	62	W +4	H +25	H +6	103	94	W +9
Portsmouth	46	11	W +35	W +10	W +9	44	33	W +11
Providence	71	217	H +146	H +158	H +192	77	249	H +172
Richmond	60	1	W +59	W +22	W +56	75	19	W +56
Scituate	35	101	H +66	H +107	H +167	53	189	H +136
Smithfield	71	117	H +46	H +84	H +106	49	162	H +113
S. Kingstown	54	59	H +5	H +17	W +30	103	67	W +36
Tiverton	40	13	W +27	H +25	W +12	66	53	W +13
Warren	9	31	H +22	H +40	H +56	39	64	H +25
Warwick	23	89	H +66	H +95	H +89	47	138	H +91
Westerly	65	17	W +48	W +81	W +94	128	14	W +114
W. Greenwich	85	19	W +66	W +30	W +76	98	40	W +58
Hand votes	334	447						
Totals	1,662	1,728	H +66	H +351	H +66	1,995	2,005	H +10

TABLE 14 (Continued)

	Ward	1763 Hopkins	Margin		Ward	1764 Hopkins	Margin	
Bristol	52	46	W	+6	45	41	W	+4
Charlestown	40	41	H	+1	48	27	W	+21
Coventry	87	76	W	+11	100	68	W	+32
Cranston	66	92	H	+26	64	101	H	+37
Cumberland	13	136	H	+123	11	130	H	+119
E. Greenwich	67	68	H	+1	77	62	W	+15
Exeter	102	56	W	+46	82	58	W	+24
Gloucester	104	127	H	+23	124	108	W	+16
Hopkinton	98	33	W	+65	98	34	W	+64
Jamestown	19	23	H	+4	16	24	H	+8
Johnston	28	51	H	+23	37	35	W	+2
Little Compton	90	30	W	+60	95	30	W	+65
Middletown	38	30	W	+8	35	32	W	+3
Newport	283	104	W	+179	279	113	W	+166
New Shoreham	25	19	W	+6	24	16	W	+8
N. Kingstown	110	88	W	+22	112	75	W	+37
N. Providence	—	—			—	—		
Portsmouth	45	40	W	+5	46	39	W	+7
Providence	70	292	H	+222	54	246	H	+192
Richmond	67	16	W	+51	72	16	W	+56
Scituate	33	236	H	+203	53	194	H	+141
Smithfield	53	161	H	+108	38	161	H	+123
S. Kingstown	88	83	W	+5	82	66	W	+16
Tiverton	70	59	W	+11	75	51	W	+24
Warren	39	73	H	+34	33	64	H	+31
Warwick	46	143	H	+97	55	111	H	+56
Westerly	107	26	W	+81	103	38	W	+65
W. Greenwich	99	61	W	+38	104	48	W	+56
Hand votes					6	4		
Totals	1,939	2,210	H	+271	1,968	1,992	H	+24

Ward	1765 Hopkins	Margin		Ward	1766 Hopkins	Margin		Ward	1767 Hopkins	Margin	
44	43	W	+1	[40]	[40]			29	55	H	+26
47	23	W	+24	47	24	W	+23	52	26	W	+26
96	82	W	+14	89	68	W	+21	88	101	H	+13
77	100	H	+23	56	91	H	+35	38	118	H	+80
37	112	H	+75	20	114	H	+94	6	169	H	+163
81	57	W	+24	78	50	W	+28	78	60	W	+18
111	36	W	+75	109	30	W	+79	107	53	W	+54
131	133	H	+2	143	103	W	+40	114	149	H	+35
98	33	W	+65	107	22	W	+85	106	34	W	+72
21	18	W	+3	19	21	H	+2	26	21	W	+5
51	32	W	+19	47	30	W	+17	34	61	H	+27
91	36	W	+55	84	32	W	+52	99	33	W	+66
45	42	W	+3	40	38	W	+2	50	44	W	+6
350	117	W	+233	325	116	W	+209	329	112	W	+217
36	12	W	+24	35	8	W	+27	41	5	W	+36
119	82	W	+37	108	81	W	+27	114	91	W	+23
—	—			48	57	H	+9	38	79	H	+41
51	30	W	+21	40	25	W	+15	49	42	W	+7
55	264	H	+209	1	194	H	+193	0	204	H	+204
83	18	W	+65	82	14	W	+68	71	31	W	+40
59	234	H	+175	48	211	H	+163	35	290	H	+255
102	162	H	+60	60	150	H	+90	53	200	H	+147
98	61	W	+37	92	58	W	+34	102	68	W	+34
74	50	W	+24	65	41	W	+24	70	50	W	+20
43	67	H	+24	30	62	H	+32	34	84	H	+50
60	125	H	+65	54	117	H	+63	48	155	H	+107
128	36	W	+92	135	23	W	+112	109	43	W	+66
112	39	W	+73	91	42	W	+49	108	55	W	+53
2	3			5	1						
2,302	2,047	W	+255	2,098	1,863	W	+235	2,028	2,433	H	+405

TABLE 14 (Continued)

	1768			1769 Wanton/ Lyndon Margin		1770			
	Wanton	Lyndon	Margin		Wanton	Ward	Margin		
Bristol	26	38	L +12	W +8	40	62	Wd +22		
Charlestown	24	38	L +14	W +22	34	16	Wn +18		
Coventry	22	103	L +81	W +56	86	71	Wn +15		
Cranston	82	33	W +49	W +73	92	47	Wn +45		
Cumberland	8	100	L +92	W +80	156	9	Wn +147		
E. Greenwich	36	77	L +41	W +17	53	70	Wd +17		
Exeter	7	55	L +48	W +30	49	72	Wd +23		
Gloucester	6	166	L +160	L +79	84	101	Wd +17		
Hopkinton	6	102	L +96	—	35	67	Wd +32		
Jamestown	17	6	W +11	W +11	24	12	Wn +12		
Johnston	26	50	L +24	W +38	22	57	Wd +35		
Little Compton	4	105	L +101	L +24	41	72	Wd +31		
Middletown	41	34	W +7	W +2	42	34	Wn +8		
Newport	126	241	L +115	L +97	225	158	Wn +67		
New Shoreham	4	11	L +7	—	—	—			
N. Kingstown	103	50	W +53	W +87	61	92	Wd +31		
N. Providence	4	52	L +48	L +9	30	17	Wn +13		
Portsmouth	26	51	L +25	W +5	60	41	Wn +19		
Providence	37	133	L +96	W +60	183	52	Wn +131		
Richmond	3	47	L +44	—	36	38	Wd +2		
Scituate	12	188	L +176	W +54	201	30	Wn +171		
Smithfield	69	184	L +115	W +22	143	36	Wn +107		
S. Kingstown	44	97	L +53	W +34	95	55	Wn +40		
Tiverton	8	81	L +73	W +13	37	43	Wd +6		
Warren	12	72	L +60	L +50	16	75	Wd +59		
Warwick	55	80	L +25	W +71	109	39	Wn +70		
Westerly	39	91	L +52	L +20	51	108	Wd +57		
W. Greenwich	18	98	L +80	W +42	65	78	Wd +13		
Totals	865	2,383	L +1,518	W +446	2,070	1,552	Wn +518		

munity. In the earliest years (1696-1714), no more than 25 percent of the adult male population voted in most cases. The only exception occurred in 1703 when the election of the first Assembly in the reign of Governor Joseph Dudley stimulated 459 citizens (34.3 percent) to cast ballots. During the decade from 1715 to 1724 (most of it within Governor Shute's administration), an average of 286 inhabitants went to the polls, approximately 16 percent of the adult men. The highest figure (454) was registered in 1719 amid conflict with the Governor on various issues. The electors taking part increased to an average of 392 over the next ten years from 1725 to 1734 as much controversy existed in the regime of Governor Burnet and the early years of Jonathan Belcher's. Yet the percentage remained roughly the same (16 percent), as the population was rising at a similar level. Both the number and percentage of voters expanded somewhat over the next few decades. From 1735 to 1744, covering the period of the Land Bank crisis, an average of 434 (18.5 percent) of the adult males turned out. This was followed by an average of 502 (22.5 percent) from 1745 to 1754, 612 (26.4 percent) from 1755 to 1764, with a drop to 555 (25.2 percent) in the years 1765 to 1774, those immediately preceding the Revolution. The two greatest tallies at any Boston election occurred in 1760 and 1763, when 997 and 1,089 persons balloted, respectively. These took place before the crisis with the mother country even began and probably reflected local conflicts between the Otis and Hutchinson factions who were vying for control of the government rather than imperial questions (see table 15).[28]

While not as abundant as Boston's, the voting figures for Connecticut tell a comparable story. The statistics show that approximately 10 to 27 percent of the adult males took part in the yearly election of governor and assistants, the higher figures being obtained when strong competition prevailed. In 1723, the earliest year with recorded numerical returns, some 1,618 freemen cast ballots, or roughly 20 percent of the men over twenty-one. The election of 1740, the first sharply contested race in the eighteenth century, brought 4,260 citizens (24.5 percent) to the polls, as Joseph Talcott won over Jared Eliot, 2,734 to 1,393, with 133 votes scattered among three other candidates. Some 4,000 to 5,000 tickets were tallied in the campaign of 1748, when competition developed over the deputy governor's post as Roger Wolcott won by a bare majority. Subsequently, about 5,200 persons participated in 1755 (20.5 percent) as Wolcott was defeated by Thomas Fitch for the governorship. Wolcott

TABLE 15
Massachusetts Voting

BOSTON, 1696-1774								
Year	No.	%	Year	No.	%	Year	No.	%
1696	134	10.2	1730	530	21.9	1752	327	14.2
1698	340	25.0	1731	474	19.1	1753	445	20.0
				450	18.1			
1699	323	23.3	1732	655	25.8	1754	603	27.1
1703	459	31.1	1733	600	23.0	1755	492	22.1
	244	16.5						
1704	206	13.7	1734	604	22.6	1756	533	23.9
1709	204	12.6	1735	517	19.0	1757	528	23.7
1711	173	10.4	1736	266	9.8	1758	369	16.6
1715	262	14.9	1737	240	8.8	1759	469	21.0
1716	376	21.1	1738	481	18.9	1760	997	44.7
1717	283	15.7	1739	635	26.2	1761	334	15.0
1718	242	13.2	1740	418	18.3	1762	629	28.2
1719	454	24.6	1741	495	22.2	1763	1,089	48.9
				280	12.6			
1721	247	13.0	1742	525	23.6	1764	449	20.1
	322	16.9						
1722	205	10.7	1743	451	20.2	1765	641	29.1
1723	275	13.9	1744	532	23.9	1766	746	33.8
1724	209	10.2	1745	342	15.3	1767	618	28.0
1725	332	15.7	1746	443	19.9	1768	440	19.9
1726	203	9.4	1747	451	20.2	1769	508	23.0
1727	204	9.1	1748	723	32.4	1770	513	23.3
	214	9.6						
1728	248	10.8	1749	684	30.7	1771	410	18.6
1729	192	8.1	1750	541	24.3	1772	723	32.8
			1751	463	20.8	1773	419	19.0
						1774	534	24.2

SALEM, 1735-1742			LYNN, 1750-1756		
Year	No.	%	Year	No.	%
1735	212	23.6	1750	126	31.7
1738	222	24.7	1751	129	32.4
	265	29.4			
1739	136	15.1	1752	148	37.2
1740	190	21.1	1753	83	20.9
1741	347	38.6	1754	98	24.4
1742	217	24.1	1756	104	26.1

had topped Fitch the previous year but lost in the rematch by around 200 votes.

No other results for Connecticut can be found until the pre-Revolutionary decade, a time of great political activity. Yet in none of the later returns did the percentage of those voting surpass any of the earlier amounts by more than a few points. Nor were most of the encounters extremely close; the winner usually outdistanced his opponent by 15 to 20 percent. In 1767, 8,323 people came out for the gubernatorial contest (24.8 percent) when William Pitkin downed Thomas Fitch, 4,777 to 3,481, with 64 going to others. The following year, 1768, a total of 7,868 appeared (23 percent) as Pitkin bested Fitch, 5,033 to 2,835, while in 1769, 7,407 balloted (22 percent) as Pitkin was again victorious by a big margin, 4,654 to 2,636, with 117 scattered. The largest number of pollers showed up in 1770, 9,771 (27.4 percent), as Jonathan Trumbull, taking over for Pitkin, edged Fitch by a few hundred votes, 4,700 to 4,266, with 805 given to various others. The margin of victory was just 4.4 percent, the smallest ever, as Trumbull took 48.1 percent of the total, Fitch, 43.7 percent. Then, as Trumbull became secure in office, the size of the annual turnouts began to decline. Only 6,382 handed in tickets in 1772 (17.4 percent), and an even smaller number did so in 1774, despite a last-ditch effort by the Old Light forces. Although no overall figures are available, the output for three towns—Goshen, Lyme, and Norwich—points to no more than 14.5 percent, or 5,400 electors colony-wide. The amount receded even further thereafter. Around 5,000 polled in 1775 (13 percent) and 4,000 in 1776 (10.5 percent), as Trumbull ran unopposed in the last two contests before independence (see table 16).[29]

Only a handful of election results are available from Maryland, however, each of the five totals represents more than half of the adult males in the particular locality, which would indicate that a majority of Marylanders went to the polls at the time of a crucial election. During the heated contest between the court and country parties in the winter of 1751-1752, 660 persons voted in Anne Arundel County (57.2 percent) and 992 did so in Baltimore County (50.3 percent). The latter turnout was said to be "as many People as ever appeared at any one Election in this Province." Actually a larger sum was recorded in Baltimore several years later in February, 1770, when more than 2,475 freeholders brought in their votes. In the capital, Annapolis, a community of approximately 150 to 200 families in the later provincial period, 120 townsmen participated in the election of the Common Council in 1759. At least 140 polled

TABLE 16

Connecticut Gubernatorial Elections, 1723-1776

	Number of Votes	Percentage		Number of Votes	Percentage
1723			**1769**		
Gurdon Saltonstall	1,618	20.0	William Pitkin	4,654	
			Thomas Fitch	2,636	
1740			Scattered	117	
Joseph Talcott	2,734			7,407	22.0
Jared Eliot	1,393				
Jonathan Law	60		**1770**		
Elisha Williams	38		Jonathan Trumbull	4,700	
Thomas Fitch	35		Thomas Fitch	4,266	
	4,260	24.5	Scattered	805	
				9,771	27.4
1748					
Jonathan Law c.4,000-5,000		23.0	**1772**		
			Jonathan Trumbull	3,879	
1755			Scattered	2,503	
Thomas Fitch	c.2,700			6,382	17.4
Roger Wolcott	c.2,500				
	5,200	20.5	**1774**		
			Jonathan Trumbull	c.5,400	14.5
1767					
William Pitkin	4,777		**1775**		
Thomas Fitch	3,481		Jonathan Trumbull	c.5,000	13.0
Scattered	64				
	8,322	24.8	**1776**		
			Jonathan Trumbull	c.4,000	10.5
1768					
William Pitkin	5,033				
Thomas Fitch	2,835				
	7,868	23.0			

for Assembly representatives five years later in 1764 when Samuel Chase, the famous Revolutionary leader, first entered politics. Chase, with 88 votes, bested Dr. George Stuart, the court candidate who had 59, while Walter Dulany, running unopposed, had 132.[30]

In New Jersey, too, few returns have been preserved, but the available results show a significant number voted at times. Amid the battle between the Assembly and Governor Lewis Morris in 1739, 458 persons (41 percent of the adult men) cast ballots in Burlington County. Fifteen years later in 1754, the time of some of "the greatest election struggles the province had ever seen," 694 freeholders went to the polls in Middlesex County, which meant practically every landowner listed for the county and 50 percent of all men. Approximately 133 males (33 percent) voted in the Cape May contest of 1761. The largest recorded turnout occurred in 1772 when 242 of the 300 adult males in the town of Perth Amboy registered their vote, more than 80 percent of those eligible.[31]

For New Hampshire, only a small quantity of reutrns have come down to us outside of the largest city, Portsmouth, but they show a considerable number of ballots being cast at times. Dover residents brought forth 109 votes in 1745, which represented more than 40 percent of the adult male population. Seventy-one inhabitants of Durham were at the polls in 1755, probably the equivalent of 40 to 50 percent of the adult men. In a combined election for Londonderry and Windham in January, 1762, some 199 voters, or about 50 percent of the males in the two towns, participated in the choice of a representative. When the results were voided because the winning candidate did not have a clear majority, 270 persons (67 percent) appeared at the rematch a short time afterward. That same year, 165 men (70 percent) delivered tickets in the combined election in Dunstable (Nashua) and Hollis. A decade later, 58 citizens participated at a local town meeting in Raymond (63 percent), and 50 did so at a similar gathering in Goffstown (80 percent). In Hampton-Falls, a town racked by religious controversy, nearly all the men (88 and 99) took part in the local elections of 1770 and 1773, respectively.[32]

In the town of Portsmouth, where almost all the results from the half-century prior to independence have been uncovered, the turnout seems to have been much lower. The figures reveal that an average of 148 freemen went to the polls in twenty-one Assembly elections, with the total never exceeding 208. The highest number appeared at the contests of 1728 and 1731, when 204 and 208 voted, and did not reach a similar plateau until the early 1760's. It would seem from the entries in the records that not very much competition occurred here, perhaps accounting for the small returns. Only twice are the losers' amounts given, and quite often each of the winning candidates had exactly the same score. No census data exist for Portsmouth before the 1760's, but according to the number of adult males at that time (about 680), no more than 30 percent took part in any of the four elections held during the decade (see table 17).[33]

Extant statistics for Delaware are even scarcer, but a few returns have been located for New Castle County. At least 564 voted in the Assembly election of 1735, 576 in 1737, 588 in 1738, and 672 in 1756. It is not clear just what percentage this represents since there are no census data available. But as New Castle was roughly as populous as neighboring Kent County, where figures are known, it would appear that the turn-outs approached 40 to 50 percent of the taxables. On the local level, many of the records for the borough elections in Wilmington have been preserved. The first such contest in 1739 attracted 96 residents to the polls, approximately 80 percent of the adult males. However, the average turnout over the next thirty-six years down to the Revolution was somewhat smaller, perhaps 35 to 40 percent. The totals varied considerably from year to year as illustrated by the highs and lows registered for each decade. For the period from 1740 to 1749, the highest was 103, the lowest 48; for 1750 to 1759, the highest was 129, the lowest was 25; for 1760 to 1769, the highest was 73, the lowest was 28; and for 1770 to 1775, the highest was 144, the lowest was 44.[34]

In the Carolinas, the few figures available indicate that except for some key elections in the decade before independence, the turnouts were generally quite sparse. The only two poll lists discovered in the North Carolina State Archives show that in the Beaufort County town of Bath, 19 persons voted in 1762 and 25 did so in 1766. However, according to the contemporary account by Herman Husband, more than 700 men (54.3

TABLE 17

Portsmouth, New Hampshire, Voting, 1717-1775

Year	Number of Votes	Year	Number of Votes	Year	Number of Votes
1717	143	1739	97	1752	187
1728	204	1740	69	1762	203
1731	208	1741	75	1762	197
1732	111	1744	170	1765	163
1733	128	1745	114	1768	107
1736	136	1746	127	1774	197
1737	137	1748	155	1775	172

percent) participated in the Orange County poll in 1769 during the Regulator troubles. In that contest, Husband and Andrew Prior topped the the court candidate, Edmund Fanning, with totals of 642 and 455, respectively, compared to the latter's 314.[35]

With the possible exception of Georgia, where almost no statistics have been found, South Carolina probably had the lowest average of any of the thirteen colonies. St. Bartholomew's Parish, containing at least 120 households, had only 23 voters at its January, 1748, election with one of the successful candidates receiving just 11 votes. More politically active St. Andrew's, the home of the Bull, Drayton, and Middleton families, shows a similar total of 23 in the election of March, 1749. Even at the famous disputed contest in St. Paul's Parish in 1762, involving the later Revolutionary leader Christopher Gadsden, merely ninety-four inhabitants participated. Indeed, one contemporary was probably not exaggerating when he claimed that in some areas the sole individuals to show up at the polls were the two churchwardens who conducted the proceedings. Only St. Philip's, the major parish in Charleston, had any substantial turnout of the electorate on a regular basis. In 1736, at least 225, approximately 40 percent of the adult males, registered their votes. Six years later in 1742, about 165 persons (30 percent) cast ballots for representatives. The greatest outpouring of voters occurred in October, 1768, when 330 voted in St. Philip's, and 304 did so in the new St. Michael's Parish, some 634 in all, or 63.4 percent of the adult male citizens (see table 18).[36]

In attempting to discern overall patterns from the voting figures examined above, it appears that turnouts were relatively stable in those places

TABLE 18

Charleston, South Carolina, Elections, 1736 and 1742

1736		1742	
Candidate	Number of Votes	Candidate	Number of Votes
B. Whitaker	225	B. Whitaker	165
C. Pinckney	193	I. Mazyck	141
I. Mazyck	188	J. Motte	137
R. Brewton	170	J. Graeme	127
O. Beale	167	J. Dart	105
J. Dart	122	A. Dupuy	105

where factionalism was limited, yet they fluctuated heavily in areas torn by partisan strife. The totals in many of the factionless Virginia counties, for instance, never wavered more than slightly. In the ten elections recorded for Essex between 1741 and 1769, the vote always fell inside the range of 318 to 377 (44.3 to 53.4 percent). The six returns listed for Richmond lay within 215 and 259 (36.6 to 44.7 percent), while the same number of regular results in Accomac were all between 482 and 561 (42.6 to 49.6 percent)—none having more than a 9.1 percent gap. On the other hand, the vote in Boston and Philadelphia, to use two examples with extensive data, jumped up and down according to the degree of competition at any particular moment. Only 183 Philadelphians participated in the city contest held in 1758, but almost 2,000 did so in 1765. The Boston high of 1,089 in 1763 plunged to 449 a year later in 1764.[37]

The relationship between the degree of factional competition and the closeness of each outcome is less in evidence. Some Virginia elections were extremely tight, whereas the vote in divided Pennsylvania and Connecticut was, except in rare cases, usually rather one-sided. Admittedly, the tallies in Rhode Island during the Ward-Hopkins struggle ran close, but those in New York seldom did; the court faction controlled some counties and the country faction held others. In 1748, despite heated controversies in the latter province, at least one-third of the Assembly seats were uncontested.[38] For the most part, factional conflict did not guarantee evenly matched races because each side would concede certain spots to their opponents and concentrate on winning a few pivotal ones.

In general, the turnout tended to be greater in large cities than in small towns or rural areas. Higher totals also prevailed in communities of heterogeneous rather than homogeneous population and in older established regions compared to those more recently settled. Furthermore, there was a gradual increase in the overall degree of participation throughout the period to the late 1760's. After 1770, the size of the vote diminished as many Americans united behind patriot candidates in response to the threat from the mother country. Looking at the era as a whole, attendance at the polls was considerable given the limited degree of political development and the wilderness conditions of the time. If we remember that the colonists were in all cases electing local and provincial officials and not intercolonial leaders, it can be strongly argued that eighteenth-century voter turnouts stand up well in comparison with those of statewide and even some national elections today.[39]

8
Voting Behavior
★★★★★★★★★★★★★★★

The determinants of voting behavior in provincial America are a difficult subject to analyze. What accounted for the size of a particular turnout? Why did some men go to the polls while others stayed home? Finally, and most importantly, what influenced persons to choose one candidate or side rather than another? Although it is beyond our means to obtain direct and completely valid responses to such questions, enough statistical and literary evidence exists to allow us to draw some tentative conclusions about the behavioral patterns followed at election time in the thirteen colonies.

Provincial voters, like twentieth-century voters, were affected by several stimuli regarding the choices to be made. Naturally, these stimuli differed to some degree from present ones. There were no national political parties or uniform system of national elections. Campaigns were brief, and the communications media played only a minor role in them. Yet voting in any age incorporates some common behavioral patterns and requires distinctive qualities of the persons taking part. As Robert Lane has written, the process of voting should be understood as "an act involving an expenditure of energy and time, the coordination of muscles and mind, scheduling the event among other events, and partaking of the nature of a positive act in other ways." Voting, he added, necessitates a decision, actually a twofold decision: to vote or not to vote and to choose a particular side. It also involves a certain "relatedness to society" and the "implementation of an emotion" as well as a rational choice.[1] Thus, if we can assume that the general kinds of influential factors were basically the same then as now, we can set up a working model to analyze early American electoral habits. Although the model cannot be fully applied given the paucity of knowledge about many aspects, the definitions and framework it provides can be very useful.

Pursuing the methods used in studies of recent voting behavior, we can divide the forces affecting participation and choice into four main types: personal attributes, ecological variables, systematic limitations, and candidates and issues.[2] Under the heading of personal characteristics one must include for the provincial period such aspects as age, occupation, family status, wealth, ethnic background, religious affiliation, and one's relation to the political system. Ecological factors would refer to societal influence upon the potential voter: the community's geographic location, its economic standing, its political development, and the composition of its population. Systematic limitations relate to many of the topics discussed earlier: the restrictions upon the suffrage, the types of officials to be chosen, the methods of balloting, the proximity to the polls. The impact of issues and the impression of the candidates would concern the ways in which these factors helped determine an individual's decision. In the analysis that follows, the influences upon voter turnout will be dealt with initially and separately from those connected with partisan choice. Through this division of the process we can see more clearly why the provincial elector acted in the manner he did.

There were, indeed, many factors in each of the four categories that affected the size of the provincial vote. The most important of the systematic variables was undoubtedly the statutes relating to the suffrage. The enactment of various restrictions according to race, religion, naturalization, residence, and property holding obviously regulated the number of potential (and thus actual) voters. The percentage of males eligible was much greater in places where land was cheap and abundant than in those areas where it was more difficult to obtain. Maryland, for example, had a far smaller count than it might have because of the inability of many persons to meet the freehold qualifications. Overall, turnout there was probably reduced 10 to 25 percent because of ineligibility. In conjunction with the franchise limitations were the restrictions upon representation, which caused even more thorough exclusion. People living in unincorporated New England towns or in the unorganized frontier regions of the southern colonies did not have a chance to exercise their right to vote.[3]

The types of officials to be chosen imposed another sort of limit. The direct election of the governor and the upper house in Rhode Island and Connecticut invariably brought out a higher proportion of voters in those two colonies than when just the lower house seats were at stake. The popular designation of county sheriff in Pennsylvania on the same ballot with the prospective Assemblymen surely inspired additional persons to go to the polls in that province. In fact, the contest for sheriff, a more localized office, was considered more crucial by many people than the selection of provincial representatives. On numerous occasions, a larger number of votes were tallied in the former race than in the latter.[4] In Boston, too, the choosing of local officials sometimes stimulated a bigger turnout than the subsequent naming of provincial officials because residents believed that the town leaders had a more important impact on their lives. For the year 1734, at least 916 were on hand for the municipal election in March, while only 604 cast ballots for House delegates in May. Two years later, 676 citizens deposited votes in the first instance, and just 266 in the second.[5] Unfortunately, few other figures are available for comparison.

The proximity of the polling place also had a large bearing on the number of electors present. The districts in which the voting site was relatively near to the majority of inhabitants normally had greater turnouts than those in which it was quite distant from them. This certainly accounts in part for the low degree of participation in South Carolina where the frontiersmen often found the balloting location impossible to reach. And as the late Charles S. Grant noted about the town of Kent, Connecticut, the persons living closest to the meetinghouse were most likely to become freemen, hence voters, whereas the persons living farthest away were least likely to be politically active.[6] Individuals residing only a short distance from the center of town generally had more contact with public affairs and knowledge of recent events compared to those who dwelled at a considerable distance. People in the backcountry, who were frequently without any news of major happenings, were even less apt to take part in the election process.

As a rule, the vote in the large cities, where the ballot box was within easy traveling distance and the people better informed, easily surpassed that of the outlying rural areas. The turnouts in New York City and Charleston were notably higher than elsewhere in their respective provinces, the vote in certain distant spots being inconsequential. The totals

in Boston and Salem, while somewhat slender by urban standards, were
probably superior to those in the majority of interior Massachusetts
towns. The percentages in Newport and Providence, seemingly low on
the basis of adult males, were ordinarily larger than in most other Rhode
Island communities if just qualified voters are considered. Similarly, in
Philadelphia, the slightly slimmer output reflected a comparatively smaller degree of eligibility rather than a lack of interest.[7]

Another fact influencing the size of the vote, sometimes connected
with urbanization, was the relative homogeneity of the population. Those
provinces whose peoples came from basically the same ethnic background
generally had less strife and smaller turnouts than those where the electorate was mixed. The rather heavy vote in the middle colonies, especially in New York and Pennsylvania, affirms the validity of this statement.
Similarly, within each colony, the towns and counties that were most
divided often had a greater degree of contention and a larger voter response. Besides the capital cities, New York and Philadelphia, which
early became places of fragmented culture, certain heterogeneous areas
such as York and Lancaster, Pennsylvania, with their sizable German and
Scotch-Irish enclaves, were noted for their extensive participation. In
fact, the returns for York and Lancaster were among the highest ones
recorded anywhere in the colony.[8]

Perhaps more important than any other factor in influencing the volume of popular response was the amount of political maturity that had
taken place. Generally those provinces that established an organized system with a refined vote-getting apparatus had bigger aggregates than the
ones that showed little tendency in this direction. As we have already
noted, colonies such as New York and Pennsylvania, with their long-
standing, coherent factions, had among the highest overall turnouts,
whereas less advanced South Carolina and Georgia had by far the lowest. Factionless Virginia may appear to be an exception to this rule but
its deep-seated tradition of individual rivalry actually grew out of the intense governor-Assembly conflict in the early eighteenth century.

Furthermore, one can measure the impact of factional rivalry upon
voter turnout by comparing provincial totals for years of political calm
with those recorded during heightened controversy. In Boston, throughout the first half of the eighteenth century, the tally was meager in normal circumstances but climbed precipitously in times of strife. The figure
went up almost 90 percent in 1719 (from 242 to 454 votes) when the

Cooke faction first attempted to gain control of the Assembly from the followers of Governor Shute. The number who took part between 1731 and 1735, the troubled portion of Jonathan Belcher's reign, was more than twice that of the late 1720's. After a few years of tranquility and limited response, the vote began to increase again in 1739 as factions reappeared. It continued to show an advance into the early 1740's, before leveling off in the later period of Governor Shirley's administration. Philadelphia County figures portray a similar correlation. When the Proprietary faction first tangled with the Quakers in 1740, the count more than tripled from 555 to 1,822. Moreover, the results remained in the latter range or higher whenever the two groups engaged in serious competition as they did in the mid-1750's and mid-1760's. Perhaps the closest connection between high totals and partisan clashes can be found in pre-Revolutionary Rhode Island. No more than 1,300 voters ever came to the polls before 1750, but in the following two decades during the Ward-Hopkins struggle the numerical vote was at least three times as high on many occasions. Then, after 1770, when division subsided, the volume returned to the low levels registered earlier.[9]

Long-standing factional competition had the effect of intensifying interest not only in an immediate campaign but in helping perpetuate involvement in subsequent contests. As people became attached to one organization or another, they felt more closely tied to the political process and showed a greater proclivity to exercise their franchise privileges again and again. During the Ward-Hopkins controversy in the mid-1760's, there was approximately an 85 percent rate of voter continuity from year to year, whereas after the conflict was removed, the continuity rate dropped to below 60 percent. Indeed, the bulk of the ballots cast in this troubled era of Rhode Island history were delivered by consistent partisans (60 to 77 percent), clearly demonstrating the intimate bond between strong party identification and frequent vote.[10]

Along with the extent of political development and factional rivalry, the degree of electioneering in any particular contest had an immense effect upon the size of the turnout. The amount of money spent, literature published, and canvassing undertaken was inevitably linked to the number of persons who went to the polls. During 1764 and 1765, when the Quaker and Proprietary factions in Pennsylvania made their biggest push to get out the vote, the largest number of electors in the colony's history cast ballots. Philadelphia especially witnessed massive participa-

tion. Similarly, in New York City where a tremendous effort was put
forth by the competing organizations in 1768, it led to the broadest as-
semblage of voters ever to appear. The higher figures for Connecticut
and Rhode Island during the pre-Revolutionary decade also reflect increased appeals to the electorate. In each colony, particularly the latter,
a much greater canvass and outlay of expenditures was made than at any
previous time.[11]

In regard to single contests, crucial issues, as well as the prevailing factional struggle, must be taken into consideration. It is difficult, of course,
to estimate the importance of an individual issue. As we know, other factors were always at work at the same time. In many cases, too, the points
in dispute were not very clear to the average voter. Nevertheless, huge
jumps in the turnout at moments when critical matters were at stake
would indicate that certain major questions were in a large way responsible for bringing additional electors to the polls. The types of issues
and their effects varied according to time and place. Some areas were
strongly influenced by colony-wide or imperial problems, others by purely local ones. The extraordinary 97 percent turnout in Watertown, Massachusetts, in 1757 was clearly the result of internal political squabbles as
were some of the high figures registered in other Bay Colony communities. One of Boston's largest totals (718) occurred at a special town meeting in July, 1740, when people voted on whether to accept Peter Faneuil's
offer to build a permanent marketplace for the city.[12]

In most places, however, broad provincial issues attracted more voters
than did local questions. The Great Awakening in Connecticut during the
1740's produced the first real contests in that colony and larger turnouts
than had ever occurred before. The subject of military spending at the
time of King George's War surely helps explain the expansion of the vote
in Portsmouth, New Hampshire, in that era. Approximately 170 men
cast ballots in 1744 compared to just 75 three years earlier, prior to the
beginning of the conflict. Military preparedness was also the issue in Pennsylvania at the start of the French and Indian War when it inspired the
heaviest outpouring of electors in Philadelphia County up to that time
(2,181 in the year 1754). That figure was soon surpassed as the movement to change Pennsylvania from a proprietary to a royal province became an even greater point of contention and brought out twice as many
persons in some counties than on any previous occasion. In Philadelphia,
at least 3,874 appeared in 1764 and 4,332 did so in 1765. Lancaster in

1765 drew almost 3,000, more than double its earlier high of 1,480, and Bucks County soared to over 1,400, nearly tripling its former mark of 522 recorded a quarter-century before.[13] Although evidence is just fragmentary, it seems that the Regulator conflict in both North and South Carolina in the late 1760's influenced many more men to go to the polls in the frontier regions of those colonies than in any prior instance. The *South Carolina Gazette* reported in 1768 that great numbers of people came down "from the back settlements to vote where it appeared to them they had a right," implying that this had never previously happened in the past.[14]

Surprisingly, however, the impact of the most important issue of all— the growing conflict with the mother country during the 1760's and 1770's—was not always in the direction of increased totals. The turnout in Virginia in 1771 was, indeed, slightly lower than the figures for 1748, 1752, and 1758. Contested elections so frequent in previous years started to diminish in number as the colony became more unified in response to the British threat. In many counties known for heavy competition, the incumbents were unanimously reelected. The same situation seems to have taken place in Maryland where disputed elections were no longer prevalent after 1767, though data here are somewhat lacking. In Boston, the average number of ballots cast dropped from 612 to 555 in the pre-Revolutionary decade. The caucus and town meeting overseers were so successful in mobilizing the populace on the patriot side that opposition became negligible and the need to vote seemed much less urgent. The output in Rhode Island and Connecticut may have been somewhat higher in the late 1760's than in the years preceding the Stamp Act, but this was primarily the result of internal political controversies, the Ward-Hopkins struggle in the former, the Susquehanna episode in the latter. Moreover, the sums registered in both these provinces began to decline after 1770 when these local problems were being resolved.[15]

To be sure, the larger vote in certain areas after 1765 was a direct outgrowth of the conflict with Great Britain as moderate and radical elements clashed head-on at the polls. More than twice the usual number came out in Charleston in October, 1768, as Christopher Gadsden and his followers triumphed over Thomas Smith and John Ward who were seeking to preserve the status quo. As a writer in the *South Carolina Gazette* aptly put it: "Upon the whole, the behaviour of the people in general evinced, that they were in no way inattentive to the importance of the present conjuncture."[16] So, too, the heavy turnout in New York City in 1768 and 1769 was in part a response to the province's handling of the Anglo-American crisis as both the DeLancey and Livingston factions became identified with pro- and anti-British positions.[17] Everywhere, as time went on, it became more difficult to separate local men from imperial measures.

There were, in addition to the institutional and ecological aspects, many personal reasons why some men went to the polls while others did not. Although evidence here is sometimes impressionistic, it still must be taken into account. For one thing, the intensity of a person's preference for a certain candidate or faction strongly affected his disposition to vote. A man who was deeply interested in the campaign and concerned about the outcome was far more likely to come out on election day than someone whose commitment was rather weak and who was not moved by the eventual result. Another crucial factor was whether one viewed voting primarily as a citizen's duty. Invariably some men cast ballots because of their strong sense of public involvement. Even in the provincial period many people looked upon voting as an important civic responsibility. They were in firm agreement with the oft-stated idea, "You are born to Liberty, and it is your Interest and Duty to preserve it."[18] Other individuals who did not maintain such an attitude were probably less apt to vote. Many writers emphasized this lack of commitment, the "criminal indifference" to who was elected, and the profound feeling of general apathy toward the electoral process.[19]

Some people were voters or nonvoters depending upon their overall perception of government. Colonists who believed that each man could understand and influence the course of political action were more frequent voters than those who looked upon it as too complex and beyond the power of the average citizen to affect. At that time (as well as in our own) it was not uncommon to hear such a statement as the following: "What can one man do against a Torrent? It is not our Business, let those who are upon the Watch look out."[20] Whether the major cause of nonparticipation was a general satisfaction with the existing system or a feeling of hopelessness about changing it is impossible to discover, though the former explanation seems the more likely one.

Beyond these attitudes, certain individual characteristics such as age, ethnic and religious affiliation, and economic standing obviously had some bearing upon a man's inclination to vote. Yet age does not appear

to have been of much significance. Although no study has been undertaken to show the relative ages of voters and nonvoters, a partial analysis of father-son participation in four Rhode Island towns indicates little
difference between the number of ballots cast by each generation. In
two cases, the fathers' vote was slightly higher; in two others, the sons
had the larger amount. Overall, the older men had a total of just seven
more than their offspring among the 450 counted.[21]

Ethnic and religious background had a somewhat greater impact. Those
who were non-English or associated with minority religious sects usually
voted on a much less regular basis than members of the majority groups.
This greater apathy was mainly a result of cultural differences and the
Old World tradition of nonparticipation. When such peoples felt their interests threatened, however, they often became extremely active. For example, the Pennsylvania Germans, at the time of the French and Indian
Wars, fearing military service and higher taxes, suddenly voted in huge
numbers. The contrast was quickly noticed by Benjamin Franklin, who
remembered when these foreign immigrants "modestly declined inter-
meddling in our elections, but now they come in droves and carry all before them, except in one or two counties."[22]

An analysis of the economic status of voters yields some surprising
results. In recent times, it has been demonstrated frequently that the
highest rate of voter participation occurs among individuals who are
wealthy and most knowledgeable about political affairs; the greatest degree of nonparticipation takes place among the poorest elements, those
least aware of issues and feeling least affected by government policies.[23]
However, group studies from the provincial era point to a somewhat opposite conclusion. A sampling of the activities of some 126 gentlemen,
lawyers, merchants, and shopkeepers in New York City by Patricia
Bonomi shows that only 60 percent of these men voted in 1768 and
46 percent in 1769.[24] On the other hand, an investigation of the mechanic or tradesmen vote in those years by Roger Champagne indicates
that 77 percent of the artisans went to the polls in the first instance
and 54.7 percent in the second.[25] Surely these were substantial differences (8.7 to 17 percent), and New York was not alone in experiencing
them. Accounts of voting in Accomac and Lancaster counties in Virginia
compiled by the Browns reveal similar disparities. From the data they
gathered on the six elections in Accomac (1738-1758), 93 percent of the
identifiable lower- and middle-class subjects voted, but only 77.8 percent

of the upper-class members did so . Meanwhile in Lancaster, 80 percent of the known lower- and middle-class electors were present at the polls in the six elections recorded (1761-1774), yet just 71.5 percent of those designated upper class participated.[26] Moreover, in Rhode Island, the eleven highest taxpayers in the town of Gloucester voted an average of 3.7 times during the five years from 1763 to 1767, while the rest of the eligible population cast 4.2 ballots in that span. Finally, Cranston's top taxpayers came out 3.1 times between 1764 and 1767, which was slightly below the 3.2 average for the remaining citizens.[27]

It is difficult to explain this smaller degree of participation among the most affluent group in that era. Perhaps because government policy in the provincial period rarely affected the upper classes to any great degree, some of these individuals did not see any pressing need to vote frequently. And possibly certain gentlemen disliked the atmosphere of noise and turbulence that was a growing part of election day proceedings. Governor William Shirley, when describing conditions at the polling place in Boston in the middle of the eighteenth century, declared that "Gentlemen, Merchants, Substantial Traders and all the better part of the Inhabitants" found it "Irksome to attend at such meetings except upon very extraordinary occasions."[28] Whatever the reasons, the fact that the richest persons did not take part as often as did other segments of the populace is surely a striking aspect of the turnout in this epoch.

The mainsprings behind partisan choice are probably not so numerous as the variables connected with voter participation. Usually several determinants influence a person to designate a particular candidate or side, they seem to be fewer than the number affecting turnout. In fact, many recent writers argue that just one factor really matters: party affiliation. Most studies of twentieth-century voting have demonstrated that partisan choice has a very close correlation to party identification and long-time partisan attitudes. It is now well established that modern voters do not for the most part make a completely unbiased appraisal each election day; rather, their decision reflects a standing commitment based on long-held views and attachments. These conditions deeply influence the manner in which an individual perceives the candidates, issues, and other political events before him. Issues themselves have been seen as having little bearing upon the voter's mind. Only cataclysmic developments such as a war or a depression have caused large-scale changes in party allegiance.[29]

But do such behavioral manifestations hold true for the provincial era when political groups were often loosely and hastily organized and lacking in modern-day vote-getting apparatus? Can they possibly pertain to those areas in which such associations were virtually nonexistent? Surely in colonies whose political life was almost wholly faction free, party loyalty had no meaning and voters based their decision upon other factors. Yet in Pennsylvania, Maryland, New York, Connecticut, and Rhode Island, where factions achieved a substantial amount of stability for a number of years, it appears that this development did have a major effect upon the voter's decision-making process.

Although we cannot demonstrate the connection between party loyalty and partisan choice in any definitive manner, we can observe numerous examples of straight-ticket voting in the provinces mentioned. A high degree of ordered rather than haphazard selection would certainly point to a considerable amount of factional identification.[30] In Pennsylvania, as the Quaker and Proprietary groups began competing against one another at the polls in 1740, the overall returns often indicate a clear-cut division between the two. For instance, the Philadelphia County totals in that year reveal that seven of the eight Quaker candidates obtained 1,070 to 1,105 votes, while the seven Proprietary opponents tallied between 731 and 807. In 1742, 1754, 1756, 1764, and 1765, other times when direct challenges were made for several seats, each side's standard-bearers always acquired fairly uniform numbers of votes. Maryland's few available statistics portray a similar outcome. The results from Baltimore and Anne Arundel counties in 1751-1752, show that, with little exception, the aggregate for all members of each slate was relatively the same. Connecticut, too, judging by the figures in the nomination lists cited before, had straight-line voting in many towns.[31]

In the province of New York, the Queens and Westchester County statistics seem to reflect even divisions along court-country lines. John Thomas and Frederick Philipse, longtime court members from Westchester, traditionally received the same approximate total, while each of their adversaries did also. Country faction stalwarts David Jones and Thomas Cornell in Queens had roughly the same count each time as did their opposition. Strictly partisan turnouts were equally common in New York City down through the 1750's but grew less so during the first two elections of the 1760's as the factions were in a state of flux. In 1761, some 51 different combinations can be found among the 1,447 ballots cast, and 84 combinations occurred among the 1,924 votes in 1768. Only in 1769 did the voters align themselves in distinct camps as 80 percent (1,225) of the 1,515 persons who went to the polls chose either a full

DeLancey or a full Livingston slate. The DeLanceys captured 768 and the Livingstons 457, with 290 votes scattered among men from both sides, though most of the latter followed a partisan trend, too.[32]

Straight-ticket voting can be seen most clearly in Rhode Island, especially during the height of the Ward-Hopkins controversy. The two lists available containing a complete tally for all offices, those of 1764 and 1766 (table 19), indicate that most people sided with one faction across the board. In almost every town the figures obtained by the Deputy Governor and each assistant usually varied from the number given to the Governor by no more than two or three votes. Overall their totals differed by fewer than 100 in a turnout of more than 2,000. In 1764, when Hopkins defeated Ward by 24 ballots, the rest of his slate succeeded by an average of 96, a difference of 72, while in 1766 when Ward won by a margin of 235, his followers triumphed by about 199, a gap of just 36.[33]

More substantial proof of fixed, party-like voting in Rhode Island comes from the actual poll lists that recorded all individual preferences. Even with the shifts in support that sometimes took place, it is clear that

TABLE 19

Rhode Island Vote for Governor and Assistants, 1764 and 1766

1764	Number of Votes	Margin	1766	Number of Votes	Margin
Stephen Hopkins	1,992	+24	Samuel Ward	2,058	+235
Joseph Wanton	2,029	+113	Elisha Brown	1,999	+139
Peleg Thurston	2,044	+101	Nicholas Easton	2,035	+171
Gideon Cornel	2,002	+43	Gideon Wanton	2,073	+248
Nicholas Tillinghast	2,035	+132	Thomas Owen	2,088	+301
Darius Sessions	1,996	+53	Stephen Rawson	2,019	+193
John Almy	1,999	+22	John Jepson	2,075	+249
Joseph Lippitt	2,041	+108	Nathaniel Searle	2,082	+163
Samuel Brownel	2,018	+85	John Burton	2,039	+198
Joseph Hazard	2,039	+121	George Nichols	2,028	+176
Thomas Church	2,023	+77	Hezekiah Babcock	2,041	+195
Jonathan Randal	—	—	Othniel Gorton	1,958	+97
Assistants' average		+96	Assistants' average		+199

a widespread and firmly established vote existed for each side in almost every community. Evidence from the four towns for which there are complete figures—Cranston, Gloucester, Johnston, and Tiverton—shows that approximately 80 percent of those who voted twice or more between 1764 and 1767 remained steadfast with one gubernatorial candidate, while only about 20 percent split their allegiance. Moreover, the data indicate that more than 60 percent backed the same man at least three times. In Tiverton, which had the highest degree of voter regularity among the four towns, about 70 percent (97 of 140) of the multiple participants cast ballots for either Ward or Hopkins three or more times during these years (see table 20).[34]

The stability of factional support in Rhode Island is further demonstrated by the returns from 1767, the year of greatest alteration in the colony totals. The aggregate figures in some towns may have differed from those of the prior election, but not the vote of those firmly attached to a particular camp. In Johnston and Gloucester, where a large-scale switch to Hopkins occurred, the change resulted primarily from the crossing over of infrequent or noncommitted voters (men who had taken part only once before or who had alternated sides in previous contests) and the influx of new electors, rather than from those who had been closely aligned with Ward earlier. Not one person in the town of Johnston and just a handful in Gloucester who had designated Ward three times (1764-1766) delivered a ticket for Hopkins in 1767.[35]

TABLE 20

Rhode Island Factional Voting, 1764-1767

Town	Voted Two or More Times	Voted for Same Man Two or More Times		Voted For Same Man Three or More Times	
	Number	Number	Percentage	Number	Percentage
Cranston	183	156	85.2	122	66.7
Gloucester	285	211	74.0	169	59.3
Johnston	95	69	72.6	48	50.5
Tiverton	140	125	89.3	97	69.3
	703	561	79.7	436	62.0

The effect of partisan alignments in creating perpetual support for certain candidates becomes more apparent when comparing the results in Rhode Island with those of faction-free Virginia. In the former, the proportion switching sides was small—as low as 2 or 3 percent in Tiverton and Cranston and no more than 17 percent in Gloucester in a typical year.[36] On the other hand, changing back and forth from one contest to the next seems to have been quite common among Virginians. Only 52 of the 113 men (46 percent) who took part in the Richmond elections of 1755, 1758, and 1761 favored victorious Landon Carter in all three instances, though 104 chose him at least once. In Lancaster, Charles Carter and Richard Mitchell comprised the winning entry in 1761 and 1765, receiving 84 votes together the first time and 138 the second, but just 47 of the 122 persons (38.5 percent) who participated on both occasions backed the two of them twice. Halifax County returns for 1768 and 1769 show that merely 57 of the 214 two-time voters (26.6 percent) chose incumbents John Lewis and Nathaniel Terry in each case. It is thus apparent that in the absence of distinct factions, polling was frequently random and haphazard; when they were present, such organizations helped channel the vote in a more orderly and consistent direction.[37]

It is easy to exaggerate the significance of partisan attachment in establishing provincial voting patterns. It is by no means clear that a faction's image was deeply impressed in people's minds or that voters always identified the candidates or themselves as connected with a faction. Furthermore, many people may have voted for a particular side on a regular basis simply because they identified it with a certain economic interest or set of cultural values. Perhaps faction itself can be seen as an important influence only in combination with other attitudes and conditions in determining partisan choice.[38]

Ecological factors, especially geographic location, were certainly major determinants of voter outlook in the Rhode Island and Connecticut gubernatorial clashes. The Ward-Hopkins struggle in Rhode Island can largely be interpreted as a sectional conflict between the southern and northern parts of the province. The Ward faction sought to maintain the preeminence of Newport as an economic, political, and cultural center, while the Hopkins group aimed at making the Providence area dominant. Although the voting figures do not reflect a complete sectional split, they do indicate that each region generally supported the organization based in their own locale. Hopkins received his highest totals in the northern towns of Cumberland, Scituate, Smithfield, and, of course, Providence, while the southern towns of Westerly, Hopkinton, Tiverton, Little Compton, and Newport gave Ward his biggest backing. Overall, approximately two-thirds of the electors in the northern environs favored Hopkins, and a similar proportion in the southern environs chose Ward (see table 21).[39]

It is more difficult to document the sectional nature of the factional division in Connecticut because of the lack of abundant statistics. However, the geographic division between Old Lights and New Lights is evident by examining the breakdown of the vote in the gubernatorial nomination for 1770. New Light sympathizer Jonathan Trumbull obtained the bulk of his total in the heavily converted eastern counties, securing 31 percent in Hartford, 21 percent in Windham, and 17 percent in New London, with less than 5 percent coming from the western conservative stronghold in Fairfield. At the same time, Old Light ex-Governor Thomas Fitch garnered 31 percent of his overall tally in Fairfield, while receiving a mere 4 percent in New London and 0.6 percent in Windham. Similar results can be observed for other Old Light leaders running for the upper house, some of whom did not acquire more than a handful of votes in certain eastern counties. Ebenezer Silliman had but 3 votes in Windham and 80 in New London, John Chester got only 5 in the former county and 64 in the latter, while Benjamin Hall was unable to gain a single vote in either of the eastern strongholds.[40] It can be argued, of course, that religion rather than geography was the key factor in producing these results. Nevertheless, geographic location undoubtedly placed a significant role in the division (see table 22).

Another factor connected with partisan choice was the candidates themselves, who were often inseparable from the factions to which they belonged. The rank and stature of those running must be considered an important part of any evaluation of a voter's selection process. Because factional leadership was frequently synonymous with a few powerful men, some persons supported a ticket mainly out of loyalty or deference to a particular individual or family. The latter had perhaps performed services for them or for the entire community or were simply considered best suited and deserving of office because of their eminent position. The willingness of certain people to offer whole-hearted backing to a prominent gentleman or a member of his family can be seen in the following instance. When the famous Indian agent Sir William Johnson of Albany announced that his son John might seek an Assembly seat in 1768, one of his friends, Richard Cartwright, wrote to him: "If there is any such intention [I] should be glad to know it. You may depend on the Interest of Cuyler's family, of Hanson's, and many more who would be glad to know it. Whatever Interest or connection I have you may command in that or anything else."[41]

Even where political factions were nonexistent, the image of the candidates definitely had a great deal of impact upon the voter's eventual decision. A gentleman dressed in fine clothes, displaying impeccable manners, and traveling about in a fancy carriage cut quite a figure. Prior to one election in Dutchess County, New York, Henry Beekman warned a friend that Cadwallader Colden's appearing at the polls would definitely influence the electors because of the councillor's "majastk presance."[42] In a

TABLE 21

Rhode Island Sectional Voting, 1763-1767

| | NORTH | | | | SOUTH | | | |
| | Ward | | Hopkins | | Ward | | Hopkins | |
Year	No.	%	No.	%	No.	%	No.	%
1763	591	29.2	1,433	70.8	1,348	66.9	667	33.1
1764	598	31.9	1,275	68.1	1,370	65.6	717	34.4
1765	755	35.8	1,354	64.2	1,547	69.1	693	30.9
1766	636	35.9	1,137	64.1	1,422	66.2	726	33.8
1767	517	23.7	1,666	76.3	1,511	66.3	768	33.7

TABLE 22

Connecticut Magistrate Nominations, 1770

| | Trumbull | | Fitch | |
| | Number of | | Number of | |
County	Votes	Percentage	Votes	Percentage
Hartford	899	30.7	459	23.2
New Haven	385	13.1	513	25.9
New London	499	17.0	85	4.3
Fairfield	140	4.8	607	30.3
Windham	618	21.1	11	0.6
Litchfield	389	13.1	304	15.4

period of strong deference toward members of the elite, it was common
for many persons to choose someone for office solely on the basis of his
wealth and social standing. As the Boston merchant, John Colman, wrote
in 1720: "In all Places . . . Great Men alwayes have their Followers, who
hang on their Skirts; and some who have no thoughts of their own, make
the Rich and Powerful their Oracle; and so it hath been among us."[43]
Several contemporaries publicly mocked the uncritical and naive manner
in which the average colonist supposedly selected his representative. According to one writer, the prospective voter made up his mind in the following way: "Sir John is a fine Gentleman, and treats People very civilly;
and my Landlord is a good Man, and has been kind: And Esquire Such a
one is our next Justice of Peace."[44] Another author humorously satirized
the manner in which a typical inhabitant was led to part with his vote.
"A squeeze by the Hand of a great Man, a few well timed Compliments;
. . . an Invitation to his Dining-Room, . . . a Glass of Wine well applied,
the Civility and good Humour of his Lady, the·Drinking a Health, inquir-
ing kindly after the Welfare of a Family, a little facecious Chat in a strain
of Freedom and Equality, have been sufficient to win the Heart of many
a Voter,"[45] he declared. Inevitably, some electors must have succumbed
to this kind of treatment.

In addition to the more subtle influences, it is clear that some men
chose a candidate because they were openly pressured into doing so. This
was especially the case in pre-Revolutionary New York and Rhode Island
where factional strife was so intense. From 1750 onward, numerous New
York pamphleteers complained about various instances where "Threats
of Hardship" were used to compel certain freemen to deliver their vote
for a particular side.[46] During the French and Indian War, James DeLancey
was said to have intimidated the opposition's supporters by threatening
to put them into the army.[47] One of the primary reasons for the paper
ballot movement in that colony in the late 1760's was to prevent "the
intollerable Tyranny of the great and opulent, who . . . have openly threatened [many of the poorer people] with the Loss of their Employment."[48]
In Rhode Island, the merchants of Providence would annually donate several thousand pounds to the Hopkins party "as may be most Usefull in
procuring the free Votes of the poorer Sort of Freemen."[49] Accounts
kept by the Brown family show that substantial amounts of sugar, wine,
codfish, cheese, and cash were distributed to voters in many communities. John Brown noted that while campaigning in Gloucester in 1765,

"their was Not Less than forty Men in town Yesterday, Freemen belonging there by Whose Return was Carried Rum Anough for a Small Guine Cargo, with Several other Necessarys."[50]

It should be reiterated, however, that such overt pressure was not very common in most of the colonies. Even in New York and Rhode Island such tactics were employed only in periods of extreme factional discord. On normal occasions, most voters could make up their minds fairly independently and did not have to contend with such strenuous outside influences. If the typical colonist designated a particular man for office, it was not usually because he was forced into making such a choice. Given the existence of deference, the use of coercion was seldom necessary. Moreover, if pressure was introduced in any contest, it was often applied more or less equally by both sides without a critical effect upon the outcome. Election figures regarding the choices made by the "poorer sort" indicate no fundamental difference in their pattern of selection from that of the other sectors of society. Indeed, studies of several Virginia counties and Rhode Island towns as well as New York City indicate very little tendency toward class voting of any kind in the provincial period. According to the Browns' analysis of numerous poll lists from Lancaster County, Virginia, men at every level "tended to scatter their votes instead of voting with any apparent degree of class solidarity." The upper classes, they concluded, did exhibit a somewhat greater degree of unity than the middle and lower classes. Yet in eleven of fourteen elections each of the groups favored the same candidates.[51]

In the three Rhode Island towns for which we have extensive data—Cranston, Tiverton, and Gloucester—there was practically no divergence whatsoever. One finds almost no difference between the overall percentage of votes received by Ward and Hopkins for the governorship during the mid-1760's and the percentage supplied by the affluent and less affluent groups in each community. Tiverton, a town in which Samuel Ward obtained 62.8 percent of the totally vote between 1764 and 1767, had 59 percent of the highest taxpayers and 58 percent of lowest taxpayers voting for Ward. In Cranston, where Stephen Hopkins won 63 percent of the tally during those same years, 61 percent of the wealthy voters were on his side, and so were 63 percent of the poorer voters. Only in Gloucester was there a slight divergence. While each candidate obtained exactly half (50 percent) of the overall turnout, Hopkins had 62 percent of the big taxpayers' share and only 42 percent of the small taxpayers' share. But even in Gloucester with so many voters switching from one side to the other every year, it is difficult to see any real class divisions at the polls (see table 23).[52]

Similarly, the data for New York City in no way imply a solid stand by any class. During the election of 1701 when the community was divided into Leislerians and anti-Leislerians, the split did not primarily result from economic factors. As Thomas Archdeacon has shown, the two groups were almost evenly distributed on the wealth scale with the exception of a slightly greater number of Leisler men in the lowest bracket.[53] The statistics from 1768 and 1769 demonstrate even more clearly the absence of

TABLE 23

Rhode Island Gubernatorial Preference in Relation to Wealth, 1764-1767[a]

Tax Paid	Hopkins Number of Voters	Percentage	Ward Number of Voters	Percentage
Tiverton				
over £3	9	40.9	13	59.1
£2-3	1		4	
£1-2	5		6	
£0-1	27	42.2	37	57.8
	42	41.2	60	58.8
Cranston				
over £3	25	61.0	16	39.0
£2-3	9		12	
£1-2	19		4	
£0-1	24	63.2	14	36.8
	77	62.6	46	37.4
Gloucester				
over £3	5	62.5	3	37.5
£2-3	11		6	
£1-2	25		22	
£0-1	42	42.5	57	57.5
	83	48.5	88	51.5

[a]Shows those voters who supported one side or the other at least twice in the four year period and whose names could be found on the tax assessment lists of 1760.

class voting. In 1769, when about 60 percent of the electorate supported the DeLancey ticket and roughly 35 to 40 percent backed the Livingston side, among the twenty-nine gentlemen designated as "Esquire," nineteen (65.5 percent) voted for the DeLanceys and ten (34.5 percent) voted for the Livingstons.[54] The vote of the mechanics was even closer to the overall tally. As table 24 indicates, no more than 3 or 4 percent separated each candidate's total percentage from his proportion of the tradesmen's vote.[55]

If in these examples there is little evidence of clear-cut class division, this does not mean that a man's wealth and professional standing played no role whatever in determining his choice at the polls. Nor does it mean that the average member of the electorate never concerned himself about immediate financial matters when preparing to cast his ballot. It merely indicates that either he did not perceive any difference in the economic

TABLE 24

Total Vote Versus Mechanic Vote
in New York City, 1768-1769

Candidate	Election of 1768 Percentage of All Voters	Percentage of Mechanic Vote
Livingston	68	66
DeLancey	62.5	60
Walton	61	58
Jauncey	54.6	52.6
Scott	45	45
Bayard	30	31
Dodge	13	12

Candidate	Election of 1769 Percentage of All Voters	Percentage of Mechanic Vote
DeLancey	61	63
Walton	61	63
Cruger	58	62
Jauncey	57.8	61
Livingston	43.9	46
Scott	42.6	46
P. V. B. Livingston	35	38.4
Van Wyck	34	37

outlook of the persons running or that other variables were more crucial
to him at that moment. To be sure, many voters were, at least on some
occasions, strongly influenced by prevailing economic conditions and
related monetary issues. Taxation was often an important question, and
men in almost every colony would at times designate candidates who
favored a lessening of the tax burden or remove those who had recommended tax increases. Although no concrete evidence is available, it is
probable that several Massachusetts legislators lost their seats because
they supported the excise tax of 1754.[56]

At certain times, people opposed any government spending they did
not think absolutely essential and would threaten to turn out those who
refused to agree with their premise. Under these conditions, the chief
executives in all the colonies had trouble financing many projects, which
would often experience lengthy delays before completion. When Governor Sharpe of Maryland wished to appropriate money to finish construc-
tion of the executive mansion in May, 1754, he was forced to postpone
it until after the upcoming House race. Most Assemblymen, he lamented,
were unwilling to do "anything generous" at the end of a session, "lest
it should induce their electors to reject them when they offer themselves
Candidates at the ensuing Election."[57]

During periods of economic difficulty, voters in several areas backed
candidates who advocated relief in the form of large-scale issuances of
paper currency. This was especially true in Rhode Island and Massachusetts in the 1730's and 1740's. Many defenders of hard money such as
Thomas Hutchinson of Boston were ousted from office by the paper-
money group, which Hutchinson said was comprised of "the needy part
of the province."[58] Robert Zemsky has shown that during the Land
Bank controversy in the Bay colony, the turnover rate in the Assembly
in 1741 was almost twice as high among opponents of the bank than
among its supporters. Only five of the fourteen incumbents (36 percent)
known to be against the scheme were reelected, whereas twenty of the
thirty-one sympathizers (61 percent) retained their seats.[59]

In Maryland and Virginia, the question of tobacco inspection laws
caused major divisions at the polls for several years in the middle of the
eighteenth century. The less affluent farmers of the Chesapeake region
feared rigid tobacco legislation would lead to tremendous hardship if
only top quality produce were acceptable. Therefore, they sought to
designate representatives who would oppose such measures. James

Littlepage of Hanover County, Virginia, was chosen to the House of Burgesses partly because he openly condemned the stringent inspection system.[60] Many Marylanders were elected on a similar platform, and those favoring strict regulations had difficulty remaining in office. After passage of the first inspection law in 1747, Governor Samuel Ogle wrote to Lord Baltimore: "As the common peoples of all Countrys hate restraint of any kind, how much soever it may be to their Advantage, the Enemies of the Law have found out their own strength" and threatened to defeat for re-election every man who supported the bill.[61]

Yet more important than economic issues in determining voting behavior is the value structure to which individuals belong and with which they identify. These values originate in the experiences of different groups and in the development of shared perspectives. Members of the same primary groups usually think alike and therefore vote alike. The most influential primary group is the family where one's outlook toward the world is first conditioned. Recent studies have shown that the majority of young people today vote as their parents do. The significance of the family was even greater in the colonial era than at present since it was a more closely knit entity and performed many more functions. Children more frequently followed in the parent's footsteps and showed greater respect for their elders. Perhaps this accounts for the larger proportion of sons having voted the same way as their fathers did than is true currently, when agreement occurs in about 60 percent of the cases. In Rhode Island, the study of father-son voting in four towns—Cranston, Gloucester, Johnston, and Tiverton—indicates that 71 percent of the identifiable sons (thirty-six of fifty-one) supported the same party their father did, over a four-year period (1764-1767). The New York City election of 1769 illustrates an even stronger intergenerational connection; thirty-seven out of forty-eight father-son combinations (77 percent) voted predominantly for the same ticket.[62]

Outside the family, religious and ethnic affiliations exerted a tremendous influence upon people's values and their attitudes toward politics. As we have come to realize each ethnic group and religious sect has its own distinctive style of behavior. This distinctiveness has frequently led to clashes at the polls between conflicting groups. In the middle colonies during the provincial era, it could form the very basis of the factional structure. New Jersey's groupings in the early 1700's, for example, were known literally as the Anglican party and the Quaker or Scottish-Quaker party by all sides. Pennsylvania's political organizations after the middle of the century were often referred to as the Quaker and Presbyterian parties.[63]

Although there is no breakdown of the Pennsylvania vote in any year, the overwhelming majority of documentary evidence points to strong identification with and bloc voting by the competing ethnic and religious groups, especially the Quakers. As early as the first decade of the eighteenth century the Quakers began to organize their members along political lines, condemning brethren who selected persons no longer attached to the Society of Friends.[64] By the 1740's, the Quaker party was regularly using their annual religious meeting to enhance political solidarity and mobilize manpower for their cause. The Quakers, according to the Anglican William Smith, "entered into Cabals in their yearly Meeting, which is convened just before the Election, and being composed of Deputies from all the monthly Meetings in the Province, is the finest Scheme that could possibly be projected, for conducting political Intrigues, under the Mask of Religion."[65]

Not only did the Quakers organize themselves for the purpose of bloc voting but they also pressured the Germans in the province to align in that fashion. The Germans were warned by the Quakers "that a militia would subject them to a bondage to governors as severe as they were formerly under to their princes in Germany, that the expenses would impoverish them, and that if any other than Quaker should be chosen upon the assembly they would be dragged down from their farms and obliged to build forts as a tribute for their being admitted to settle in the province."[66] The Germans, who had not previously participated in the political life of the colony, began coming to the polls in great numbers to elect Quaker candidates. It was estimated that several hundred Germans handed in tickets for the Quaker party in the Philadelphia County election of 1754 at the outset of the French and Indian War. The strength of this group was even more powerfully felt in the Lancaster region where, it was claimed, "the Germans . . . carry everything in that Country that goes by Vote."[67] A few years later, opponents succeeded in splitting the German populace to a certain degree, but overall they did not make significant inroads. Somehow the Quakers managed to convince the vast majority of the need to continue their faction in office.

By the 1760's, another group in Pennsylvania began to organize politically: the Presbyterians. Tired of being, despite their large numbers, "a Body of very little Weight and Consequence," this sect, like the Quakers, started holding annual meetings in order to promote their religious and civic interests. Acting in conjunction with the Proprietary faction, they sought to make gains in the Quaker-dominated Assembly and block the movement to establish a royal colony. During the election of 1764, one contemporary noted that in the quest for votes, the Presbyterians "made use of every artifice in their power that they could invent to obtain them, the Ministers having been remarkably vigilant in the affr & stir'd themselves more than was ever known before."[68] As a result of such efforts, these opponents of Crown government captured the province's Presbyterian elements "to a man."[69]

Ethnic and religious divisions in New York were similarly important. In several parts of the colony, especially the counties along the Hudson River, the conflict between the English and Dutch was often the foremost determinant in provincial elections. Although the Dutch government had been eliminated in 1664, many Dutch people continued to resent English rule down to the end of the colonial period and were loath to choose anyone but Dutchmen to the legislature. Practically all the persons elected from Albany and Ulster counties, the Dutch strongholds, were non-English.[70] Segmentation of Dutch and English can best be documented in New York City. The early political factions, especially those formed after Leisler's rebellion in 1689, closely followed lines of national origins. In the municipal election of 1701, the Dutch inhabitants gave overwhelming support to the Leislerian group, with 111 of 133 known Hollanders (83 percent) casting ballots for that side. Meanwhile, the English, plus a considerable number of French, were almost entirely united behind the other side, 99 of 109 votes going to the anti-Leislerians.[71]

The split between Dutch and English continued in New York City down to the middle of the eighteenth century. Even though no figures are available, it would appear from the vigorous partisan appeals by the Morrisites in the 1730's and the DeLanceys in the 1740's that the Dutch remained fairly solidified and persisted in voting as a bloc. However, the gradual assimilation of the group, as well as the growth of divisions within their ranks, led to a situation where in the election of 1761 the Dutch vote practically mirrored the English vote. Subsequently, in the famous contest between the Livingstons and the DeLanceys in 1769, a sampling of 100 Dutch names shows 50 percent supporting the Livingston candidates with 45 percent backing the DeLancey men, definitely not a startling difference.[72]

By the late 1760's, religious conflict between Anglicans and Dissenters replaced ethnic distinctions as most crucial. Especially at issue was the question of incorporating the Presbyterian church. Opponents, such as the High Church leader Reverend Samuel Auchmuty, saw the Livingston or Presbyterian faction as dangerous to the Anglican interest. "Every One that has any loyalty, or regard for the Established Church of the Nation, must think himself in Duty bound to oppose the ambitious Scheme of a most restless and turbulent sect."[73] The more credulous Anglicans were led to believe that if Dissenters such as John Morin Scott got into the Assembly, "the ruin of their church was inevitable."[74] Although there is no full record of the Anglicans and Presbyterians in colonial New York City by which to analyze their political connection, the religiously oriented partisanship that existed is evident. A comparison of the membership in a group called the Society of Dissenters with the list of voters in the election of 1769 shows that of the fourteen who took part, all of them, with one exception, followed a straight Livingston ticket.[75]

In most of New England, because of the greater homogeneity of the population, ethnic origin or religious affiliation had less meaning at election time. In the eighteenth century, Massachusetts, New Hampshire, and Rhode Island experienced little of the religious-based factional controversy that occurred in the middle colonies. Only a few isolated regions within these provinces had heavy concentrations of settlers who were not of the majority faith. Yet in these areas serious division did take place, at least on the local level. Towns such as Bellingham and Swansea in Massachusetts, both with large numbers of Baptists, often exhibited sharp electoral splits along religious lines. Deeply divided Londonderry, Hampton-Falls, and Newton, New Hampshire, frequently became involved in similar disputes. At the Newton town meeting in March, 1769, there was a great deal of "tumult and confusion" over the choice of local officers, especially the moderator. The old selectmen, who were in charge, "declared that they did not care who was Chosen for Moderator provided they would Chuse the [new] Select Men as follows vizt. One Quaker, One Baptist and One Congregationalist—but that if they did not Choose 'em in that manner they would purge the House."[76]

Tiverton, one of the few towns in the colony of Rhode Island containing a Congregational church and a Baptist church, affords the best evidence of religiously determined voter response in this section. Fragmentary records reveal that practically all of the identifiable voters (fourteen of fifteen) associated with the Congregationalists overwhelmingly supported Samuel Ward during the Ward-Hopkins controversy: forty-six of the forty-seven proxies delivered by these men from 1764 to 1767 went to Ward. Meanwhile, the majority of Baptists sided with Stephen Hopkins. Probably the Baptists believed that Hopkins, himself a member of a dissenting group, the Quakers, would be most sympathetic to their cause. The backing for Hopkins was not as strong, but six out of ten gave him at least a plurality of their ballots, and several gave much more.[77]

Connecticut proved an exception to the overall picture of relative religious harmony in New England. As a reaction to the Great Awakening of the 1740's, a large part of the colony became divided politically by ecclesiastical controversy and separated into Old Lights and New Lights. During the early stages of the Awakening several councilmen and Assemblymen were not reelected because of their espousal of New Light doctrines. Hezekiah Huntington, for example, was ousted from his position as assistant in 1743 upon becoming a New Light. Later on, when the two sides became more evenly matched, many Old Lights were rejected from office too. Indeed, by 1763, the New Lights had become a majority in the lower house and were moving toward control of the upper house. William Samuel Johnson lamented: "The N. L. within my short memory were a small party merely a religious one [but] in this short period by their continual struggles they have acquired such an Influence as to be nearly the ruling part of the Government."[78]

Another outgrowth of the Congregational split in Connecticut was the emergence of an Anglican political faction in many towns. Because each of the two main protagonists had trouble gaining a majority of voters, they sought alliances with the Anglicans in order to obtain at least some power. Through such collaboration, fifty-five Churchmen were chosen to the Assembly by twenty-five Connecticut communities in the period after 1740. In Stratford, twenty-one of the twenty-eight elections between 1743 and 1772 resulted in the choice of one Old Light Congregationalist and one Anglican deputy. Pastor Samuel Johnson noted in 1767 that "the Church [of England] got the ascendant by joining the Tomlinson interest [First Church] and Capt. Nichols [Christ Church]."[79]

In Virginia, religious influence upon voting behavior seems to have been less in evidence than in colonies farther north. The eastern counties were traditionally Anglican while the majority of the Dissenters settled

primarily in certain inland regions. However, even in areas with considerable enclaves of Presbyterians and other minority sects, there does not
seem to have been any significant degree of bloc voting. Comparing a
list of Presbyterian petitioners in Essex County in 1758 with the election poll of that year shows a many-sided split among the twenty-seven
who participated in the balloting. Five different combinations can be
distinguished with no more than ten individuals voting for any single
pair. Using the same list for the contest in 1761, there was a three-way
division among twenty-nine voters, with twelve backing one duo, ten
another, and seven opting for the third arrangement.[80] Similarly, in Lancaster County in the 1760's, no pattern of Presbyterian partisanship can
be determined. Presbyterians whose names can be ascertained supported
the same Assembly candidates as the majority of the inhabitants.[81] Perhaps the religious factor would have been more telling if an issue had
arisen centering upon some type of church-related controversy. To be
sure, Presbyterians and other groups did exert political pressure at times
if an episode in Hanover County is any indication. During the 1750's,
Reverend William Dawson, an Anglican official, noted that the Dissenters
began extracting numerous concessions from men seeking office. It had
become a matter of public notoriety, he said, that they "exacted Bonds
from the candidates to serve and stand by their Interests, before they
would suffer them to be elected Burgesses, a most unjustified and un-
precedented thing."[82]

Ultimately, it is impossible to make any definitive statements about
the colonists' voting behavior. In general, as Edmund Morgan has written, they did not wish to be bothered with voting unless they thought
the government was up to something worth being bothered about. What
stirred people to go to the polls varied from place to place, as did the
reasons for their choosing particular candidates, though the degree of
political development in a province plus a person's value structure and
ethno-cultural background seem to have had a great influence.[83]

Epilogue

★★★★★★★★★★★★★★

In the provincial period, an American voting system slowly began to emerg
While most of the election practices introduced were English in origin, con
ditions in the New World prevented the development of a purely English p
tern. The unsettled wilderness environment hindered the creation of politi
cal institutions in the exact form as in the homeland. Together with the lac
of strict controls exercised by the London government, it fostered change
from the very outset. Although the Crown eventually tried to limit the
scope of some of the innovations, it proved difficult to contain a movement already started. The existence of thirteen separate colonies also
operated against the establishment of traditional British procedures. Divergence naturally resulted from the formation of thirteen individual legislatures instead of a single Parliament, especially when those bodies were
initiated by various private groups. The presence of peoples with differing
religious and ethnic backgrounds, often holding new ideas about how elections should be carried out, guaranteed further departures and led to even
wider experimentation.

More than anything else, early American voting was characterized by
a great deal of variety. Each colony and region had its own particular
methods of doing things, and each, furthermore, made significant alterations over the course of time. Marked differences could be found in the
qualifications for voters and officeholders from very stringent to very
lenient. There were several distinct types of balloting, including viva voce,
paper tickets, or a combination of the two. Most variable were the kinds
of electioneering and voting behavior exhibited. Whereas apathy existed
in numerous areas, there was growing interest and participation in others.
The lower South experienced few real contests, though the upper tier,
Virginia and Maryland, sometimes had the most heated competition seen
anywhere. Heavy treating and violence at the polls were more common
here than in any other section. New England's campaigning style was

somewhat more subdued, yet its elections were often hard fought, most notably in pre-Revolutionary Connecticut and Rhode Island. The middle colonies took part in the liveliest politics of all. Ethnic conflict, organized factions, and vigorous electioneering efforts were frequently the rule. Everywhere, however, the political scene was dominated by the gentlemen class, from mobilizing the voters in the role of faction leaders to winning the election in the role of candidates.

Nevertheless, the election process, though influenced to a considerable extent by an elite group, was less aristocratic than its counterpart in England.[1] America possessed no rotten boroughs and few seats from which a man could be automatically chosen to office. The adoption of residence requirements for voting and officeholding helped establish actual representation in America in contrast to the virtual representation practiced across the sea. In addition, the colonial voter was able to exhibit far more independence at the polls. The provincial electorate was broader and less easy to manipulate. Fewer candidates resorted to direct pressure and the outright purchase of votes, both common occurrences in England. Many American visitors to the British Isles were shocked by the unsavory methods employed by all sides in parliamentary elections. "The whole depends upon Intrigue, Party, Interest, and Money," declared William Samuel Johnson of Connecticut.[2]

Not only was the American voting system more democratic than England's, it was growing more so on the eve of the Revolution. Even before the new nation was established, evidences of progressive change were already apparent. Several colonial spokesmen, influenced by the ideals surrounding the struggle with the mother country, began advocating an expansion of the suffrage. As early as 1765, James Otis stated that each individual by nature had "his life and liberty" and should have the right to vote regardless of whether he owned property.[3] A decade later, New Jersey inhabitants were calling for an end to landholding qualifications, insisting that all taxpayers be permitted to choose delegates to the legislature and to the provincial congress.[4] In April, 1776, as militia companies were being formed, a Philadelphian exclaimed that "every man in the country who manifests a disposition to venture his all for the defence of its Liberty should have a voice in its Councils."[5] Shortly after independence, Pennsylvania established full suffrage for adult male taxpayers, and a number of other states reduced their requirements.

In addition to calling for an extension of the franchise, some writers began questioning the idea of electing only wealthy gentlemen to office,

arguing that individuals of humble circumstances were just as well suited.
The amount of riches that someone possessed was no indication of his
ability. As the author of "The People the Best Governors" put it, "social
virtue and knowledge" was "the best and only necessary qualification"
for a government post.[6] "Democritus," writing in the *Massachusetts Spy*,
urged voters "to choose men that have learnt to get their living by honest
industry, and that will be content with as small an income as the general-
ity of those who pay for their services." Such a person, he said, "knows
the wants of the poor, and can judge pretty well what the community can
bear of public burdens."[7] Undoubtedly these pleas had effect since, as
Jackson T. Main has convincingly demonstrated, successful candidates
for public office increasingly came from the ranks of the artisan and
middling-farmer class.[8]

The means by which a candidate obtained election were also further
democratized. Nominations tended to be more broadly based with a wider spectrum of the populace—especially artisans in the cities—taking part.
Large-scale caucuses or mass public meetings became standard procedures
in certain places, and even nominating conventions were held in a few
locales. With the growth of more permanent factions, the dimensions of
electioneering were expanded, bringing more people into contact with
the political process. Placing items in the press, open-air gatherings, and
door-to-door canvassing were becoming very important vote-getting techniques. Newspapers played an increasingly vital role, printing articles on
major issues, supporting particular causes or parties, and listing slates of
candidates.

Other parts of the election machinery were being democratized too.
New election districts were established with representation based on population instead of wealth. Several states instituted annual elections as a
check against corrupt officeholders. Stronger laws against bribery were
enacted, making free and open contests more possible. Secret balloting
became more widespread, protecting the voter from undue pressure.
Many judicial and administrative positions once appointed by the Crown
became elective. The principle of rotation in office was put into practice
in certain states. The Pennsylvania Constitution of 1776, for example,
limited a sheriff's tenure to three years and barred his being rechosen
during the four years immediately afterward.[9]

All in all, the voting process was moving in the direction of more popular control, embodying many ideas present in the Declaration of Independence and other writings of the Revolutionary era.

Notes

★★★★★★★★★★★★★★

CHAPTER 1

1. For development of new techniques in the Revolutionary and early national periods, see William N. Chambers, *Political Parties in a New Nation: The American Experience, 1776-1809* (New York, 1963), and George D. Luetscher, *Early Political Machinery in the United States* (Philadelphia, 1903).

2. *South Carolina Gazette*, October 5, 1765. See also ibid., March 6, 1749, February 7, 1771.

3. *A Letter to the Freeholders and Other Inhabitants of This Province* (Boston, 1742), p. 1. See also *A Letter to the Inhabitants of the Province of Massachusetts Bay* (Boston, 1751), p. 3; Andrew Fletcher [pseud.], *Vincit Amor Patriae* (New York, 1732), p. 2; *Advice to the Freeholders and Electors of Pennsylvania* (Philadelphia, 1735), p. 3.

4. Michael Zuckerman, *Peaceable Kingdoms: New England Towns in the Eighteenth Century* (New York, 1970); Robert E. Brown, *Middle-Class Democracy and the Revolution in Massachusetts, 1691-1780* (Ithaca, 1955).

5. *New England Courant*, April 30, 1722.

6. Richard J. Hooker, ed., *The Carolina Backcountry on the Eve of the Revolution* (Chapel Hill, 1953), p. 188. See also pp. 178-179, 183, 205-206.

7. Chambers, *Political Parties*, pp. 26-27. Benjamin Franklin noted that the Germans in early eighteenth-century Pennsylvania showed little interest in provincial politics. See his letter to Peter Collinson, May 9, 1753, in Leonard W. Labaree et al., eds., *The Papers of Benjamin Franklin* (New Haven, 1959-), 4: 484.

8. For the institutional structure of colonial government, see Leonard W. Labaree, *Royal Government in America* (New Haven, 1930), and Evarts B. Greene, *The Provincial Governor in the English Colonies of North America* (New York, 1898). For the parish vestry in Virginia, see Charles S. Sydnor, *Gentlemen Freeholders: Political Practices in Washington's Virginia* (Chapel Hill, 1952), pp. 90-93.

9. [John Trenchard and William Gordon], "Second Address to the Freeholders. . . ," *Cato's Letters,* 5th ed. (London, 1748), 3:12. See also Richard Buel, Jr., "Democracy and the American Revolution: A Frame of Reference," *William and Mary Quarterly,* 3d ser., 21 (July 1964): 165-190; J. R. Pole, "Historians and the Problem of Early American Democracy," *American Historical Review* 67 (April 1962): 626-646; William R. Brock, *The Evolution of American Democracy* (New York, 1970), p. 14.

10. James Wilson, *Considerations on the Nature and Extent of the Legislative Authority of the British Parliament* (1774), in Robert G. McCloskey, ed., *The Works of James Wilson* (Cambridge, 1967), 2:727.

11. *South Carolina Gazette,* October 30, 1736.

12. *Maryland Gazette,* November 13, 1751.

13. *South Carolina Gazette,* March 6, 1749.

14. *New York Journal,* Supplement, February 26, 1768.

15. John Kirkpatrick to George Washington, July 6, 21, 1758, in Stanislaus M. Hamilton, ed., *Letters to Washington and Accompanying Papers* (Boston and New York, 1898-1902), 2:345-346, 379.

16. John Brown to Joseph Winsor, April 8, 1765, Brown Papers, L & P, 58-70, RIP, John Carter Brown Library, Providence.

17. Theodore G. Tappert and John W. Doberstein, trans., *The Journals of Henry Melchior Muhlenberg* (Philadelphia, 1945), 2:517.

18. Jasper Yeates to Col. James Burd, October 6, 1773, in Thomas Balch, ed., *Letters and Papers Relating Chiefly to the Provincial History of Pennsylvania* (Philadelphia, 1855), p. 232.

19. Thomas J. Wertenbaker, *Give Me Liberty: The Struggle for Self-Government in Virginia* (Philadelphia, 1958), pp. 9ff.; Charles M. Andrews, *The Colonial Period of American History* (New Haven, 1934-1938), 1:185.

20. George D. Langdon, Jr., *Pilgrim Colony: A History of New Plymouth, 1620-1691* (New Haven, 1966), pp. 90-99.

21. For New York (New Netherlands), see Andrews, *Colonial Period,* 3:chaps. 2-3. For Massachusetts, see Thomas J. Wertenbaker, *Puritan Oligarchy* (New York, 1947), chap. 8. For Connecticut and Rhode Island, see Andrews, *Colonial Period,* 2:chaps. 1-4. To be sure, some important contests did take place prior to 1689, such as those at the time of Bacon's

Rebellion (1676) in Virginia. See Edmund S. Morgan, *American Slavery, American Freedom* (New York, 1975), pp. 261-262.

22. Alison G. Olson, *Anglo-American Politics, 1660-1775: The Relationship Between Parties in England and Colonial America* (New York, 1973), pp. 79-80, 138-139.

23. Localism is emphasized in Zuckerman, *Peaceable Kingdoms,* and J. R. Pole, *Political Representation in England and the Origins of the American Republic* (London, 1966), pp. 38-54. For specific cases where local disputes led to heated contests, see James D. Phillips, *Salem in the Eighteenth Century* (Boston, 1937), pp. 102-112; James R. Trumbull, *History of Northampton, Massachusetts* (Northampton, 1901-1902), 2:34-35.

24. Lucille B. Griffith, *The Virginia House of Burgesses, 1750-1774,* rev. ed. (University, Ala., 1970), p. 62; Douglas S. Freeman, *George Washington: A Biography* (New York, 1948-1957), 2:147.

25. Lucius R. Paige, *A History of Cambridge, Massachusetts, 1630-1877* (Cambridge, 1877), pp. 130-131. For other examples of personal feuds, see Clifford K. Shipton, *Biographical Sketches of Those Who Attended Harvard College (Sibley's Harvard Graduates)* (Boston, 1873-1975), 6:159-164; Griffith, *Virginia House of Burgesses,* pp. 87-88; Robert E. and B. Katherine Brown, *Virginia, 1705-1786: Democracy or Aristocracy?* (East Lansing, 1964), p. 187.

26. For a brief discussion of early party or factional formation, see Bernard Bailyn, *The Origins of American Politics* (New York, 1968), pp. 64, 106-124. See also Jackson T. Main, *Political Parties before the Constitution* (New York, 1973), chap. 1. The quote is taken from James Otis, *A Vindication of the Conduct of the House of Representatives* (Boston, 1762), p. iv.

27. Jack P. Greene, *The Quest for Power: The Lower Houses of Assembly in the Southern Royal Colonies, 1689-1776* (Chapel Hill, 1963).

28. Bailyn, *Origins,* pp. 125-130; Patricia U. Bonomi, "The Middle Colonies: Embryo of the New Political Order," in Alden T. Vaughan and George A. Billias, eds., *Perspectives on Early American History* (New York, 1973), pp. 63-92. Although the word *party* usually connotes a less personal and more permanent form of political organization than *faction,* the two were often used interchangeably by eighteenth-century writers and are sometimes so used in this work. See Richard Hofstadter, *The Idea of a Party System: The Rise of Legitimate Opposition in the United States, 1780-1840* (Berkeley, 1969), chap. 1.

29. "Pennsylvania Assembly Committee: Report on the Proprietor's Answer (1753)," in *Franklin Papers,* 5:47.

30. Main, *Political Parties,* pp. xvii-xviii.

31. William W. Abbot, *The Royal Governors of Georgia* (Chapel Hill, 1959), pp. 10-11.

32. Ibid., pp. 39-40; Joseph Ottolenghe to Benjamin Martin, November 30, 1754, unpublished Georgia Colonial Records, 27:86-90, Georgia State Archives, Atlanta.

33. Abbot, *Royal Governors,* p. 10.

34. Ibid., pp. 145-146.

35. The most authoritative study of South Carolina provincial politics is M. Eugene Sirmans, *Colonial South Carolina: A Political History, 1663-1763* (Chapel Hill, 1966).

36. Alexander Hewatt, *An Historical Account of the Rise and Progress of the Colonies of South Carolina and Georgia* (London, 1779), 1:150.

37. William J. Rivers, *A Sketch of the History of South Carolina to the Close of the Proprietary Government, 1719* (Charleston, 1856), p. 459. See also Sirmans, *Colonial South Carolina,* pp. 83-84.

38. Sirmans, *Colonial South Carolina,* pp. 107, 123.

39. Ibid., p. 245; Robert M. Weir, " 'The Harmony We Were Famous For': An Interpretation of Pre-Revolutionary South Carolina Politics," *William and Mary Quarterly,* 3d ser., 26 (October 1969): 473-501.

40. *South Carolina Gazette,* February 25, 1749.

41. Sirmans, *Colonial South Carolina,* p. 245; Richard Walsh, *Charleston Sons of Liberty: A Study of the Artisans 1763-1789* (Columbia, 1959), chap. 2; Weir, " ' The Harmony We Were Famous For.' "

42. The most up-to-date study of the political life in this province is found in Hugh T. Lefler and William S. Powell, *Colonial North Carolina: A History* (New York, 1973).

43. Gov. George Burrington to the Lower House, July 18, 1733, in William L. Saunders, ed., *The Colonial Records of North Carolina, 1662-1776* (Raleigh, 1886-1890), 3:560.

44. Lefler and Powell, *Colonial North Carolina,* pp. 118-125.

45. Ibid., pp. 217-234; John S. Bassett, "The Regulators of North Carolina, 1765-1771," American Historical Association, *Annual Report, 1894* (Washington, D.C., 1895).

46. Richard L. Morton, *Colonial Virginia* (Chapel Hill, 1960), contains a competent survey of Virginia's politics. See also Wertenbaker, *Give Me Liberty.*

47. Morton, *Colonial Virginia,* 2: chaps. 1-8.

48. Wertenbaker, *Give Me Liberty,* pp. 171-172. On the Spotswood regime, see also *The Official Letters of Alexander Spotswood* (Richmond, 1882-1885).

49. Quoted in Wertenbaker, *Give Me Liberty*, p. 180. See also Morton, *Colonial Virginia*, 2:506n.

50. These conclusions are drawn chiefly from Sydnor, *Gentlemen Freeholders*, and Griffith, *Virginia House of Burgesses*.

51. Charles A. Barker, *The Background to the Revolution in Maryland* (New Haven, 1940), esp. chaps. 5, 7; David C. Skaggs, *Roots of Maryland's Democracy* (Westport, Conn., 1973).

52. Barker, *Background*, chap. 5; Aubrey C. Land, *The Dulanys of Maryland: A Biographical Study of Daniel Dulany, the Elder (1685-1753) and Daniel Dulany, the Younger (1722-1797)* (Baltimore, 1955), p. 225.

53. Disputed elections in Maryland are recorded in W. H. Browne et al., eds., *Archives of Maryland* (Baltimore, 1883-1972), vols. 36, 39, 44, 46, 50, 55, 56, 58, 59, 61, 62, 63.

54. Skaggs, *Roots of Maryland's Democracy*, pp. 113-131; *Maryland Gazette*, May 20, 1773.

55. The best study of political life in early Pennsylvania is Gary B. Nash, *Quakers and Politics: Pennsylvania, 1681-1726* (Princeton, 1968). See also Roy N. Lokken, *David Lloyd, Colonial Lawmaker* (Seattle, 1959); Frederick B. Tolles, *James Logan and the Culture of Provincial America* (Boston, 1957); Thomas Wendel, "The Keith-Lloyd Alliance: Factional and Coalition Politics in Colonial Pennsylvania," *Pennsylvania Magazine of History and Biography* 92 (July 1968): 289-305.

56. This summary is based primarily on Theodore G. Thayer, *Pennsylvania Politics and the Growth of Democracy, 1740-1776* (Harrisburg, 1953), chap. 2.

57. Ibid., chaps. 2-5; William S. Hanna, *Benjamin Franklin and Pennsylvania Politics* (Stanford, 1964); James H. Hutson, *Pennsylvania Politics, 1746-1770: The Movement for Royal Government and Its Consequences* (Princeton, 1972); Benjamin H. Newcomb, *Franklin and Galloway* (New Haven, 1972); John J. Zimmerman, "Benjamin Franklin and the Quaker Party, 1755-1756," *William and Mary Quarterly*, 3d ser., 17 (July 1960): 291-313.

58. Hutson, *Pennsylvania Politics*, pp. 170-177; Benjamin H. Newcomb, "Effects of the Stamp Act on Colonial Pennsylvania Politics," *William and Mary Quarterly.*, 3d ser., 23 (April 1966): 257-272.

59. Hutson, *Pennsylvania Politics*, pp. 210-243; David Hawke, *In the Midst of a Revolution* (Philadelphia, 1961); Newcomb, *Franklin and Galloway*, chaps. 7-10.

60. Robert W. Johannsen, "The Conflict between the Three Lower Counties on the Delaware and the Province of Pennsylvania, 1682-1704," *Delaware History* 5 (1952): 96-132.

61. Richard S. Rodney, "Delaware under Governor Keith, 1717-1726," *Delaware History* 3 (1948): 1-25; Harold B. Hancock, ed., " ' Fare Weather and Good Health,' The Journal of Caesar Rodney, 1727-1729," ibid. 10 (1962): 69.

62. George H. Ryden, ed., *Letters to and from Caesar Rodney, 1756-1783* (Philadelphia, 1933); Harold B. Hancock, "Thomas Robinson: Delaware Loyalist," *Delaware History* 4 (1950-1951): 1-36.

63. Quoted in Donald L. Kemmerer, *Path to Freedom: The Struggle for Self-Government in Colonial New Jersey, 1703-1776* (Princeton, 1940). For New Jersey politics, see also Richard P. McCormick, *New Jersey from Colony to State, 1609-1789* (Princeton, 1964), and John E. Pomfret, *Colonial New Jersey: A History* (New York, 1973).

64. Lewis Morris to Sir Charles Wager, October 1739, in W. A. Whitehead, ed., *The Papers of Lewis Morris,* New Jersey Historical Society, *Collections* (1852), 4:61. See also Lewis Morris to Benjamin Smith, January 3, 1740, ibid., p. 73. For this era in general, see Pomfret, *Colonial New Jersey,* chap. 7.

65. W. A. Whitehead et al., eds., *New Jersey Archives* (Newark, 1880-190 1st ser., 19:382; Pomfret, *Colonial New Jersey,* chap. 7.

66. *New Jersey Archives,* 1st ser., 26: 191-192, 209-210; 28: 98, 100; Edgar J. Fisher, *New Jersey as a Royal Province, 1738-1776* (New York, 1911), p. 94; J. R. Pole, "Suffrage Reform and the American Revolution in New Jersey," New Jersey Historical Society, *Proceedings* 74 (July 1956): 173-194.

67. The most important survey of provincial politics in New York is Patricia U. Bonomi, *A Factious People: Politics and Society in Colonial New York* (New York, 1971). See also the collected articles of Milton M. Klein, *The Politics of Diversity: Essays in the History of Colonial New York* (Port Washington, 1974).

68. Edmund B. O'Callaghan and Berthold Fernow, eds., *Documents Relative to the Colonial History of the State of New York* (Albany, 1853-1887), 4: 218, 223, 384, 395, 507-508. See also Bonomi, *A Factious People,* pp. 75-78, and Thomas A. Archdeacon, "The Age of Leisler—New York City, 1689-1710: A Social and Demographic Interpretation," in Jacob Judd and Irwin H. Polishook, eds., *Aspects of Early New York Society and Politics* (Tarrytown, 1974), pp. 63-82, the latter emphasizing the Dutch-English split.

69. Stanely N. Katz, *Newcastle's New York: Anglo-American Politics, 1732-1753* (Cambridge, 1968), chap. 4; Bonomi, *A Factious People,* chaps. 3-4. The details of the Westchester County election appear in the *New York Weekly Journal,* November 5, 1733.

70. Bonomi, *A Factious People,* chap. 5; Katz, *Newcastle's New York,* chap. 6-7.

71. Philanthropos [pseud.], *A Few Observations on the Conduct of the General Assembly of New-York* (New York, 1768); Roger Champagne, "Family Politics versus Constitutional Principles: The New York Assembly Elections of 1768 and 1769," *William and Mary Quarterly,* 3d ser., 20 (January 1963): 57-79; Bonomi, *A Factious People,* chap. 7.

72. There is no general survey of New England politics in the provincial period except for the somewhat dated James T. Adams, *Revolutionary New England, 1691-1776* (Boston, 1923).

73. "Account of the Government of the New England Colonies," *The Letters and Papers of Cadwallader Colden,* New York Historical Society, *Collections* (1918-1937), 67: 247. A brief study of Connecticut elections appears in Robert J. Dinkin, "Elections in Colonial Connecticut," *Connecticut Historical Society Bulletin* 37 (January 1972): 17-20. See also Oscar Zeichner, *Connecticut's Years of Controversy, 1750-1776* (Chapel Hill, 1949), chap. 1.

74. Dinkin, "Elections," p. 18; Zeichner, *Connecticut,* chap. 2; Richard L. Bushman, *From Puritan to Yankee: Character and Social Order in Connecticut, 1690-1765* (Cambridge, 1967), esp. pp. 268-270.

75. Dinkin, "Elections," pp. 19-20; Zeichner, *Connecticut,* chap. 6; Samuel Johnson to William Samuel Johnson, April 24, 1767, in Herbert and Carol Schneider, eds., *Samuel Johnson, His Career and Writings* (New York, 1929), 1: 400.

76. Zeichner, *Connecticut,* chaps. 6-8.

77. John Adams to William Tudor, February 4, 1817, in Charles F. Adams, ed., *The Works of John Adams* (Boston, 1850-1856), 10: 242. For the early provincial years, see Timothy H. Breen, *The Character of the Good Ruler: A Study of Puritan Political Ideas in New England, 1630-1730* (New Haven, 1970), chaps. 5-7; Richard S. Dunn, *Puritans and Yankees: The Winthrop Dynasty of New England, 1630-1717* (Princeton, 1962), pp. 278-283.

78. Thomas Lechmere to John Winthrop, March 13, 1721, Winthrop Papers, IX, Massachusetts Historical Society, Boston. See also G. B. Warden, *Boston, 1689-1776* (Boston, 1970), pp. 92-94.

79. For this period, see Robert Zemsky, *Merchants, Farmers, and River Gods: An Essay in Eighteenth-Century American Politics* (Boston, 1971), chap. 5; George A. Billias, *The Massachusetts Land Bankers of 1740* (Orono, 1959); Thomas Hutchinson, *The History of Massachusetts Bay Colony,* ed. Lawrence S. Mayo (Cambridge, 1936), 2: 300.

80. For the Shirley regime, see John A. Schutz, *William Shirley: King's*

Governor of Massachusetts (Chapel Hill, 1961); Zemsky, *Merchants, Farmers, and River Gods,* chap. 6; Paul S. Boyer, "Borrowed Rhetoric: The Massachusetts Excise Controversy of 1754," *William and Mary Quarterly,* 3d ser., 21 (July 1964): 328-351.

81. The pre-Revolutionary decade is treated in Ellen E. Brennan, *Plural Office-Holding in Massachusetts, 1760-1780* (Chapel Hill, 1945); John J. Waters, Jr., *The Otis Family in Provincial and Revolutionary Massachusetts* (Chapel Hill, 1968), chaps. 7-9.

82. In 1701, for example, one of the representatives from the town of Hampton was chosen with just six votes, whereas the number of free-holders was "neer 200." Joseph Smith to John Usher, September 22, 1701, in W. N. Sainsbury et al., eds., *Calender of State Papers, Colonial Series, America and West Indies, 1702-1703* (London, 1913), p. 436. See also William H. Fry, *New Hampshire as a Royal Province* (New York, 1908

83. The Belcher-Dunbar dispute is fully treated in Joseph J. Malone, *Pine Trees and Politics* (Seattle, 1963), chap. 6.

84. Gov. Jonathan Belcher to Henry Sherburne, August 21, 1732, Belcher Mss., Letter-Book, Massachusetts Historical Society.

85. For the Benning Wentworth regime, see Jere Daniell, *Experiment in Republicanism: New Hampshire Politics and the American Revolution, 1741-1794* (Cambridge, 1970), chap. 1. See also Nathaniel Bouton et al., eds., *Documents and Records Relating to New Hampshire* (Concord and Manchester, 1867-1941), vols. 9-13).

86. Daniell, *Experiment in Republicanism,* chaps. 2-4; Richard F. Upton, *Revolutionary New Hampshire* (Hanover, 1936), chaps. 1-2.

87. Sydney V. James, *Colonial Rhode Island: A History* (New York, 1975); David S. Lovejoy, *Rhode Island Politics and the American Revolution, 1760-1776* (Providence, 1958), chap. 1.

88. Gov. William Wanton to the General Assembly, April 1733, in Gertrude S. Kimball, ed., *The Correspondence of the Colonial Governors of Rhode Island, 1723-1775* (Boston and New York, 1902-1903), 1: 37.

89. James, *Colonial Rhode Island,* chap. 8; Lovejoy, *Rhode Island Politics,* pp. 6-9.

90. James, *Colonial Rhode Island,* chaps. 11-12; Lovejoy, *Rhode Island Politics,* pp. 9-14; Mack E. Thompson, "The Ward-Hopkins Controversy and the American Revolution in Rhode Island: An Interpretation," *William and Mary Quarterly,* 3d ser., 16 (July 1959): 363-375.

91. Samuel Ward to Peter Philips, March 16, 1764, Rhode Island Historical Society Manuscripts, II, 101, Rhode Island Historical Society, Providenc

92. James, *Colonial Rhode Island,* chap. 12; Lovejoy, *Rhode Island Politics,* pp. 152-153.

CHAPTER 2

1. The most up-to-date study of the suffrage in provincial America is Chilton Williamson, *American Suffrage from Property to Democracy, 1760-1860* (Princeton, 1960). Still valuable in many ways are three older works: Albert E. McKinley, *The Suffrage Franchise in the Thirteen English Colonies in America* (Philadelphia, 1905); Kirk H. Porter, *Suffrage in the United States* (Chicago, 1918); Cortlandt F. Bishop, *History of Elections in the American Colonies* (New York, 1893).

2. McKinley, *Suffrage Franchise,* p. 1.

3. Porter, *Suffrage,* p. 1.

4. Thomas Cooper and D. J. McCord, eds., *Statutes at Large of South Carolina* (Columbia, 1836-1841), 2: 683. See also William W. Hening, ed., *The Statutes at Large . . . of Virginia* (Richmond, 1809-1823), 2: 280.

5. Porter, *Suffrage,* pp. 4-5.

6. John Adams to James Sullivan, May 26, 1776, in Charles F. Adams, ed. *The Works of John Adams* (Boston, 1850-1856), 9: 376.

7. Williamson, *American Suffrage,* p. 15; McKinley, *Suffrage Franchise,* pp. 35, 146, 270, 473-474.

8. Mary S. Benson, *Women in Eighteenth-Century America* (New York, 1935), pp. 244-249.

9. *New York Gazette,* June 6, 1737.

10. Mary P. Clarke, *Parliamentary Privilege in the American Colonies* (New Haven, 1943), p. 151. Women could vote for a time in New Jersey during the early national period; see Edward R. Turner, "Women's Suffrage in New Jersey, 1790-1807," *Smith College Studies in History,* vol. 1, no. 4, July 1916.

11. Williamson, *American Suffrage,* p. 15; McKinley, *Suffrage Franchise,* pp. 35, 111, 146, 172, 212, 270, 282, 474.

12. John Adams to James Sullivan, May 26, 1776, in Adams, ed. *Works,* 9: 377.

13. McKinley, *Suffrage Franchise,* pp. 324, 374.

14. William L. Saunders, ed., *The Colonial Records of North Carolina, 1662-1776* (Raleigh, 1886-1890), 1: 696; Nathaniel Bouton et al., eds., *Documents and Records Relating to New Hampshire* (Concord and Manchester, 1867-1941), 9: 152, 12: 30-31; Massachusetts Archives, 8: 277-278, Statehouse, Boston; Samuel Hazard et al., eds., *Pennsylvania Archives* (Philadelphia and Harrisburg, 1852-1935), 8th ser., 4: 3280.

15. Massachusetts Archives, 8: 277-278; Robert E. Brown, *Middle-Class Democracy and the Revolution in Massachusetts, 1691-1780* (Ithaca, 1955), p. 40.

16. Warren Brown, *History of the Town of Hampton-Falls, New Hampshire* (Manchester, 1900), pp. 63-65.

17. McKinley, *Suffrage Franchise*, p. 474.

18. Ibid., pp. 304, 353-354, 475-476; Bishop, *History of Elections*, p. 60; Charles S. Sydnor, *Gentlemen Freeholders: Political Practices in Washington's Virginia* (Chapel Hill, 1952), p. 28.

19. Williamson, *American Suffrage*, pp. 15-16; McKinley, *Suffrage Franchise*, pp. 35, 70-76, 157-158, 214, 451. Catholics who were not recusants could vote in Virginia; see H. R. McIlwaine and J. P. Kennedy, eds., *Journals of the House of Burgesses, 1761-1765* (Richmond, 1907), pp. 126-130.

20. W. H. Browne et al., eds., *Archives of Maryland* (Baltimore, 1883-1972), 33: 288. See also John T. Ellis, *Catholics in Colonial America* (Baltimore, 1965), p. 346; Charles A. Barker, *The Background to the Revolution in Maryland* (New Haven, 1940), pp. 43-44, 172.

21. Jacob R. Marcus, *The Colonial American Jew, 1492-1776* (Detroit, 1970), 1: 397-474, 509-510.

22. Milton M. Klein, *The Politics of Diversity: Essays in the History of Colonial New York* (Port Washington, 1974), p. 24; Jacob R. Marcus, *Early American Jewry* (Philadelphia, 1951-1953), 2: 230.

23. Samuel G. Arnold, *History of the State of Rhode Island* (New York, 1859-1860), 2: 494. No Jewish name appears on any of the Newport poll lists available; see Deputies and Freemen, Rhode Island State Archives, Providence.

24. Winthrop D. Jordan, *White over Black : American Attitudes Toward the Negro, 1550-1812* (Chapel Hill, 1968), pp. 126-127. See also Emil Olbrich, *The Development of Sentiment on Negro Suffrage to 1860* (Madison, 1912); Stephen B. Weeks, "The History of Negro Suffrage in the South," *Political Science Quarterly* 9 (1894): 671-703.

25. Brown, *Middle-Class Democracy*, pp. 40-43.

26. Saunders, ed., *Colonial Records of North Carolina*, 2: 903, 908, 4: 251.

27. Cooper and McCord, eds., *South Carolina Statutes*, 2: 683; Saunders, ed., *Colonial Records of North Carolina*, 2: 214-215; McKinley, *Suffrage Franchise*, p. 474.

28. Richard West to Lords of Trade, January 10, 1724, in Emory G. Evans, ed., "A Question of Complexion: Documents Concerning the Negro and the Franchise in Eighteenth-Century Virginia," *Virginia Magazine of History and Biography* 71 (October 1963): 413.

29. Gov. William Gooch to Alured Popple, May 18, 1736, in ibid., 414; Jordan, *White over Black*, p. 127.

30. Allen D. Candler, ed., *Colonial Records of the State of Georgia*

(Atlanta, 1904-1916), 18: 465.

31. Richard B. Morris, *Government and Labor in Early America* (New York, 1945), pp. 503-506; Robert E. and B. Katherine Brown, *Virginia, 1705-1786: Democracy or Aristocracy?* (East Lansing, 1964), pp. 143-144.

32. McKinley, *Suffrage Franchise,* pp. 92, 270, 279, 374, 474-475.

33. Ibid., pp. 131-135; Williamson, *American Suffrage,* p. 53; M. Eugene Sirmans, *Colonial South Carolina: A Political History, 1663-1763* (Chapel Hill, 1966), pp. 61-62.

34. Williamson, *American Suffrage,* pp. 51-53.

35. William Smith, *A Brief State of the Province of Pennsylvania* (London, 1755), p. 40.

36. Bishop, *History of Elections,* pp. 67, 270, 278, 281.

37. *New York Gazette,* September 19, 26, 1737; Edmund B. O'Callaghan and Berthold Fernow, eds., *Documents Relative to the Colonial History of the State of New York* (Albany, 1853-1887), 6: 56n.; McKinley, *Suffrage Franchise,* pp. 215-217.

38. William Smith, Jr., *The History of the Province of New-York,* ed. Michael Kammen (Cambridge, 1972), 2: 35.

39. See *A Copy of the Poll List of the Election for Representatives for the City and County of New-York . . . MDCCLXVIII* (New York, 1880), and *A Copy of the Poll List of the Election for Representatives for the City and County of New-York . . . MDCCLXIX* (New York, 1880). The disallowance probably stemmed from objections to the bill's clause calling for the end of nonresident officeholding. McKinley, *Suffrage Franchise,* p. 216n.

40. Brown and Brown, *Virginia,* p. 152. Sydnor, *Gentlemen Freeholders,* pp. 34-35, claims nonresidents were a "significant force" in Virginia elections but gives scant evidence of this.

41. J. W. Gough, *John Locke's Political Philosophy,* 2d ed. (Oxford, 1973), pp. 88-89; M. Seliger, *The Liberal Politics of John Locke* (New York, 1968), pp. 284-287; J. R. Pole, *Political Representation in England and the Origins of the American Republic* (London, 1966), pt. 1.

42. Baron de Montesquieu, *The Spirit of the Laws* (New York, 1949), 2: 155.

43. See Chilton Williamson, "American Suffrage and Sir William Blackstone," *Political Science Quarterly* 68 (December 1953): 552-557.

44. Robert G. McCloskey, ed., *The Works of James Wilson* (Cambridge, 1967), 2: 725.

45. John Adams to James Sullivan, May 26, 1776, in Adams, ed., *Works,* 9: 376.

46. *Pennsylvania Gazette,* December 8, 1737.

47. Williamson, *American Suffrage,* chap. 5.

48. Hening, ed., *Statutes of Virginia,* 2: 280.

49. John R. Bartlett, ed., *Records of the Colony of Rhode Island and Providence Plantations* (Providence, 1856-1865), 2: 113. See also McKinley, *Suffrage Franchise,* pp. 449-453.

50. Leonard W. Labaree, ed., *Royal Instructions to British Colonial Governors* (New York, 1935), 1: 93.

51. Gov. Burrington to Lords of Trade, September 4, 1731, in Saunders, ed., *Colonial Records of North Carolina,* 3: 207. See also McKinley, *Suffrage Franchise,* pp. 96-100.

52. Williamson, *American Suffrage,* pp. 14-15; Sirmans, *Colonial South Carolina,* pp. 239-240.

53. Williamson, *American Suffrage,* pp. 12-14; Brown, *Middle-Class Democracy,* p. 25.

54. Fifty acres in western Pennsylvania in the 1760s cost only two to three pounds; Theodore G. Thayer, *Pennsylvania Politics and the Growth of Democracy, 1740-1776* (Harrisburg, 1953), p. 6. See also Williamson, *American Suffrage,* pp. 12-14. Lifetime leaseholders and even those possessing short-term leases could vote in Virginia; Brown and Brown, *Virginia,* pp. 126, 131, 144-145.

55. J. Franklin Jameson, *The American Revolution Considered as a Social Movement* (Princeton, 1926), pp. 39-40; Brown and Brown, *Virginia,* p. 132.

56. Williamson, *American Suffrage,* pp. 13-14; Joseph Anderson, ed., *The Town and City of Waterbury, Connecticut* (New Haven, 1896), 1: 303-309.

57. Williamson, *American Suffrage,* pp. 32-33.

58. Ibid., pp. 17-18; McKinley, *Suffrage Franchise,* p. 114n.

59. Klein, *Politics of Diversity,* pp. 21-22.

60. James T. Adams, *Revolutionary New England, 1691-1776* (Boston, 1923), p. 195.

61. Brown, *Middle-Class Democracy,* chap. 5; *Watertown Records* (Watertown, 1894-1906), 2: 202ff.; *Town of Weston, Records of the First Precinct, 1746-1754 and of the Town, 1754-1803* (Boston, 1893), pp. 35-36ff.

62. Thomas Jefferson to John Hambden Pleasants, August 19, 1824, in Andrew A. Lipscomb and Albert E. Bergh, eds., *The Writings of Thomas Jefferson* (Washington, D.C., 1903-1904), 16: 28. See also Thomas Jefferson, *Notes on the State of Virginia,* ed. William Peden (Chapel Hill, 1955), p. 118.

63. Gov. Robert Dinwiddie to the Lords of Trade, February 23, 1756,

in R. A. Brock, ed., *The Official Records of Robert Dinwiddie* (Richmond, 1883-1884), 2: 345.

64. Ezra Stiles to Benjamin Gale, October 1, 1766, Stiles Papers, Yale University Library, New Haven.

65. Brown, *Middle-Class Democracy,* chap. 1; Benjamin Franklin to Dr. Joshua Babcock, January 13, 1772, in Albert H. Smyth, ed., *The Writings of Benjamin Franklin* (New York, 1905-1907), 5: 362-363.

66. J. Franklin Jameson, "Did the Fathers Vote?" *New England Magazine,* n.s., 1 (January 1890): 484-490, and "Virginia Voting in the Colonial Period, 1744-1774," *The Nation* 56 (April 27, 1893): 309-310.

67. Carl Becker, *The History of Political Parties in the Province of New York, 1760-1776* (Madison, 1909), p. 11, and *The United States: An Experiment in Democracy* (New York, 1920), pp. 35-36.

68. Clinton L. Rossiter, *Seedtime of the Republic: The Origin of the American Tradition of Liberty* (New York, 1953), p. 20.

69. Brown, *Middle-Class Democracy,* chap. 2; Brown and Brown, *Virginia,* chap. 7; Richard P. McCormick, *The History of Voting in New Jersey: A Study of the Development of Election Machinery, 1664-1911* (New Brunswick, 1953), pp. 61-63; Klein, *Politics of Diversity,* pp. 20-26, 42; David S. Lovejoy, *Rhode Island Politics and the American Revolution, 1760-1776* (Providence, 1958), pp. 15-17. This material is ably summarized in Jack P. Greene, "Changing Interpretations of Early American Politics," in Ray A. Billington, ed., *The Reinterpretation of Early American History* (San Marino, 1966), pp. 151-184.

70. Williamson, *American Suffrage,* p. 38.

71. Brown, *Middle-Class Democracy,* p. 50.

72. Benjamin W. Labaree, *Patriots and Partisans: The Merchants of Newburyport, 1764-1815* (Cambridge, 1962), p. 13; James Henretta, "Economic Development and Social Structure in Colonial Boston," *William and Mary Quarterly.,* 3d ser., 22 (January 1965): 75-91; Brown, *Middle-Class Democracy,* p. 65; Joseph B. Felt, "Statistics on Population in Massachusetts," in American Statistical Association, *Collections* (Boston, 1847), 1: 152-154; Kenneth A. Lockridge, "Land, Population and the Evolution of New England Society, 1630-1790," *Past and Present* 39 (April 1968): 62-80. Population figures for the various colonies, unless otherwise indicated, are taken from Evarts B. Greene and Virginia D. Harrington, *American Population before the Federal Census of 1790* (New York, 1932), and W. S. Rossiter, *A Century of Population Growth, 1790-1900* (Washington, D.C., 1909).

73. William H. Fry, *New Hampshire as a Royal Province* (New York, 1908), p. 135n; Bouton et al., eds., *Documents and Records Relating to*

New Hampshire, 9: 211, 685-687, 12: 83-84; Williamson, *American Suffrage,* p. 25; Charles J. Fox, *History of the Old Township of Dunstable* (Nashua, 1846), p. 158; Levi W. Leonard and Josiah L. Seward, *The History of Dublin, New Hampshire* (Dublin, 1920), pp. 158-159.

74. Lawrence H. Gipson claimed that no more than one-fourth of the adult males in New Haven were freemen. See his *Jared Ingersoll, A Study in American Loyalism in Relation to British Colonial Government* (New Haven, 1920), p. 19. Sources for other Connecticut freemen are Anderson, ed., *Waterbury,* 1: 303-309; Groton, Conn., "Grand Lists for the Town of Groton," Connecticut State Library, Hartford; *History of Litchfield County, Connecticut* (Philadelphia, 1881), p. 527; Charles S. Grant, *Democracy in the Connecticut Frontier Town of Kent* (New York, 1961), p. 111: Clarence W. Bowen, *The History of Woodstock, Connecticut* (Norwood, Mass., 1926-1932), 1: 108.

75. Lovejoy, *Rhode Island Politics,* p. 16; Rhode Island Colony Records (Mss.), VI, Rhode Island State Archives, Providence.

76. *Providence Gazette,* January 2, 1768.

77. Roger Champagne, "Liberty Boys and Mechanics of New York City, 1764-1774," *Labor History* 8 (Spring 1967): 125: Edmund B. O'Callaghan, *The Documentary History of the State of New York* (Albany, 1849-1851), 1: 694-695, 2: 200-208.

78. E. Marie Becker, "The 801 Westchester County Freeholders of 1763 *New-York Historical Society Quarterly* 35 (July 1951): 296; *New York Gazette* (Weyman's), March 2, 1761; *New York Gazette and Weekly Mercury,* March 21, 1768.

79. Williamson, *American Suffrage,* pp. 33-34; *The Scotch-Irish of Northampton County, Pennsylvania* (Easton, 1926), pp. 27-31; David Hawke, *In the Midst of a Revolution* (Philadelphia, 1961), pp. 33-34, 34n.

80. McCormick, *History of Voting,* p. 63; J. P. Snell, *History of Hunterdon and Somerset Counties, New Jersey* (Philadelphia, 1881), p. 815; New Jersey Historical Society, *Proceedings,* 2d ser., 13: 29-34, 3d ser., 1: 103-109.

81. David C. Skaggs, *Roots of Maryland's Democracy* (Westport, Conn., 1973), pp. 39-52.

82. Lucille B. Griffith, *The Virginia House of Burgesses, 1750-1774,* rev. ed. (University, Ala., 1970), pp. 54-60; Brown and Brown, Virginia, chap. 7; Jackson T. Main, "The Distribution of Property in Post-Revolutionary Virginia," *Mississippi Valley Historical Review* 41 (September 1954): 241-258.

83. Jackson T. Main, *The Social Structure of Revolutionary America* (Princeton 1965), pp. 60-63; McKinley, *Suffrage Franchise,* pp. 112-115.

84. Sirmans, *Colonial South Carolina*, pp. 239-240; Main, *Social Structure*, pp. 64-65; *South Carolina Gazette*, October 10, 1768.

85. Gov. James Wright to the Lords of Trade, December 26, 1768, quoted in Williamson, *American Suffrage*, p. 31.

86. Thomas Hutchinson to Lord Hillsborough, May 29, 1772, quoted in Brown, *Middle-Class Democracy*, p. 60.

87. "A Serious Address to the People of Pennsylvania on the Present Situation of Their Affairs," *Pennsylvania Packet*, December 5, 1778, in Philip S. Foner, ed., *The Complete Writings of Thomas Paine* (New York, 1945), 2: 287-288.

88. David Dunbar to William Popple, June 5, 1730, in *Calendar of State Papers, Colonial Series, America and West Indies, 1730* (London, 1937), p. 132. Some thirty-eight Quakers were excluded by the sheriff in the Westchester County, New York, election of 1733 as part of the attempt to defeat Lewis Morris. See *New York Weekly Journal*, November 5, 1733.

89. Saunders, ed., *Colonial Records of North Carolina*, 6: 366-367.

90. See Clarke, *Parliamentary Privilege*, chap. 4. On one occasion, the published election announcement in the Boston newspapers specifically mentions that "an exact Scrutiny will be made as to the Qualification of Voters." *Boston News-Letter*, May 2, 1745; *Boston Gazette*, April 30, 1745.

91. Richard J. Hooker, ed., *The Carolina Backcountry on the Eve of the Revolution* (Chapel Hill, 1953), p. 166.

92. William Douglass, *A Summary, Historical and Political, of the . . . British Settlements in North America* (London, 1755), 1: 504.

93. *New Hampshire Gazette*, March 18, 1774; Jere Daniell, *Experiment in Republicanism: New Hampshire Politics and the American Revolution, 1741-1794* (Cambridge, 1970), p. 78.

94. J. H. Plumb, "The Growth of the Electorate in England from 1600 to 1715," *Past and Present* 45 (November 1969): 111.

CHAPTER 3

1. The hypothesis that American officeholders were unhappy with their situation is strongly argued in James K. Martin, *Men in Rebellion: Higher Governmental Leaders and the Coming of the American Revolution* (New Brunswick, 1973).

2. Mary P. Clarke, *Parliamentary Privilege in the American Colonies* (New Haven, 1943), esp. chaps. 4-5; Jack P. Greene, *The Quest for Power:*

The Lower Houses of Assembly in the Southern Royal Colonies, 1689-1776 (Chapel Hill, 1963), chap. 9.

3. William L. Saunders, ed., *The Colonial Records of North Carolina, 1662-1776* (Raleigh, 1886-1890), 2: 884-885; Jacob R. Marcus, *The Colonial American Jew, 1492-1776* (Detroit, 1970), 1: 509-511.

4. Cortlandt F. Bishop, *History of Elections in the American Colonies* (New York, 1893), p. 278; Albert S. Batchellor, ed., *Laws of New Hampshire* (Concord, 1913), 2: 402-403; Thomas Cooper and D. J. McCord, eds, *Statutes at Large of South Carolina* (Columbia, 1836-1841), 2: 683; Samuel Allinson, ed., *Acts of the General Assembly of the Province of New Jersey, 1702-1776* (Burlington, 1776), p. 6.

5. Albert E. McKinley, *The Suffrage Franchise in the Thirteen English Colonies in America* (Philadelphia, 1905), pp. 169-171; William W. Abbot, *The Royal Governors of Georgia* (Chapel Hill, 1959), p. 11.

6. Clarke, *Parliamentary Privilege*, pp. 163-164; David C. Skaggs, *Roots of Maryland's Democracy* (Westport, Conn., 1973), pp. 75-76; Edgar J. Fisher, *New Jersey as a Royal Province, 1738-1776* (New York, 1911), p. 87.

7. William S. Hanna, *Benjamin Franklin and Pennsylvania Politics* (Stanford, 1964), p. 3; Patricia U. Bonomi, *A Factious People: Politics and Society in Colonial New York* (New York, 1971), pp. 24-27, 49-51; Arthur H. Hirsch, *The Huguenots of Colonial South Carolina* (Durham, 1928), chaps. 5-6; Wayne L. Bockelman and Owen S. Ireland, "The Internal Revolution in Pennsylvania: An Ethnic-Religious Interpretation," *Pennsylvania History* 41 (April 1974), 125-159.

8. William Douglass, *A Summary, Historical and Political, of the . . . British Settlements in North America* (London, 1755), 1: 507; Bernard Bailyn, *The Origins of American Politics* (New York, 1968), pp. 84-86; Hubert Phillips, *The Development of a Residence Qualification for Representatives in Colonial Legislatures* (Cincinnati, 1921). In New York, the Livingstons and others manipulated the residency requirement for political purposes, sometimes supporting it, sometimes opposing it. See Bonomi, *A Factious People*, pp. 258-259.

9. Walter Clarke, ed., *The State Records of North Carolina* (Winston and Goldsboro, 1886-1914), 23: 208.

10. Greene, *Quest for Power*, pp. 186-188; Clarke, *Parliamentary Privilege*, pp. 159-162.

11. Theodore G. Thayer, *Pennsylvania Politics and the Growth of Democracy, 1740-1776* (Harrisburg, 1953), appendix 1, p. 206; *The Colonial Laws of New York* (Albany, 1894-1896), 2: 835-837; *North Carolina Historical and Genealogical Register* 3 (April 1903): 136; Wil-

liam W. Hening, ed., *The Statutes at Large . . . of Virginia* (Richmond, 1809-1823), 3: 236; William H. Fry, *New Hampshire as a Royal Province* (New York, 1908), p. 135.

12. John Winthrop, "A Modell of Christian Charity," *Winthrop Papers* (Boston, 1931), 2: 282; Edmund S. Morgan, ed., *Puritan Political Ideas, 1558-1794* (Indianapolis and New York, 1965), pp. xv-xvii.

13. Charles Chauncy, *Civil Magistrates* (Boston, 1747), pp. 30-31.

14. Daniel Lewis, *Good Rulers* (Boston, 1748), p. 9.

15. Many of the ideas emphasized in the writings below first appeared in the works of English liberal journalists such as Trenchard and Gordon; see Caroline Robbins, *The Eighteenth-Century Commonwealthman* (Cambridge, 1959). See also Jackson T. Main, "Government by the People: The American Revolution and the Democratization of the Legislatures," *William and Mary Quarterly*, 3d ser., 23 (July 1966): 391-392.

16. *Maryland Gazette*, December 3, 1767.

17. *A Letter to the Freeholders and Other Inhabitants of this Province* (Boston, 1742), p. 5.

18. *A Letter to the Inhabitants of the Province of Massachusetts Bay* (Boston, 1751), p. 5.

19. *New York Weekly Journal*, May 23, 1737. See also *A Letter to the Freemen and Freeholders of the City of New York; Relating to the Approaching Election* (New York, 1752), p. 11.

20. *South Carolina Gazette*, October 30, 1736. See also John Sydney [pseud.], *According to My Promise* (New York, 1734), p. 4; *To the Free-Holders of the Province of Pennsylvania* (Philadelphia, 1742).

21. *New York Weekly Journal*, March 5, 1739. See also *Boston Evening-Post*, May 14, 1759, April 27, 1761; Americanus [pseud.], *A Letter to the Freeholders* (Boston, 1739), p. 9.

22. *New Hampshire Gazette*, March 25, 1774.

23. *Pennsylvania Journal*, September 30, 1756.

24. William Livingston et al., *The Independent Reflector*, ed. Milton M. Klein (Cambridge, 1963), p. 281. See also Bailyn, *Origins*, p. 143.

25. *English Advice to the Freeholders &c. of the Province of Massachusetts Bay* (Boston, 1722), p. 2.

26. *An Address to the Freeholders* (Boston, 1751), p. 6.

27. Timothy Wheelwright [pseud.], *Two Letters on Election of Aldermen* (New York, 1734), p. 3.

28. *South Carolina Gazette*, October 30, 1736.

29. *Boston Evening-Post*, May 7, 1750. See also *An Address to the Freeholders*, p. 6.

30. *South Carolina Gazette*, October 5, 1765.

31. Memorial of Gov. Samuel Shute to King George I, August 1723, in *Calendar of State Papers, Colonial Series, America and West Indies, 1722-1723* (London, 1934), pp. 325-326; Carl Bridenbaugh, ed., *Gentleman's Progress: The Itinerarium of Dr. Alexander Hamilton, 1744* (Chapel Hill, 1948), p. 31. See also Douglass, *Summary,* 1: 507; Douglass Adair and John A. Schutz, eds., *Peter Oliver's Origin and Progress of the American Rebellion* (San Marino, 1961), p. 27.

32. Robert E. and B. Katherine Brown, *Virginia, 1705-1786: Democracy or Aristocracy?* (East Lansing, 1964), pp. 225-227.

33. Robert Munford, *The Candidates; or, the Humours of a Virginia Election,* ed. Jay B. Hubbell and Douglass Adair (Williamsburg, 1948).

34. Edward Holyoke, *Integrity and Religion to be Principally Regarded* . . . (Boston, 1736), pp. 19-20. See also "Massachusettensis," Letter III, *Massachusetts Gazette and Boston Post-Boy,* December 26, 1774.

35. Robert Kennedy, *To the Worthy Tradesmen, Artificers, Mechanics, &c. Electors for the City and County of Philadelphia* (Philadelphia, 1770).

36. Roger Champagne, "Liberty Boys and Mechanics of New York City, 1764-1774," *Labor History* 8 (Spring 1967): 125; Brown and Brown, *Virginia,* p. 227.

37. William Eddis, *Letters from America,* ed. Aubrey C. Land (Cambridge, 1969), p. 64.

38. Main, "Government by the People," pp. 393-397.

39. John Adams, *A Defense of the Constitutions of Government of the United States* (1787), in Charles F. Adams, ed., *The Works of John Adams* (Boston, 1850-1856), 4: 393.

40. Main, "Government by the People," p. 397.

41. Bruce C. Daniels, "Large Town Officeholding in Eighteenth Century Connecticut: The Growth of Oligarchy," *Journal of American Studies* 9 (April 1975): 9. See also William F. Willingham, "Deference Democracy and Town Government in Windham, Connecticut, 1755-1786," *William and Mary Quarterly,* 3d ser., 30 (July 1973): 407; Charles S. Grant, *Democracy in the Frontier Town of Kent* (New York, 1961), pp. 150-152. On the other hand, Patricia U. Bonomi found most of the high officials in eighteenth-century Kingston, New York, were of "the middling sort." See "Local Government in Colonial New York: A Base for Republicanism," in Jacob Judd and Irwin H. Polishook, eds., *Aspects of Early New York. Society and Politics* (Tarrytown, 1974), p. 34.

42. Henry A. Hazen, *History of Billerica, Massachusetts* (Boston, 1883), pp. 247-251; E. V. Bigelow, *A Narrative History of the Town of Cohasset* (Cohasset, 1898), pp. 275-276; *Early Records of Dedham* (Dedham, 1906-

1936), 6: 384-390; Lucius R. Paige, *History of Hardwick, Massachusetts* (Boston, 1883), pp. 295-298; *Town Records of Manchester* (Salem, 1889), 2: 195-200; *Milton Town Records, 1662-1729* (Milton, 1930), pp. 375-377; Alfred M. Copeland, *A History of the Town of Murrayfield, Massachusetts* (Springfield, 1892), p. 57; Josiah C. Kent, *Northborough History* (Newton, 1921), p. 18; George F. Clark, *A History of the Town of Norton* (Boston, 1859), pp. 221-222; George F. Daniels, *History of the Town of Oxford, Massachusetts* (Worcester, 1892), pp. 261-266; Francis E. Blake, *History of the Town of Princeton* (Boston, 1915), 1: 130; *Watertown Records* (Watertown, 1894-1906), 5: 161; *Town of Weston, Records of the First Precinct, 1746-1754 and of the Town, 1754-1803* (Boston, 1893), pp. 14-19.

43. Thomas Hutchinson to Israel Williams, May 19, 1749, Israel Williams Papers, Massachusetts Historical Society, Boston.

44. Robert Lane, *Political Life* (New York, 1964), p. 101.

45. Sir Lewis Namier, *The Structure of Politics at the Accession of George III,* 2d ed. (London, 1957), chap. 1.

46. Admiral Sir George Rodney to Lord George Germain, quoted in ibid., p. 1.

47. Henry Beekman to Henry Livingston, May 15, 1745, quoted in Philip L. White, *The Beekmans of New York in Politics and Commerce, 1647-1877* (New York, 1956), p. 199.

48. Robert A. Rutland, *George Mason, Reluctant Statesman* (Charlottesville, 1961), p. 25, and Rutland, ed., *The Papers of George Mason, 1725-1792* (Chapel Hill, 1970), 1: 159.

49. Joseph Galloway, *A True and Impartial State of the Province of Pennsylvania* (Philadelphia, 1759), p. 53; Hening, ed., *Statutes of Virginia,* 4: 279; Thayer, *Pennsylvania Politics,* p. 7; Abner C. Goodell, et al., eds., *Acts and Resolves . . . of the Province of Massachusetts Bay* (Boston, 1869-1922), 1: 89, 740, 2: 406, 3: 22, 206, 241, 295, 370; M. Eugene Sirmans, *Colonial South Carolina: A Political History, 1663-1763* (Chapel Hill, 1966), p. 245; Edward Shippen, Jr., to Edward Shippen, Sr., September 19, 1756, in Thomas Balch, ed., *Letters and Papers Relating Chiefly to to the Provincial History of Pennsylvania* (Philadelphia, 1855), pp. 63-64.

50. Gov. Jonathan Belcher to John Stoddard, April 15, 1734, Belcher Mss. Letter-Book, Massachusetts Historical Society, Boston. See sketch of Stoddard in Clifford K. Shipton, *Biographical Sketches of Those Who Attended Harvard College (Sibley's Harvard Graduates)* (Boston, 1873-1975), 5: 96-106.

51. William Smith to Philip Schuyler, January 18, 1768, quoted in Don R. Gerlach, *Philip Schuyler and the American Revolution in New York, 1733-1777* (Lincoln, 1964), p. 143.

52. On patronage in the American colonies, see Bailyn, *Origins,* pp. 72-80; Martin, *Men in Rebellion,* chap. 2.

53. Charles J. Stille', *The Life and Times of John Dickinson, 1732-1808* (Philadelphia, 1891), p. 38.

54. For the career of James DeLancey, see Stanley N. Katz, *Newcastle's New York: Anglo-American Politics,* 1732-1753 (Cambridge, 1968), chaps. 7-8; Bonomi, *A Factious People,* chap. 5.

55. Thomas Jefferson to John Adams, October 28, 1813, in Lester J. Cappon, ed., *The Adams-Jefferson Letters* (Chapel Hill, 1959), 2: 389.

56. Ellen E. Brennan, *Plural Office-Holding in Massachusetts, 1760-1780* (Chapel Hill, 1945), pp. 33-34, 72-73.

57. Lawrence H. Leder, *Robert Livingston, 1654-1728, and the Politics of New York* (Chapel Hill, 1961), p. 205; Bonomi, *A Factious People,* pp. 205-206; George A. Billias, *The Massachusetts Land Bankers of 1740* (Orono, 1959), pp. 4-5; Jere Daniell, *Experiment in Republicanism: New Hampshire Politics and the American Revolution, 1741-1794* (Cambridge, 1970), pp. 24-25.

58. Quoted in Charles Hudson, *History of the Town of Marlborough, Massachusetts* (Boston, 1862), p. 191.

59. New York figures are based on the list in Bonomi, *A Factious People,* appendix C, pp. 295-311; New Jersey's are derived from New Jersey Historical Society, *Proceedings,* 1st ser., 5: 24-33. For Massachusetts, see Michael Zuckerman, *Peaceable Kingdoms: New England Towns in the Eighteenth Century* (New York, 1970), appendix 8, pp. 278-279; for Virginia, see Brown and Brown, *Virginia,* pp. 227-230; for South Carolina, see Sirmans, *Colonial South Carolina,* pp. 245-246.

60. Carl Bridenbaugh, *Seat of Empire: The Role of Williamsburg in the Eighteenth Century* (Charlottesville, 1950), p. 10; Dumas Malone, *Jefferson the Virginian* (Boston, 1948), p. 130.

61. Jack P. Greene, ed., *The Diary of Colonel Landon Carter of Sabine Hall, 1752-1778* (Charlottesville, 1965), 1: 25.

62. George Washington to Col. James Wood, July 1758, in John C. Fitzpatrick, ed., *The Writings of George Washington* (Washington, D.C., 1930-1944), 2: 251.

63. Benjamin Franklin, *The Autobiography of Benjamin Franklin,* ed. Max Farrand (Berkeley, 1949), p. 147.

64. Lyman H. Butterfield et al., eds., *Diary and Autobiography of John Adams* (Cambridge, 1961), 3: 294.

65. Malone, *Jefferson,* p. 131.
66. Franklin, *Autobiography,* p. 147.

CHAPTER 4

1. The only attempt at a general treatment of this subject is the brief and sketchy summary in Frederick W. Dallinger, *Nominations for Elective Office in the United States* (New York, 1897), pp. 4-8. The sole study of a particular colony is Carl Becker, "Nominations in Colonial New York," *American Historical Review* 6 (January 1901): 260-275. For the post-1776 era, see William N. Chambers, *Political Parties in a New Nation: The American Experience, 1776-1809* (New York, 1963), pp. 21-22.

2. David Van der Heyden to Sir William Johnson, February 3, 1761, in James Sullivan and Alexander C. Flick, eds., *The Papers of Sir William Johnson* (Albany, 1921-1965), 3: 325.

3. *Pennsylvania Journal,* September 19, 1754. Similar statements can be found in any Philadelphia newspaper in the quarter-century before the Revolution.

4. See, for example, Philip L. White, *The Beekmans of New York in Politics and Commerce, 1647-1877* (New York, 1956), p. 199.

5. *Connecticut Courant,* March 5, 1770. Bruce C. Daniels, in "Connecticut's Villages Become Mature Towns," *William and Mary Quarterly,* 3d ser., 34 (January 1977), 95-96, notes that in a few towns the selectmen made nominations.

6. A partial list of printed New England town records appears in Frank Freidel, ed., *Harvard Guide to American History,* rev. ed. (Cambridge, 1974), 1: 79-85. See also Michael Zuckerman *Peaceable Kingdoms: New England Towns in the Eighteenth Century* (New York, 1970), pp. 166-169.

7. George F. Clark, *A History of the Town of Norton* (Boston, 1859), p. 281n. See also John Adams's first election in Braintree (1766) and in Boston (1770): Lyman H. Butterfield et al., eds., *Diary and Autobiography of John Adams* (Cambridge, 1961), 1: 302, 3: 294.

8. *South Carolina Gazette,* November 13, 1736, January 6, 1749, October 26, 1760, April 4, 1761, February 13, 1762; J. H. Easterby and Ruth S. Green, eds., *The Colonial Records of South Carolina,* Series I: *The Journal of the Commons House of Assembly, 1736-1750* (Columbia, 1951-1962), 1: viii, 4: 15-16, 5: 22. See also M. Eugene Sirmans, *Colonial South Carolina: A Political History, 1663-1763* (Chapel Hill, 1966), p. 246.

9. Becker, "Nominations," p. 265; Douglas S. Freeman, *George Washington, A Biography* (New York, 1948-1957), 2: 147; George H. Ryden, ed., *Letters to and from Caesar Rodney, 1756-1783* (Philadelphia, 1933), pp. 27, 46, 50-51, 64; Patricia U. Bonomi, *A Factious People: Politics and Society in Colonial New York* (New York, 1971), p. 190; Nicholas Varga, "Election Procedures and Practices in Colonial New York," *New York History* 41 (July 1960): 259-261; John S. Bassett, "Suffrage in the State of North Carolina (1776-1861)," American Historical Association *Annual Report, 1895* (Washington, D.C., 1896), 272.

10. Sir William Johnson to Philip Schuyler, February 29, 1768, in Sullivan and Flick, eds., *The Papers of Sir William Johnson* 6: 127.

11. Varga, "Election Procedures," p. 261, claims that there was a "broad canvass," which included "the civil and military officers of the county, the local clergy, as well as some of the more 'civic-minded' freeholders," but gives little evidence of such extensive numbers being consulted.

12. Cadwallader Colden to Gov. George Clinton, January 1748, in *The Letters and Papers of Cadwallader Colden,* New-York Historical Society, *Collections* (1918-1937), 53: 3.

13. Abraham Ten Broeck to James Duane, February 22, 1768, James Duane Papers, New-York Historical Society, New York. See also Sir William Johnson to the Voters of Canajoharie, July 1750, in Sullivan and Flick, eds., *Johnson Papers,* 6: 293-294; *New York Gazette or Weekly Post-Boy,* January 9, 1769; David S. Lovejoy, *Rhode Island Politics and the American Revolution, 1760-1776* (Providence, 1958), pp. 22-24; John Adams to James Warren, May 12, 1776, in *The Warren-Adams Letters* Massachusetts Historical Society, *Collections* (1917), 72: 243.

14. Robert E. and B. Katherine Brown, *Virginia, 1705-1786: Democracy or Aristocracy?* (East Lansing, 1964), pp. 157-158.

15. Charles S. Sydnor, *Gentlemen Freeholders: Political Practices in Washington's Virginia* (Chapel Hill, 1952), pp. 75-77; Bassett, "Suffrage," p. 272; Becker, "Nominations."

16. George Washington to John Augustine Washington, May 28, 1755, in John C. Fitzpatrick, ed., *The Writings of George Washington* (Washington, D.C., 1930-1944), 1: 130-131.

17. Sydnor, *Gentlemen Freeholders,* pp. 67-69; Freeman, *George Washington,* 2: 147, 317-318; Brown and Brown, *Virginia,* pp. 159-160.

18. Capt. Robert Stewart to George Washington, February 13, 1761, in Stanislaus Hamilton, ed., *Letters to Washington and Accompanying Paper* (Boston and New York, 1898-1902), 3: 202.

19. For an excellent description of the newly developing political practices in eighteenth-century American cities, see Gary B. Nash, "The Trans-

formation of Urban Politics, 1700-1765," *Journal of American History* 60 (December 1973): 605-632. See also Carl Bridenbaugh, *Cities in Revolt: Urban Life in America, 1743-1776* (New York, 1955), pp. 6-13, 221-224.

20. Only the Boston caucus and its origins have been subjected to any critical study; see G. B. Warden, "The Caucus and Democracy in Colonial Boston," *New England Quarterly* 43 (March 1970): 19-45; Alan and Katherine Day, "Another Look at the Boston 'Caucus,' " *Journal of American Studies* 5 (April 1971): 19-42.

21. John Pickering, *A Vocabulary, or Collection of Words and Phrases . . . Peculiar to the United States of America* (Boston, 1816), p. 57; Warden, "Caucus," pp. 19-20; Butterfield, ed. *Diary and Autobiography,* 1: 239n-240n.

22. *South Carolina Gazette,* April 5, 1735.

23. Ibid., October 30, 1736.

24. William Gordon, *The History of the Rise, Progress and Establishment of the Independence of the United States of America* (London, 1788), 1: 365.

25. Warden, "Caucus," pp. 21-22.

26. Ibid., pp. 22-23.

27. Butterfield et al., eds., *Diary and Autobiography,* 1: 238.

28. *Boston Evening-Post,* March 14, 1763; Day and Day, "Another Look," p. 21.

29. *Boston Evening-Post,* May 4, 1764.

30. Earl of Bellomont to the Lords of Trade, April 27, 1699, in Edmund B. O'Callaghan and Berthold Fernow, eds., *Documents Relative to the Colonial History of the State of New York* (Albany, 1853-1887), 4: 508. Varga, "Election Procedures," p. 262, states that the practice of using tickets soon disappeared.

31. Stanley N. Katz, *Newcastle's New York: Anglo-American Politics, 1732-1753* (Cambridge, 1968), pp. 63-70; *New York Weekly Journal,* September 30, 1734. See also James Alexander, *A Brief Narrative of the Case and Trial of John Peter Zenger,* ed. Stanley N. Katz (Cambridge, 1963), pp. 5-7, 131-132.

32. *New York Gazette,* February 27, 1739; Carl Becker, *The History of Political Parties in the Province of New York, 1760-1776* (Madison, 1909), p. 18.

33. *New York Gazette,* February 3, 17, 1752; Becker, *History of Political Parties,* p. 18.

34. James Logan to William Penn, December 20, 1706, March 6, 1709, Isaac Norris to James Logan, August 29, 1710, in Edward Armstrong, ed., *The Correspondence of William Penn and James Logan* (Philadelphia, 1872), 2: 188, 336, 427.

35. [James Logan], *A Dialogue Shewing What's Therein to be Found* (Philadelphia, 1725), pp. 30-31. See also *To the Freeholders and Freemen, A Further Information* (Philadelphia, 1727).

36. Quoted in Thomas Wendel, "The Keith-Lloyd Alliance: Faction and Coalition Politics in Colonial Pennsylvania," *Pennsylvania Magazine of History and Biography* 92 (July 1968): 300. See also Gary B. Nash, *Quakers and Politics: Pennsylvania, 1681-1726* (Princeton, 1968), p. 234; Roy N. Lokken, *David Lloyd, Colonial Lawmaker* (Seattle, 1959), p. 226.

37. Issac Norris to James Logan, August 29, 1710, in Armstrong, ed., *The Correspondence of William Penn and James Logan*, 2: 427; James Logan to Isaac Taylor, September 25, 1724, *Pennsylvania Magazine of History and Biography* 35 (1911): 274-275.

38. Zuckerman, *Peaceable Kingdoms,* pp. 167, 172.

39. Theodore G. Thayer, *Pennsylvania Politics and the Growth of Democracy, 1740-1776* (Harrisburg, 1953), p. 16. See also Sister Joan de Lourdes Leonard, "Elections in Colonial Pennsylvania," *William and Mary Quarterly,* 3d ser., 11 (October 1954): 387-389; William S. Hanna, *Benjamin Franklin and Pennsylvania Politics* (Stanford, 1964), p. 207; Dietmar Rothermund, *The Layman's Progress: Religious and Political Experience in Colonial Pennsylvania, 1740-1770* (Philadelphia, 1961), p. 73.

40. Thomas Penn to T. Jackson, [1740], quoted in Hanna, *Benjamin Franklin,* p. 207. For similar sentiments, see William Smith, *A Brief State of the Province of Pennsylvania* (London, 1755), p. 28.

41. Edward Shippen, Jr., to Edward Shippen, Sr., September 19, 1756, in Thomas Balch, ed., *Letters and Papers Relating Chiefly to the Provincial History of Pennsylvania* (Philadelphia, 1855), p. 64.

42. John Smith Diary, September 25, 1750, in Albert C. Myers, ed., *The Courtship of Hannah Logan* (Philadelphia, 1904), p. 296. See also ibid., pp. 312-313.

43. Edward Shippen to Joseph Shippen, Jr. [September 1756], quoted in Hanna, *Benjamin Franklin,* p. 115.

44. *Pennsylvania Gazette,* September 12, 19, 1754.

45. Leonard W. Labaree et al., eds., *The Papers of Benjamin Franklin* (New Haven, 1959-), 7: 34-35.

46. Richard Peters to Thomas Penn, October 2, 1756, in *Pennsylvania Magazine of History and Biography* 31 (1907): 246-247; Hanna, *Benjamin Franklin,* p. 114. For another attempt at a combined ticket, see Leonard, "Elections in Colonial Pennsylvania," p. 388.

47. Samuel Purviance to Col. James Burd, September 10, 1764, in Balch, ed., *Letters and Papers,* pp. 204-205.

48. Samuel Purviance to Col. James Burd, September 20, 1765, in ibid., pp. 210-211.

49. Quoted in Wayne L. Bockelman, "Local Politics in Lancaster County, Pennsylvania," *Pennsylvania Magazine of History and Biography* 97 (January 1973): 71, 72.

50. Nicholas Brown to Joseph Wanton, April 7, 1765, Brown Papers, P-W2, John Carter Brown Library, Providence.

51. Lovejoy, Rhode Island Politics, pp. 22-24; Gertrude S. Kimball, ed., *The Correspondence of the Colonial Governors of Rhode Island, 1723-1775* (Boston and New York, 1902-1903), 2: 323-325.

52. Moses Brown to Joseph Wanton, April 9, 1770, Moses Brown Papers, 1: 105, Rhode Island Historical Society (RIHS), Providence. See also Joseph Wanton to Moses Brown, April 8, 1770, ibid., p. 104; Josias Lyndon to Samuel Ward, March 31, 1769, Ward Manuscripts, Box 1, no. 83, RIHS.

53. Thomas Greene to Moses Brown, April 11, 1770, Moses Brown Papers, 1: 105, RIHS.

54. Joseph Wanton to Moses Brown, April 11, 1770, ibid., p. 106.

55. Lovejoy, *Rhode Island Politics,* p. 24.

56. Rhode Island Proxes, 1758, RIHS.

57. Rhode Island Proxes, 1767, RIHS.

58. James H. Trumbull and Charles J. Hoadly, eds., *Public Records of the Colony of Connecticut, 1636-1776* (Hartford, 1850-1890), 4: 223; 5: 39.

59. "Statistics on Elections," Connecticut Historical Society, Hartford. See also Robert J. Dinkin, "The Nomination of Governor and Assistants in Colonial Connecticut," *Connecticut Historical Society Bulletin* 36 (July 1971): 92-96.

60. Dinkin, "Nomination," pp. 93-96.

61. The only full account of this meeting is found in the *Connecticut Courant*, March 31, 1766. See also Lawrence H. Gipson, *Jared Ingersoll, A Study in American Loyalism in Relation to British Colonial Government* (New Haven, 1920), pp. 218-221. Gipson referred to this event as the first convention in Connecticut history, apparently not realizing that it was the first anywhere in the colonies.

62. *Connecticut Courant,* March 31, 1766.

63. Robert J. Taylor, ed., *The Susquehanna Company Papers* (Ithaca, 1962-1971), 5: xxxiv; Edith A. Bailey, "Influences Toward Radicalism in Connecticut, 1754-1775," *Smith College Studies in History* 5 (July 1920): 216-218; *Connecticut Courant,* February 22, 1774.

64. *Connecticut Gazette,* April 22, 1774; *Connecticut Courant,* May 3, 1774; Bailey, "Influences Toward Radicalism," pp. 221-222. Silas

Deane referred to the Middletown convention as the "present mad proceedings," in a letter to Jonathan Trumbull, March 21, 1774, in Taylor, ed., *Susquehanna Papers*, 5: 345.

65. William L. Saunders, ed., *Colonial Records of North Carolina, 1662-1776* (Raleigh, 1886-1890), 7: 671.

66. Ibid., p. 725; John S. Bassett, "The Regulators of North Carolina, 1765-1771," American Historical Association, *Annual Report, 1894* (Washington, D.C., 1895), p. 172.

67. Richard Walsh, *Charleston's Sons of Liberty: A Study of the Artisans, 1763-1789* (Columbia, 1959), pp. 31-32.

68. *South Carolina Gazette*, October 10, 1768; Arthur M. Schlesinger, *The Colonial Merchants and the American Revolution* (New York, 1918), p. 140.

69. Becker, *Political Parties*, p. 18.

70. Ibid., p. 19; *New York Gazette or Weekly Post-Boy*, January 9, 1769.

71. Bonomi, *A Factious People*, p. 251; Becker, *Political Parties*, p. 19; *New York Mercury*, January 9, 1769.

72. For the expansion of the Boston caucus, see Day and Day, "Another Look," pp. 20-25; Richard Frothingham, *Life and Times of Joseph Warren* (Boston, 1865), pp. 50-51; Esther Forbes, *Paul Revere and the World He Lived In* (Boston, 1942), pp. 119ff.; John Cary, *Joseph Warren* (Urbana, 1961), pp. 55, 126; Butterfield et al., eds., *Diary and Autobiography*, 1: 239n.-240n.

73. John Eliot, *A Biographical Dictionary, Containing a Brief Account of the First Settlers and Other Eminent Characters . . . in New England* (Salem, 1809), p. 472. Day and Day, "Another Look," pp. 29-34, conclude that despite the presence of some artisans, the caucus was still dominated by merchants and lawyers.

74. "Proceedings of the North End Caucus," in Elbridge H. Goss, *The Life of Colonel Paul Revere* (Boston, 1891), 2: 637-638.

75. *Pennsylvania Gazette*, September 27, 1770. See also ibid., August 19, 1772; Charles H. Lincoln, *The Revolutionary Movement in Pennsylvania* (Philadelphia, 1901), chap. 5.

76. Charles S. Olton, "Philadelphia's Mechanics in the First Decade of Revolution 1765-1775," *Journal of American History* 59 (September 1972): 322. See also R. A. Ryerson, "Political Mobilization and the American Revolution: The Resistance Movement in Philadelphia, 1765 to 1776," *William and Mary Quarterly*, 3d ser., 31 (October 1974): 565-588.

77. Olton, "Philadelphia's Mechanics," pp. 322-326, 313n.; Hawke, *In the Midst*, pp. 23, 28, 100. For meetings of the Philadelphia caucus

in this era, see William Duane, ed., *Extracts from the Diary of Christopher Marshall* (Albany, 1877), pp. 66, 67.

CHAPTER 5

1. See supra, p. 57.
2. On this point see Alden T. Vaughan, "The Character of Colonial Politics," in Richard W. Leopold, Arthur S. Link, and Stanley Coben, eds., *Problems in American History,* 3d ed. (Englewood Cliffs, 1966), p. 62.
3. For electioneering by DeLancey, see Patricia U. Bonomi, *A Factious People: Politics and Society in Colonial New York* (New York, 1971), pp. 161-162; for Allen, see Penn Papers, Historical Society of Pennsylvania, Philadelphia; for Hopkins, see Brown Papers, John Carter Brown Library (JCBL), Providence; for Bordley, see Stephen Bordley Letter Book, 1740-1747, Maryland Historical Society, Baltimore.
4. Stephen Bordley to Thomas Bordley, November 18, 1745, Bordley Letter Book, 1740-1747, Maryland Historical Society.
5. Stephen Bordley to John Bordley, October 30, 1745, ibid.
6. Gov. George Clinton to the Lords of Trade, July 30, 1750, in Edmund B. O'Callaghan and Berthold Fernow, eds., *Documents Relative to the Colonial History of the State of New York* (New York, 1853-1887), 6: 578; Bonomi, *A Factious People,* p. 162.
7. Samuel Purviance to Col. James Burd, September 10, 20, 1764, in Thomas Balch, ed., *Letters and Papers Relating Chiefly to the Provincial History of Pennsylvania* (Philadelphia, 1855), pp. 204-205, 208-209.
8. See Moses Brown to Nicholas Brown, April 16, 1764, March 25, 1766, Brown Papers, P-P6, JCBL; ibid., April 9, 1770, Moses Brown Papers, I, 105, Rhode Island Historical Society, Providence.
9. Letter of Joshua Gee, October 5, 1721, quoted in Thomas J. Wertenbaker, *Give Me Liberty: The Struggle for Self-Government in Virginia* (Philadelphia, 1958), p. 172. For another example of the use of patronage to gain votes, see Donald L. Kemmerer, *Path to Freedom: The Struggle for Self-Government in Colonial New Jersey, 1703-1776* (Princeton, 1940), pp. 159-160.
10. Bernard Bailyn, *The Origins of American Politics* (New York, 1968), p. 109; Jere Daniell, *Experiment in Republicanism: New Hampshire Politics and the American Revolution, 1741-1794* (Cambridge, 1970), p. 10.
11. Gov. Jonathan Belcher to Richard Waldron, September 16, 1734, in *Belcher Papers,* Massachusetts Historical Society, *Collections,* 6th ser.

(1894), 7: 120; See also Nathaniel Bouton et al., eds., *Documents and Records Relating to New Hampshire* (Concord and Manchester, 1867-1941), 4: 875.

12. John Rutherford to Sir William Johnson, January 7, 1748, in James Sullivan and Alexander Flick, eds., *The Papers of Sir William Johnson* (Albany, 1921-1965), 1: 127.

13. "Humble Address of the Assembly of North Carolina," May 23, 1760, in William L. Saunders, ed., *Colonial Records of North Carolina, 1662-1776* (Raleigh, 1886-1890), 6: 414.

14. Jonathan Belcher, for example, wrote letters to his supporters urging them to seek office, but he himself did not become actively involved in any Massachusetts campaign. See Belcher to John Stoddard, April 15, 1734, Belcher Mss. Letter-Book, Massachusetts Historical Society, Boston, and in general, *Belcher Papers*, vols. 6-7.

15. Charles S. Sydnor, *Gentlemen Freeholders: Political Practices in Washington's Virginia* (Chapel Hill, 1952), p. 48.

16. Capt. Robert Stewart to George Washington, February 13, 1761, in Stanislaus M. Hamilton, ed., *Letters to Washington and Accompanying Papers* (Boston and New York, 1898-1902), 3: 201-202. See also Lucille B. Griffith, *The Virginia House of Burgesses, 1750-1774*, rev. ed. (University, Ala., 1970), pp. 61-62.

17. Sydnor, *Gentlemen Freeholders*, pp. 43-44; Griffith, *Virginia House of Burgesses*, pp. 61-62.

18. William Parsons to Richard Peters, September 1752, in John W. Jordan, "James Burnside of Northampton County, Pennsylvania," *Pennsylvania Magazine of History and Biography* 21 (1897): 118. See also James Alexander to Cadwallader Colden, May 5, 1728, *Letters and Papers of Cadwallader Colden,* New-York Historical Society, *Collections* (1917), 50: 260; Griffith, *Virginia House of Burgesses*, p. 75.

19. Jack P. Greene, ed. *The Diary of Landon Carter of Sabine Hall, 1752-1778* (Charlottesville, 1965), 2: 1008-1009; Sydnor, *Gentlemen Freeholders*, pp. 44-45.

20. Sydnor, *Gentlemen Freeholders*, p. 43; Griffith, *Virginia House of Burgesses*, p. 75.

21. Cadwallader Colden to Gov. George Clinton, February 19, 1749, *Colden Papers,* New-York Historical Society, *Collections* (1920), 53: 102. For the political role of taverns in early America, see Carl Bridenbaugh, *Cities in the Wilderness: The First Century of Urban Life in America, 1625-1742* (New York, 1938), pp. 426-427; Michael Zuckerman, *Peaceable Kingdoms: New England Towns in the Eighteenth Century* (New York, 1970), pp. 173-175.

22. Charles F. Adams, ed., *The Works of John Adams* (Boston, 1850-1856), 2: 112.

23. John Smith Diary, October 1, 1750, quoted in Sister Joan de Lourdes Leonard, "Elections in Colonial Pennsylvania," *William and Mary Quarterly*, 3rd Ser., 11 (October 1954): 389. See also ibid., p. 391; *Pennsylvania Evening Post*, April 27, 1776.

24. Andrew Belcher to Edmund Quincy, May 6, 1762, quoted in Robert Zemsky, *Merchants, Farmers, and River Gods: An Essay on Eighteenth-Century American Politics* (Boston, 1971), p. 242.

25. *The Freeholders and Freemen of the City and County* . . . (New York, 1769); *Maryland Gazette*, May 13, 1773; H. W. Sellers, "Charles Willson Peale, Artist-Soldier," *Pennsylvania Magazine of History and Biography* 38 (1914): 262.

26. Jacob Ten Eyck and Volkert Douw to Sir William Johnson, February 3, 1761, in Sullivan and Flick, eds., *Johnson Papers*, 3: 324.

27. John Duncan to Sir William Johnson, November 19, 1763, in ibid., 13: 302.

28. "Reverend James Moir," in Gaston Lichtenstein, *When Tarboro Was Incorporated.* (Richmond, 1910), pp. 17-18; J. Kelly Turner and Jonathan L. Bridgers, Jr., *History of Edgecombe County, North Carolina* (Raleigh, 1920), pp. 58-59. For other examples of clerical involvement in electioneering, see *Boston Weekly Post-Boy*, May 11, 1741; Philip L. White, *The Beekmans of New York in Politics and Commerce, 1647-1877* (New York, 1956), p. 198.

29. Samuel A. Peters, *General History of Connecticut,* ed. Samuel J. McCormick (Freeport, New York, 1969), p. 222.

30. Griffith, *Virginia House of Burgesses,* p. 64; Sydnor, *Gentlemen Freeholders,* pp. 68-69; Hamilton, ed., *Letters to Washington,* 2: 345-346, 349, 379, 381-382, 384, 3: 201-202.

31. *Georgia Gazette,* May 11, 1768; William W. Abbot, *The Royal Governors of Georgia* (Chapel Hill, 1959), p. 11.

32. Quoted in Leonard, "Elections in Colonial Pennsylvania," p. 386. See also I. Daniel Rupp, *History of Lancaster County* (Lancaster, 1844), p. 264.

33. Edward Shippen, Jr., to Edward Shippen, Sr., September 14, 1756, in Balch, ed., *Letters and Papers,* pp. 62-63.

34. Gov. Horatio Sharpe to Lord Baltimore, June 6, 1754, "The Correspondence of Governor Horatio Sharpe, 1753-1771," in W. H. Browne et al., eds., *Archives of Maryland* (Baltimore, 1883-1972), 6: 68.

35. *Pennsylvania Gazette,* September 20, 1759. See also Leonard, "Elections in Colonial Pennsylvania," pp. 389-390.

36. For the best discussion of treating, see Sydnor, *Gentlemen Free-holders*, pp. 51-59. See also Leonard, "Elections in Colonial Pennsylvania," pp. 385, 397; Nicholas Varga, "Election Procedures in Colonial New York" *New York History* 41 (July 1960): 264-265; Julian P. Boyd, "The Sheriff in Colonial North Carolina," *North Carolina Historical Review* 5 (April 1928): 179.

37. *American Weekly Mercury,* September 25, 1729; Sydnor, *Gentlemen Freeholders,* p. 51; Nicholas Cresswell, *The Journal of Nicholas Cresswell, 1774-1777* (London, 1925), p. 28.

38. Henry Beekman to Henry Livingston, January 23, 1752, "A Packet of Old Letters," Dutchess County Historical Society, *Yearbook,* 1921, pp. 35-36; Kemmerer, *Path to Freedom,* p. 38. See also Bonomi, *A Factious People,* p. 244.

39. *Connecticut Courant,* March 5, 1770; Peters, *General History,* p. 222.

40. *Boston Evening-Post,* May 14, 1759.

41. Lyman H. Butterfield et al., eds., *Diary and Autobiography of John Adams* (Cambridge, 1961), 1: 277.

42. Robert Livingston to Abraham Yates, Jr., February 8, 1761, quoted in Milton M. Klein, *The Politics of Diversity: Essays in the History of Colonial New York* (Port Washington, 1974), p. 19.

43. Douglass Adair, ed., "James Madison's Autobiography," *William and Mary Quarterly,* 3d ser., 2 (April 1945): 199-200.

44. Sydnor, *Gentlemen Freeholders,* p. 58; George Washington to Colonel James Wood, July 1758, in John C. Fitzpatrick, ed., *The Writings of George Washington* (Washington, D.C., 1930-1944), 2: 251.

45. *New York Gazette,* June 6, 1737.

46. "Report of the Committee of Elections and Privileges," in Browne et al., eds., *Archives of Maryland,* 46: 282-283. See also ibid., pp. 263-264.

47. Ibid., 61: 417-418, 378-379.

48. *Maryland Gazette,* July 14, 1768.

49. Margaret B. Klapthor and Paul D. Brown, *The History of Charles County, Maryland* (LaPlata, Md., 1958), p. 50; David C. Skaggs, *Roots of Maryland's Democracy* (Westport, Conn., 1973), p. 24.

50. *Virginia Gazette* (Purdie & Dixon), July 7, 1774, quoted in Sydnor, *Gentlemen Freeholders,* pp. 55-56.

51. Thomas Jefferson to James Madison, March 5, 1795, quoted in ibid., p. 56.

52. Griffith, *Virginia House of Burgesses,* p. 64; Varga, "Election Procedures," p. 260; James DeLancey to Benjamin Stout, March 7, 1768,

DeLancey Papers, Box 1, New-York Historical Society; David S. Love-joy, *Rhode Island Politics and the American Revolution, 1760-1776* (Providence, 1958), pp. 24-25; Election Proxes, 1765, Brown Papers, JCBL.

53. Isaac Sharpless, *A Quaker Experiment in Government* (Philadelphia, 1898), pp. 75n.-76n.; Thomas Lechmere to John Winthrop, IV, May 4, 1719, Winthrop Papers, IX, Massachusetts Historical Society; Bouton et al., eds., *New Hampshire Documents*, 13: 102-103, 226; William Livingston et al., *The Independent Reflector*, ed. Milton M. Klein (Cambridge, 1963), pp. 278-284.

54. [Archibald Kennedy], *An Essay on the Government of the Colonies* (New York, 1752), p. 34.

55. Butterfield et al., eds., *Diary and Autobiography*, 1: 333.

56. "Antilon's First Letter," in *Maryland and the Empire, 1773: The Antilon-First Citizen Letters*, ed. Peter S. Onuf (Baltimore, 1974), p. 50. See also *Maryland Gazette*, May 13, 1773; *A Tooth-Full of Advice* (New York, 1768); *The Occasionalist* (New York, 1768); Zuckerman, *Peaceable Kingdoms*, p. 170.

57. "Petition from Watertown," Massachusetts Archives, 117: 306-307, quoted in Zuckerman, *Peaceable Kingdoms*, p. 172.

58. For good discussions of the development of the colonial newspaper, see Arthur M. Schlesinger, *Prelude to Independence: The Newspaper War on Britain 1764-1776* (New York, 1958), chap. 3; Daniel Boorstin, *The Americans: The Colonial Experience* (New York, 1958), chap. 51.

59. *South Carolina Gazette*, March 17, 1733.

60. *New York Gazette*, February 27, 1739. See also *New York Weekly Post-Boy*, October 17, 1743, June 24, 1745.

61. *Pennsylvania Journal*, August 16, 1744.

62. Ibid., August 23, 1744. See further advertisements by Scull in *Pennsylvania Gazette*, September 12, 19, 1745, September 11, 18, 25, 1746.

63. *New York Evening-Post*, January 11, 1748.

64. The *Providence Gazette*, for example, started carrying advertisements for Henry Ward, who was seeking the post of provincial secretary, beginning in 1767. See the issues of April 11, 1767, April 15, 1769, and April 14, 1770.

65. *Pennsylvania Gazette*, September 29, 1737.

66. *Boston Evening-Post*, February 3, April 28, 1766; *Boston Gazette*, March 31, April 14, May 5, 1766; Ellen E. Brennan, *Plural Office-Holding in Massachusetts, 1760-1780* (Chapel Hill, 1945), pp. 78-79.

67. *To the Freeholders and Freemen of the City and County of New York* (New York, 1768). See also *A Political Creed for the Day* (New York, 1768).

68. Jack Bowling and Tom Hatchway [pseud.], *A Card* (New York, 1768).

69. Titus Hosmer to Jared Ingersoll, April 14, 1767, "Jared Ingersoll Papers," ed. Franklin B. Dexter, *Papers of the New Haven County Historical Society* (1918), 9: 404.

70. See John S. Bassett, "The Regulators of North Carolina, 1765-1771," American Historical Association, *Annual Report, 1894* (Washington, D.C., 1895). For an excellent discussion of provincial pamphlet literature, see Bernard Bailyn, *Pamphlets of the American Revolution, 1750-1776, vol. I: 1750-1765* (Cambridge, 1965), introduction, and also Gary B. Nash, "The Transformation of Urban Politics, 1700-1765," *Journal of American History* 60 (December 1973): 616-617.

71. John Barnard, *The Throne Established by Righteousness. . .* (Boston, 1734), p. 59.

72. John Colman, *The Distressed State of the Town of Boston &c. Considered* (Boston, 1720), pp. 8-9. For additional pamphlets on the Land Bank question, see Andrew M. Davis, *Colonial Currency Reprints, 1682-1751* (New York, 1910-1911).

73. Nash, "Transformation of Urban Politics," p. 617.

74. Bouton et al., eds., *New Hampshire Documents,* 13: 699. For a brief survey of fagot voting, see Chilton Williamson, *American Suffrage from Property to Democracy, 1760-1860* (Princeton, 1960), pp. 50-51.

75. Gov. George Clinton to Robert Hunter Morris, August 29, 1750, quoted in Bonomi, *A Factious People,* p. 162.

76. William Allen to Thomas Penn, October 21, 1764, quoted in James H. Hutson, *Pennsylvania Politics, 1746-1770: The Movement for Royal Government and Its Consequences* (Princeton, 1972), p. 170n. For the use of similar tactics in Massachusetts, see *Reflections upon Reflections: or More News from Robinson Cruso's Island in a Dialogue Between a Country Representative and a Boston Gentleman* (Boston, 1720), reprinted in Davis, *Colonial Currency Reprints,* 2: 116.

77. Sydnor, *Gentlemen Freeholders,* p. 43.

78. *New York Gazette* (Weyman's), February 2, 1761.

79. *New York Weekly Journal,* October 24, 1743; *New York Weekly Post-Boy,* September 3, 1750; *Maryland Gazette,* January 25, 1759; *Boston Evening-Post,* May 14, 1759, April 27, 1761. Isaac Royall of Charlestown, Mass., frequently contributed his stipend to charity; see Charlestown Town Records, VII, City Hall, Boston.

80. William Tudor, *The Life of James Otis* (Boston, 1823), pp. 91-92.

81. "Brief of Mr. Jauncey's Defence against the Charge of Bribery and Corruption made against him by Mr. Scott," November 1768, James Duane Papers, New-York Historical Society.

82. Nicholas Brown to Joseph Wanton, April 7, 1765, Brown Papers, P-W2, JCBL.

83. George Jackson et al. to Beriah Brown, April 10, 1767, in James N. Arnold, ed., *The Narragansett Historical Register* (Providence, 1882-1891), 2: 110.

84. Nicholas Brown to Richard Greene, April 10, 1767, Brown Papers, P-P6, JCBL.

85. Ezra Stiles, *Extracts from the Itineraries and Other Miscellanies of Ezra Stiles, D.D., L.L.D. 1755-1794,* ed. Franklin B. Dexter (New Haven, 1916), p. 103.

86. Robert Rogers, *A Concise Account of North America* (1765; reprint ed., New York, 1966), pp. 57-58.

87. George Washington to Capt. Van Swearingen, May 15, 1761, Fitzpatrick, ed., *Washington*, 2: 359.

88. Sydnor, *Gentlemen Freeholders*, pp. 68-69.

89. In 1761, for example, 416 of the 1,447 voters (28.7 percent), designated fewer than the normal number of candidates. See *A Copy of the Poll List of the Election of Representatives for the City and County of New York . . . MDCCLXI* (New York, 1880).

90. *Connecticut Courant*, April 6, 1767.

91. Hendrick Frey to Sir William Johnson, February 2, 1752, in Sullivan and Flick, eds., *Johnson Papers*, 1: 363.

92. Charles Pettit to Joseph Reed, November 3, 1764, in William B. Reed, *Life and Correspondence of Joseph Reed* (Philadelphia, 1847), 1: 36-37.

93. On this point, see Gordon S. Wood, "Revolution and the Political Integration of the Enslaved and Disenfranchised," in *America's Continuing Revolution* (Washington, D.C., 1975), p. 102.

CHAPTER 6

1. Many of the legal aspects of the actual voting process are treated in Cortlandt F. Bishop, *History of Elections in the American Colonies* (New York, 1893), chap. 3, and Mary P. Clarke, *Parliamentary Privilege in the American Colonies* (New Haven, 1943), chap. 4.

2. Bishop, *History of Elections,* pp. 99-101; Clarke, *Parliamentary*

Privilege, p. 232; Evarts B. Greene, *The Provincial Governor in the English Colonies of North America* (New York, 1898), pp. 145-146.

3. Bishop, *History of Elections,* pp. 100-101.

4. Alexander Campbell, [psued.], *Maxima Libertatis Custodia Est* (New York, 1732), p. 2. See also *Vincit Amor Patriae* (New York, 1732), p. 2; *O Liberty thou Goddess Heavenly Bright* (New York, 1732), p. 2; Edmund B. O'Callaghan and Berthold Fernow, eds., *Documents Relative to the Colonial History of the State of New York* (Albany, 1853-1887), 6: 130; Patricia U. Bonomi, *A Factious People: Politics and Society in Colonial New York* (New York, 1971), pp. 124-125.

5. New York Assemblies listed in Bonomi, *A Factious People,* appendix C, pp. 295-311; New Jersey Assemblies listed in New Jersey Historical Society, *Proceedings,* 1st ser., 5: 24-33.

6. These data are compiled from the various printed Assembly journals and colonial records.

7. Bishop, *History of Elections,* pp. 106-113; Albert E. McKinley, *The Suffrage Franchise in the Thirteen English Colonies in America* (Philadelphia, 1905), p. 96.

8. The writ is printed in Bishop, *History of Elections,* p. 240. For other examples, see ibid., appendix A.

9. Ibid., pp. 103-104.

10. *A Letter to the Freemen and Freeholders of the City of New York* (New York, 1752), p. 8.

11. Bishop, *History of Elections,* p. 108.

12. See, for example, W. H. Browne et al., eds., *Archives of Maryland* (Baltimore, 1883-1972), 46: 263-264, 662, 62: 56-57.

13. Bishop, *History of Elections,* pp. 110-112.

14. Payne Kilbourne, *Sketches and Chronicles of the Town of Litchfield, Connecticut* (Hartford, 1859), p. 58.

15. Bishop, *History of Elections,* pp. 111-112.

16. *Maryland Gazette,* February 22, 1749, October 30, November 20, 1751, November 7, 1754, August 25, 1757; *Georgia Gazette,* April 20, May 4, 1768.

17. *Boston News-Letter,* May 3, 1744, May 2, 1745, May 10, 1750; *Boston Gazette,* May 1, 1744, April 30, 1745.

18. *New York Gazette* (Weyman's), February 2, 1761.

19. William Moore, *A Preface to a Memorial . . .* (Philadelphia, 1757), p. 1. See also William L. Saunders, ed., *Colonial Records of North Carolina, 1662-1776* (Raleigh, 1886-1890), 4: 118.

20. Nathaniel Bouton et al., eds., *Documents and Records Relating to New Hampshire* (Concord and Manchester, 1867-1941), 9: 152.

21. See Massachusetts Archives, Statehouse, Boston, 115: 50-53.

22. Bishop, *History of Elections,* pp. 108-109, 269-272.

23. *Georgia Gazette,* May 4, 1768.

24. Bishop, *History of Elections,* p. 109.

25. J. Thomas Scharf, *History of Baltimore City and County* (Philadelphia, 1881), p. 40.

26. Samuel Allinson, ed., *Acts of the General Assembly of the Province of New Jersey* (Burlington, 1776), p. 69; Donald L. Kemmerer, *Path to Freedom: The Struggle for Colonial Self-Government in Colonial New Jersey, 1703-1776* (Princeton, 1940), p. 38.

27. *New York Gazette and Weekly Mercury,* December 11, 1769. See also Michael N. D'Innocenzo, Jr., "Voting in Colonial New York" (Master's thesis, Columbia University, 1959), p. 38.

28. Sister Joan de Lourdes Leonard, "Elections in Colonial Pennsylvania," *William and Mary Quarterly,* 3rd ser., 11 (October 1954): 393; Charles S. Sydnor, *Gentlemen Freeholders: Political Practices in Washington's Virginia* (Chapel Hill, 1952), pp. 18, 52; Richard P. McCormick, *The History of Voting in New Jersey: A Study of the Development of Election Machinery, 1664-1911* (New Brunswick, 1953), p. 62; Richard J. Hooker, ed., *The Carolina Backcountry on the Eve of the Revolution* (Chapel Hill, 1953), p. 166.

29. Sydnor, *Gentlemen Freeholders,* p. 44; Lucille B. Griffith, *The Virginia House of Burgesses, 1750-1774,* rev. ed. (University, Ala., 1970), p. 53.

30. Bishop, *History of Elections,* pp. 101-105; Robert E. and B. Katherine Brown, *Virginia, 1705-1786: Democracy or Aristocracy?* (East Lansing, 1964), p. 152.

31. Sir William Johnson to Rev. Dr. [Samuel] Auchmuty, January 25, 1769, in Edmund B. O'Callaghan, ed., *The Documentary History of the State of New York* (Albany, 1849-1851), 4: 253-254; Sir William Johnson to Goldsbrow Banyar, January 29, 1769, in James Sullivan and Alexander C. Flick, eds., *The Papers of Sir William Johnson* (Albany, 1921-1965), 12: 692; Nicholas Varga, "Election Procedures and Practices in Colonial New York," *New York History* 41 (July 1960): 258-259.

32. Leonard, "Elections in Colonial Pennsylvania," p. 398.

33. *Maryland Gazette,* September 22, 1757, December 6, 1764; David C. Skaggs, *Roots of Maryland's Democracy* (Westport, Conn., 1973), p. 21.

34. *Maryland Gazette,* October 5, 1758, December 3, 10, 17, 1767.

35. *New York Gazette* (Weyman's), February 23, 1761; *Copy of the Poll List . . . MDCCLXIX* (New York, 1880); *Pennsylvania Magazine of*

History and Biography 18 (1894): 185-193; Franklin Papers, American Philosophical Society, Philadelphia, LXIX, 97.

36. Bishop, *History of Elections,* pp. 113-114.

37. *New York Weekly Journal,* November 5, 1733.

38. *Maryland Gazette,* May 27, 1773.

39. Lyman H. Butterfield et al., eds., *Diary and Autobiography of John Adams* (Cambridge, 1961), 1: 303.

40. Salem Town Records, May 17, 1729, quoted in James D. Phillips, *Salem in the Eighteenth Century* (Boston, 1937), p. 99.

41. Sydnor, *Gentlemen Freeholders,* pp. 24-25; Douglas S. Freeman, *George Washington: A Biography* (New York, 1948-1957), 2: 146-147.

42. *Maryland Gazette,* December 19, 1754.

43. Brown and Brown, *Virginia,* p. 153.

44. "Petition of Thomas Wade," November 29, 1773, in Julian P. Boyd, "The Sheriff in Colonial North Carolina," *North Carolina Historical Review,* 5 (April 1928), 176-177.

45. Samuel Hazard et al., eds. *Pennsylvania Archives* (Philadelphia and Harrisburg, 1852-1935), 1st ser., 2: 50-52; John Gibson, ed., *History of York County, Pennsylvania* (Chicago, 1886), pp. 309-310; Leonard, "Elections in Colonial Pennsylvania," pp. 398-399.

46. *Minutes of the Provincial Council of Pennsylvania* (Philadelphia, 1838-1853), 4: 620-622. See also Norman S. Cohen, "The Philadelphia Election Riot of 1742," *Pennsylvania Magazine of History and Biography* 92 (July 1968): 306-319.

47. *American Weekly Mercury,* October 19, 1738. See also *New Jersey Archives,* 1st ser., 26: 209.

48. Nicholas Cresswell, *The Journal of Nicholas Cresswell, 1774-1777* (London, 1925), p. 28.

49. Cadwallader Colden to Mrs. Colden, September 11, 1737, *Letters and Papers of Cadwallader Colden,* New-York Historical Society, *Collection* (1918), 51: 179.

50. Peter R. Livingston to Philip Schuyler, January 16, 1769, quoted in Bonomi, *A Factious People,* p. 253.

51. Boyd, "Sheriff in North Carolina," pp. 151-181; Sydnor, *Gentlemen Freeholders,* pp. 71-72.

52. Saunders, ed., *Colonial Records of North Carolina,* 4: 494-495.

53. Brown and Brown, *Virginia,* pp. 160-161.

54. W. H. Browne et al., eds., *Archives of Maryland* (Baltimore, 1883-1972), 62: 56-57.

55. A good brief survey of the methods of balloting is Charles S. Sydnor and Noble E. Cunningham, Jr., "Voting in Early America," *American*

Heritage 4 (Fall 1952): 6-8. For paper balloting in local New York elections, see Marius Schoonmaker, *The History of Kingston, New York* (New York, 1888), pp. 201-202.

56. Worthington C. Ford, "Voting with Beans and Corn," Massachusetts Historical Society, *Proceedings* (January 1924), 57: 232.

57. Bishop, *History of Elections,* pp. 143-144, 166-168.

58. Sydnor and Cunningham, "Voting in Early America," pp. 6, 8.

59. Sydnor, *Gentlemen Freeholders,* pp. 20-24.

60. *New York Gazette or Weekly Post-Boy,* September 3, 1750. See also Cadwallader Colden to the Earl of Hillsborough, April 25, 1768, in O'Callaghan and Fernow, eds., *Documents Relative to the Colonial History of New York,* 8: 61.

61. *New York Gazette,* March 20, 1739.

62. Sydnor, *Gentlemen Freeholders,* p. 25; McCormick, *History of Voting,* p. 59.

63. Gov. James Glen to the Board of Trade, October 10, 1748, in Jack P. Greene, ed., *Settlements to Society 1584-1763* (New York, 1966), p. 362. See also *Pennsylvania Journal,* Supplement, March 25, 1756; Sydnor and Cunningham, "Voting in Early America," p. 6.

64. Baron de Montesquieu, *The Spirit of the Laws* (New York, 1949), 1: 155.

65. *The Mode of Elections Considered* (New York, 1769).

66. Sydnor and Cunningham, "Voting in Early America," p. 7.

67. Michael Zuckerman, *Peaceable Kingdoms: New England Towns in the Eighteenth Century* (New York, 1970), p. 177.

68. Ibid., pp. 183-184. The law in Massachusetts authorized that either constable or selectmen preside; see ibid., p. 318.

69. Sydnor and Cunningham, "Voting in Early America," p. 7.

70. Bishop, *History of Elections,* pp. 127-136.

71. See the collection of proxes in RIHS. See also David S. Lovejoy, *Rhode Island Politics and the American Revolution, 1760-1776* (Providence, 1958), pp. 23-24. For evidence of Connecticut tickets, see Taylor, ed., *Susquehanna Papers,* 6: 156; *Connecticut Courant,* May 3, 1774.

72. Sydnor and Cunningham, "Voting in Early America," pp. 6-7.

73. McKinley, *Suffrage Franchise,* pp. 270-271. The "hundred" was a subdivision used in several English and American counties.

74. Thomas Cooper and D. J. McCord, eds., *Statutes at Large of South Carolina* (Columbia, 1836-1841), 2: 683; Bishop, *History of Elections,* pp. 174-175.

75. Bishop, *History of Elections,* pp. 173-174.

76. Fletcher, *Vincit Amor Patriae,* p. 2.

77. *Queries Humbly Offered to the Freeholders in the County of Westchester* (New York, 1750).

78. Bonomi, *A Factious People*, p. 275; *To the Freeholders . . .* (New York, 1770). See also *All the Real Friends of Liberty* (New York, 1770).

79. Bonomi, *A Factious People*, p. 275.

80. Bishop, *History of Elections*, pp. 176-177.

81. Ibid., pp. 177-178.

82. *Pennsylvania Archives*, 8th ser., 4: 3280, 3288. Leonard, "Elections in Colonial Pennsylvania," pp. 396, 399-400.

83. Massachusetts Archives, 117: 296-297.

84. Ibid., p. 392.

85. Clarke, *Parliamentary Privilege*, chap. 4, esp. pp. 151-152.

86. Browne et al., eds., *Archives of Maryland*, 36: 198, 207-208, 214-215, 39: 228, 235, 44: 74-75, 113, 46: 263-264, 429-430, 653, 655, 660, 662, 50: 168-169, 55: xxxiii-xxxv, 56: 163, 165, 58: xvi, 59: lxiii-lxv, 61: 378-379, 62: 56-57, 63: xv-xvii.

87. Clarke, *Parliamentary Privilege*, pp. 134-148; Bishop, *History of Elections*, pp. 188-189; Sydnor, *Gentlemen Freeholders*, pp. 13-15, 48.

88. *Archives of Maryland*, 50: xii; Clarke, *Parliamentary Privilege*, p. 149.

89. Bishop, *History of Elections*, pp. 178-179; *Notes of Debates in the Federal Convention of 1787 Reported by James Madison* (Athens, Ohio, 1966), p. 592; Christopher Collier, *Roger Sherman's Connecticut* (Middletown, 1971), pp. 248-250.

90. *New York Weekly Post-Boy*, September 3, 1750. See also *New York Weekly Journal*, November 5, 1733; Cadwallader Colden to Mrs. Colden, September 11, 1737, *Colden Papers*, New-York Historical Society, *Collections* (1918), 51: 179.

91. W. A. Whitehead et al., eds., *New Jersey Archives* (Newark, 1880-1906), 1st ser., 26: 210. See also *South Carolina Gazette*, October 11, 1760, March 28, 1761.

92. Charles Smith to George Washington, July 24, 1758, in Stanislaus M. Hamilton, ed., *Letters to Washington and Accompanying Papers* (Boston and New York, 1898-1902), 2: 384.

CHAPTER 7

1. Albert E. McKinley, *The Suffrage Franchise in the Thirteen English Colonies in America* (Philadelphia, 1905), p. 487. This lack of data did not stop him from making a generalization, however, as he estimated

the average turnout to be just 2 percent of the population (10 percent of the adult males), a gross understatement, though one still included in some textbooks. See John C. Miller, *This New Man, The American* (New York, 1974), p. 598.

2. Daniel J. Boorstin, *The Decline of Radicalism: Reflections on America Today* (New York, 1969), chap. 1.

3. Evarts B. Greene and Virginia D. Harrington, *American Population Before the Federal Census of 1790* (New York, 1932), p. xxiii.

4. As several colonies present tax and population data on adult males with age sixteen as determining manhood, one-fourth of the figure given has been subtracted in order to account for those between ages sixteen and twenty-one. In the interest of brevity, the method of computation for each percentage is omitted. Unless otherwise indicated, calculations were based on statistics in ibid. and W. S. Rossiter, *A Century of Population Growth, 1790-1900* (Washington, D.C., 1909).

5. Virginia election returns (tables 4 and 5) are taken from Lucille B. Griffith, *The Virginia House of Burgesses, 1750-1774,* rev. ed., (University, Ala., 1970), appendix 1, with corrections and additions from Robert E. and B. Katherine Brown, *Virginia, 1705-1786: Democracy or Aristocracy?* (East Lansing, 1964). See also Charles S. Sydnor, *Gentlemen Freeholders: Political Practices in Washington's Virginia* (Chapel Hill, 1952), pp. 137-140.

6. The foregoing is based on figures in Griffith, *Virginia House of Burgesses,* appendix 1.

7. New York County returns (tables 6 and 8) are taken from the following sources: 1699: Edmund B. O'Callaghan and Berthold Fernow, eds., *Documents Relative to the Colonial History of the State of New York* (Albany, 1853-1887), 4: 508; 1701: *Minutes of the Common Council of the City of New York, 1675-1776* (New York, 1905), 2: 163-178; 1734: *New York Weekly Journal,* October 7, 1734; 1737: Valentine's *Manual of the Corporation* (New York, 1869), p. 851; 1739: *New York Gazette,* March 20, 1739; 1745: *New York Evening-Post,* June 24, 1745; 1761: *New York Gazette* (Weyman's), February 23, 1761, *Copy of the Poll List . . . MDCCLXI* (New York, 1880); 1768: *New York Gazette and Weekly Mercury,* March 14, 1768, *Copy of the Poll List . . . MDCCLXVIII* (New York, 1880); 1769: *Copy of the Poll List . . . MDCCLXIX* (New York, 1880).

8. Cadwallader Colden to Mrs. Colden, September 11, 1737, *Colden Papers,* New-York Historical Society, *Collections* (1918), 51: 179.

9. *New York Gazette or Weekly Post-Boy,* September 3, 1750.

10. For this point, the author is indebted Patricia U. Bonomi, New York University.

11. Queens County returns (table 7) are found in the following: *To the Honourable House of Representatives*... (New York, 1698); 1737: *New York Gazette,* June 6, 1737; 1739: ibid., March 20, 1739; 1748: *New York Weekly Journal,* February 8, 1748; 1750: *New York Gazette or Weekly Post-Boy,* September 3, 1750; 1761: ibid., February 26, 1761; *New York Gazette* (Weyman's), April 29, 1761; 1768: *New York Gazette and Weekly Mercury,* March 21, 1768.

12. Westchester County results are as follows: 1733: *New York Weekly Journal,* November 5, 1733; 1750: *New York Gazette or Weekly Post-Boy,* September 3, 1750; 1761: ibid., March 5, 1761; 1768: *New York Gazette and Weekly Mercury,* March 21, 1768. Other sources for New York returns (table 8) are Albany, 1739: *The Annals of Albany* (Albany, 1854-1871), 3: 132; Ulster, 1748: *Colden Papers,* New-York Historical Society, *Collections* (1920), 53: 8; Richmond, 1761: James Duane Papers, X, New-York Historical Society; Dutchess, 1769: *New York Gazette and Weekly Mercury,* February 20, 1769.

13. Pennsylvania returns (tables 9 and 10) are taken from the sources listed below: Philadelphia County, 1727-1739: John F. Watson, *Annals of Philadelphia, and Pennsylvania,* rev. ed. (Philadelphia, 1887), 2: 402-403; 1740-1764: "Isaac Norris Journals," Rosenbach Foundation, Philadelphia; 1765-1766: Franklin Papers, American Philosophical Society, Philadelphia, LXIX, 96, 98; 1771: Benjamin Newcomb, *Franklin and Galloway* (New Haven, 1972), p. 222n.; 1774: Lyman H. Butterfield, ed., *Adams Family Correspondence* (Cambridge, 1963), 1: 165; 1775: William Duane, ed., *Extracts from the Diary of Christopher Marshall* (Albany, 1877), p. 44. For results from Bucks, Chester, Lancaster, and York, see *Pennsylvania Magazine of History and Biography* 7 (1883), 74; *American Weekly Mercury,* October 9, 1738, October 4, 1739, October 2, 1740; *Pennsylvania Gazette,* October 7, 1742; *Pennsylvania Archives,* 6th ser., 11: 215, 415-416, 8th ser., 4: 3288.

14. *Pennsylvania Gazette,* October 7, 1742.

15. The figures for the losing candidates appear only in the Isaac Norris Journals and not in any published account.

16. See table 10.

17. See table 9.

18. Ezra Stiles, *Extracts from the Itineraries and Other Miscellanies of Ezra Stiles, D.D., L.L.D., 1755-1794,* ed. Franklin B. Dexter (New Haven, 1916), p. 103.

19. Rhode Island data (tables 11-14) come from the following sources: 1758, 1759, 1764, 1770: Moses Brown Miscellaneous Mss., B-814, Box 2, Rhode Island Historical Society (RIHS), Providence; 1760: Stiles, *Itineraries,* p. 103; 1761: Ward Mss., Box 1, 1725-1770, RIHS; 1762:

General Assembly Reports (1751-1765), 2: 120, Rhode Island State Archives (RISA); 1765: Brown Papers, P-P6, L63-71M, John Carter Brown Library (JCBL); 1766: ibid., L & P, 58-70, RIP, L63-71M, JCBL; 1768: General Assembly Reports (1766-1768), 3: 21, RISA. Many of the actual town voting lists for the years 1763-1768, giving the name of every voter, are preserved in a collection known as Deputies and Freemen, RISA. Where discrepancies exist these official lists were used. See also *Providence Gazette,* April 18, 1767, April 23, 1768, April 22, 1769, April 21, 1770.

20. Newport Town Records, Newport Historical Society, Newport; North Kingstown Records, Town Hall, Wickford. For a few other scattered figures after 1770, see Exeter Papers, Box 15, RIHS; Johnston Town Meeting Records, RIHS; Warren Town Meeting Records, Town Hall, Warren.

21. Johnston was not incorporated until 1759, North Providence in 1765. Rossiter, *A Century of Population Growth,* p. 163. Table 12 voting statistics are from Deputies and Freemen, RISA.

22. Among the proxes Ward acquired 1,328 to 1,281 for Hopkins, a margin of 47, but the latter had 113 more hand votes. Hand delivered ballots were outlawed after 1760, see above, p. 137.

23. The *Providence Gazette,* April 18, 1767, gives Hopkins a margin of 414.

24. See table 14.

25. Ibid.

26. A number of Boston figures prior to 1715 are noted in *The Diary of Samuel Sewall,* Massachusetts Historical Society, *Collections,* 5th ser. (1878-1882), vols. 5-7. After 1715, totals are regularly listed in *Reports of the Record Commissioners of the City of Boston* (Boston, 1876-1909), vols. 8, 12, 16, 18. Salem results are found in Fitch E. Oliver, ed., *The Diaries of Benjamin Lynde and Benjamin Lynde, Jr.* (Boston, 1880), pp. 143, 153-154, 156, 161-163; Lynn results are published in *Records of Ye Towne Meetings of Lyn* (Lynn, 1949-1966), 5: 38, 42, 47, 51-52, 58, 68.

27. The sources for other Massachusetts returns are Cambridge, 1740: *Boston Gazette,* May 12, 1740; Woburn, 1742: *Boston Weekly Post-Boy,* May 10, 1742; Dorchester, 1750 and 1751: Dorchester Town Records, May 7, 1750, May 15, 1751, City Hall, Boston; Watertown, 1757: Massachusetts Archives, Statehouse, Boston, 117: 291-301; Weston, 1773: ibid., 50: 452-455.

28. *Reports of the Record Commissioners,* vols. 8, 12, 16, 18.

29. Most of the Connecticut figures (table 15) are listed in Robert J. Dinkin, "Elections in Colonial Connecticut," *Connecticut Historical So-*

ciety Bulletin 37 (January 1972): 20. The sources for each year's data are as follows: 1723: Simeon E. Baldwin, "The Early History of the Ballot in Connecticut," American Historical Association, *Papers* (1890), 4: 41 1740: "Statistics on Elections," Connecticut Historical Society, Hartford; 1748: Connecticut Historical Society, *Collections,* 15: 249; 1755: ibid., 16: xxxii; 1767: Stiles, *Itineraries,* p. 63; 1768: *Connecticut Courant,* May 16, 1768; 1769: Taylor, ed., *Susquehanna Papers,* 3: 226; 1770: "Statistics on Elections," 1772: ibid.; 1774: Oscar Zeichner, *Connecticut's Years of Controversy, 1750-1776* (Chapel Hill, 1949), p. 156; Taylor, ed., *Susquehanna Papers,* 6: 202, 214; 1775: Samuel Gray to Joseph Trumbull, Joseph Trumbull Papers, Connecticut State Library: 1776: Gov. Jonathan Trumbull to Joseph Trumbull, May 13, 1776, ibid.

30. Maryland voting statistics are taken from the *Maryland Gazette,* November 27, 1751, March 12, 1752, January 11, 1759, November 29, 1764; Thomas Scharf, *History of Baltimore City and County* (Philadelphia, 1881), p. 40.

31. Most New Jersey results are noted in Donald L. Kemmerer, "The Suffrage Franchise in Colonial New Jersey," New Jersey Historical Society *Proceedings* (1934): 52: 170. See also *New Jersey Archives,* 1st ser., 19: 382, 28: 100.

32. Most of the scattered New Hampshire returns are found in Nathaniel Bouton et al., eds., *Documents and Records Relating to New Hampshire* (Concord and Manchester, 1867-1941), 11: 516, 579, 12: 30-31, 148, 447-449, 627-629. A few others are located in George W. Brown, ed., *Early Records of Londonderry, Windham, and Derry, N.H., 1719-1762* (Manchester, 1908), pp. 370-371; Joseph Fullonton, *The History of Raymond, New Hampshire* (Dover, 1875), p. 39.

33. Portsmouth voting figures (table 17) have been extracted from the Portsmouth Town Records, Portsmouth City Hall. I am deeply indebted to Gerald Foss of Rye, New Hampshire, for transcribing this material for me.

34. New Castle totals appear in the following sources: 1735: *American Weekly Mercury,* October 9, 1735; 1737: ibid., October 6, 1737; 1738: ibid., October 5, 1738; 1756: *Pennsylvania Archives,* 6th ser., 11: 475. Wilmington records are included in Ernest S. Griffith, *A History of American City Government; The Colonial Period* (New York, 1938), p. 211n.

35. Bath Poll List, 1762 and 1766, Legislative Papers, North Carolina Department of Archives and History, Raleigh; Archibald Henderson, ed., "Herman Husband's Continuation of the Imperial Relation," *North Carolina Historical Review* 18 (January 1941): 65.

36. For South Carolina results, see *South Carolina Journals, 1736-1739,* viii; ibid., *1742-1744,* 7; ibid., *1748,* 7; ibid., *1749-1750,* 6; Richard Walsh, ed., *The Writings of Christopher Gadsden, 1746-1805* (Columbia, 1966), p. 38; *South Carolina Gazette,* October 10, 1768. Only nineteen persons voted in the Savannah, Georgia, election of 1772. Georgia Historical Society, *Collections* (1904), 6: 168.

37. See tables 5, 9, and 16.

38. *New York Evening-Post,* January 25, 1748.

39. Approximately 40 to 65 percent vote in national elections today and less than 40 percent in local elections. See Michael Lipsky et al., *American Government Today* (Del Mar, 1974), p. 405.

CHAPTER 8

1. Robert Lane, *Political Life* (New York, 1964), pp. 46-47. See also Angus Campbell, Philip E. Converse, Warren E. Miller, and Donald E. Stokes, *The American Voter* (New York, 1960); Seymour M. Lipset, *Political Man* (Garden City, 1960).

2. Angus Campbell et al., *The American Voter,* esp. chap. 2, and the model applied by Edward M. Cook, Jr., "Rhode Island Voters in an Era of Partisan Realignment, 1760-1800: Towards a Model for the Study of Individual Voting Behavior" (Paper delivered at the American Historical Association Convention, San Francisco, December 28, 1973).

3. See chap. 2 above.

4. For example, see the Philadelphia County election results of 1750 when more than 2,000 votes were cast in the sheriff's race, but only about 1,800 in the contest for Assemblymen. John Smith Diary, October 2, 1750, in Albert C. Myers, ed., *The Courtship of Hannah Logan* (Philadelphia, 1904), p. 297. See also Theodore G. Thayer, *Pennsylvania Politics and the Growth of Democracy, 1740-1776* (Harrisburg, 1953), p. 7.

5. *Reports of the Record Commissioners of the City of Boston* (Boston, 1876-1909), 12: 57, 83, 136-137.

6. Charles S. Grant, *Democracy in the Connecticut Frontier Town of Kent* (New York, 1961), p. 113.

7. See figures in chap. 7 above.

8. See table 9.

9. See figures in chap. 7 above.

10. Continuity rate is based on returns from Cranston, Gloucester, Johnston, Tiverton, and Warren. Voter frequency of partisans taken from Cook, "Rhode Island Voters," p. 16. See also Campbell et al., *The American Voter,* p. 125.

11. Gary B. Nash, "The Transformation of Urban Politics, 1700-1765," *Journal of American History* 60 (December 1973): 630-631; Patricia U. Bonomi, *A Factious People: Politics and Society in Colonial New York* (New York, 1971), pp. 239-244; David S. Lovejoy, *Rhode Island Politics and the American Revolution, 1760-1776* (Providence, 1958), pp. 24-25; Oscar Zeichner, *Connecticut's Years of Controversy, 1750-1776* (Chapel Hill, 1949), chap. 6.

12. Robert Zemsky, *Merchants, Farmers, and River Gods: An Essay on Eighteenth-Century American Politics* (Boston, 1971), pp. 244-246; Michae Zuckerman, *Peaceable Kingdoms: New England Towns in the Eighteenth Century* (New York, 1970), p. 172; *Report of the Record Commissioners,* 12: 260.

13. See tables 9 and 17.

14. *South Carolina Gazette,* October 10, 1768. See also Richard M. Brown, *The South Carolina Regulators: The Story of the First Vigilante Movement* (Cambridge, 1963); Richard J. Hooker, ed., *The Carolina Backcountry on the Eve of the Revolution* (Chapel Hill, 1953).

15. See figures in chap. 7 above. See also Robert E. and B. Katherine Brown, *Virginia, 1705-1786: Democracy or Aristocracy?* (East Lansing, 1964), p. 188; *Maryland Gazette,* May 27, 1773.

16. *South Carolina Gazette,* October 10, 1768.

17. Bonomi, *A Factious People,* pp. 277-278; Leopold S. Launitz-Schurer, Jr., "Whig-Loyalists: The DeLanceys of New York," *New-York Historical Society Quarterly* 56 (July 1972): 179-198.

18. Phileleutheros (pseud.), *Address to the Freeholders* (Boston, 1751), p. 3; Americanus (pseud.), *A Letter to the Freeholders* (Boston, 1739), p. 3; Timothy Wheelwright (pseud.), *Two Letters on Election of Alderman* (New York, 1734), p. 3; *The Occasionalist* (New York, 1768). See also Campbell et al., *The American Voter,* pp. 105-110.

19. *A Letter to the Inhabitants of the Province of Massachusetts Bay* (Boston, 1751), p. 3. See also supra, p. 4.

20. Andrew Fletcher (pseud.), *Vincit Amor Patriae* (New York, 1732), p. 1.

21. Data based on returns in Cranston, Gloucester, Johnston, and Tiverton, 1764-1767, Deputies and Freemen, Rhode Island State Archives (RISA); Johnston Town Records, Rhode Island Historical Society (RIHS), Providence.

22. Benjamin Franklin to Peter Collinson, May 9, 1753, in Leonard W. Labaree et al., eds., *The Papers of Benjamin Franklin* (New Haven, 1959-), 4: 484.

23. Robert Lane, *Political Life* (New York, 1964), chap. 16.

24. Patricia U. Bonomi, "Political Patterns in Colonial New York City: The General Assembly Election of 1768," *Political Science Quarterly* 81 (September 1966): 432-447.

25. Roger Champagne, "Liberty Boys and Mechanics of New York City, 1764-1774," *Labor History* 8 (Spring 1967): 124-132.

26. Percentages derived from Brown and Brown, *Virginia,* chap. 7, tables B and C.

27. Figures extracted from Cranston and Gloucester voting lists, Deputies and Freemen, RISA, and Tax Assessment Lists, 1760, RISA.

28. Gov. William Shirley to the Lords of Trade, December 1, 1747, in Charles H. Lincoln, ed., *The Correspondence of William Shirley* (New York, 1912), 1: 418. See also James K. Hosmer, *The Life of Thomas Hutchinson* (Boston, 1896), pp. 206, 231.

29. Campbell et al., *The American Voter,* esp. chap. 6. See also Paul F. Lazarsfeld, Bernard Berelson, and Hazel Gaudet, *The People's Choice,* 2d ed. (New York, 1948). Norman Nie et al., *The Changing American Voter* (Cambridge, 1976), sees party influence lessening in recent elections.

30. Richard P. McCormick, "Ethno-Cultural Interpretations of Nineteenth Century American Voting Behavior," *Political Science Quarterly* 89 (June 1974): 351-378, emphasizes that straight-ticket voting does not necessarily imply the existence of parties.

31. For Pennsylvania, see table 10; for Maryland, the *Maryland Gazette,* November 27, 1751, March 12, 1752; for Connecticut, see Robert J. Dinkin, "Nominations in Colonial Connecticut," *Connecticut Historical Society Bulletin* 36 (July 1971): 95-96.

32. See figures in chap. 7 above and *Copy of the Poll List. . . MDCCLXI, . . . MDCCLXVIII, . . . MDCCLXIX* (New York, 1880).

33. The results for the year 1764 are in Moses Brown Miscellaneous Mss., B-814, Box 2, Rhode Island Historical Society, Providence, those for 1766 in Brown Papers, L & P, 58-70, RIP John Carter Brown Library (JCBL).

34. Figures for table 20 are derived from voter lists in Deputies and Freemen, RISA.

35. See voter lists in ibid.

36. Ibid. The years 1764 and 1765 were compared in this sample.

37. For the Richmond and Halifax statistics, see tables in Brown and Brown, *Virginia,* pp. 161, 202; Lancaster poll lists in Lancaster Deed Book, 16: 222-223, 18: 42-43, Virginia State Library (VSL), Richmond.

38. See models presented in Campbell et al., *The American Voter.*

39. Figures in table 21 based on voter lists in Deputies and Freemen, RISA.

40. Zeichner, *Connecticut,* p. 125; Nomination List, October 1770, "Statistics on Elections," Connecticut Historical Society, Hartford.

41. Richard Cartwright to Sir William Johnson, January 8, 1768, in James Sullivan and Alexander C. Flick, eds., *The Papers of Sir William Johnson* (Albany, 1921-1965), 12: 408. Other examples are quoted in Carl Becker "Nominations in Colonial New York," *American Historical Review* 6 (January 1901): 260-275.

42. Henry Beekman to Henry Livingston, November 26, 1747, in Dutchess County Historical Society, *Yearbook,* 1921, p. 32. The importance of the candidate's image today is discussed in Lane, *Political Life,* pp. 24-25, 307-308.

43. John Colman, *The Distressed State of the Town of Boston &c. Considered* (Boston, 1720), p. 6.

44. *Boston Evening-Post,* May 14, 1759. See also *Advice to the Freeholders and Electors of Pennsylvania* (Philadelphia, 1735), pp. 3-4.

45. *New York Gazette or Weekly Post-Boy,* February 5, 1761. See also Willem Johonas Van Dore Manadus [pseud.], *To the Freeholders and Freemen of the City and County of New-York* (New York, 1768); *New York Journal* (Holt's), February 18, 1768.

46. *Queries Humbly Offered to the Freeholders in the County of Westchester* (New York, 1750). See also William Livingston et al., *The Independent Reflector,* ed. Milton M. Klein (Cambridge, 1963), p. 65: *New York Gazette or Weekly Post-Boy,* February 15, 1768.

47. *New York Journal* (Holt's), April 12, 1770.

48. *All the Real Friends of Liberty* (New York, 1770).

49. "List of subscriptions to the Political Campaign in Rhode Island," Brown Papers, L & P, 58-70, RIP, JCBL.

50. Nicholas Brown & Co. to Joseph Wanton, April 7, 1765, Brown Papers, P-W2, JCBL. See also James B. Hedges, *The Browns of Providence Plantations,* vol. 1: *The Colonial Years* (Cambridge, 1952), pp. 190-191; Lovejoy, *Rhode Island Politics,* pp. 83-84.

51. Brown and Brown, *Virginia,* chap. 9, esp. p. 187.

52. Figures in table 23 based on material in Deputies and Freemen, RISA, and Tax Assessment Lists, 1760, RISA.

53. Thomas A. Archdeacon, "The Age of Leisler—New York City, 1689-1710: A Social and Demographic Interpretation," in Jacob Judd and Irwin H. Polishook, eds., *Aspects of Early New York Society and Politics* (Tarrytown, 1974), p. 78.

54. Figures compiled from *Copy of the Poll List . . . MDCCLXIX.*

55. Champagne, "Liberty Boys and Mechanics," p. 132.

56. See Paul S. Boyer, "Borrowed Rhetoric: The Massachusetts Ex-

cise Controversy of 1754," *William and Mary Quarterly,* 3d ser., 21 (July 1964): 328-351.

57. Gov. Horatio Sharpe to Lord Baltimore, May 2, 1754, in W. H. Browne et al., eds., *Archives of Maryland* (Baltimore, 1883-1972), 6: 56.

58. Thomas Hutchinson, *The History of the Massachusetts Bay Colony,* ed. Lawrence S. Mayo (Cambridge, 1936), 2: 300.

59. Zemsky, *Merchants, Farmers, and River Gods,* pp. 247-248.

60. Charles S. Sydnor, *Gentlemen Freeholders: Political Practices in Washington's Virginia* (Chapel Hill, 1952), pp. 43-44, 47-48.

61. Gov. Samuel Ogle to Lord Baltimore, February 12, 1749, in Browne et al., eds., *Archives of Maryland,* 44: 699. See also Vertrees J. Wyckoff, *Tobacco Regulation in Colonial Maryland* (Baltimore, 1936), chap. 8.

62. For recent parent-child voting patterns, see David O. Sears, "Political Behavior," in Gardner Lindzey and Elliot Aronson, eds., *The Handbook of Social Psychology,* 2d ed. (Reading, 1969), p. 377. Rhode Island figures based on voter lists in Deputies and Freemen, RISA. New York figures from *Copy of the Poll List . . . MDCCLXIX.*

63. The religiously based party conflicts in early eighteenth century New Jersey are described in John E. Pomfret, *Colonial New Jersey: A History* (New York, 1973), chap. 6. For Pennsylvania's clashes, see James H. Hutson, *Pennsylvania Politics, 1746-1770: The Movement for Royal Government and Its Consequences* (Princeton, 1972).

64. See statement of the Quaker yearly meeting, January, 1710, quoted in Hermann Wellenreuther, *Glaube und Politik in Pennsylvania, 1681-1776* (Koln, 1972), p. 171.

65. William Smith, *A Brief State of the Province of Pennsylvania* (London, 1755), p. 28.

66. Gov. George Thomas to John Penn, October 20, 1740, quoted in J. Paul Selsam, *The Pennsylvania Constitution of 1776* (Philadelphia, 1936), p. 23. See also Thayer, *Pennsylvania Politics,* p. 16.

67. Quoted in Carl Bridenbaugh, *Mitre and Sceptre: Transatlantic Faiths, Ideas, Personalities, and Politics, 1689-1775* (New York, 1962), p. 251. See also Smith, *A Brief State,* p. 29; Thayer, *Pennsylvania Politics,* p. 41; Arthur D. Graeff, *The Relations between the Pennsylvania Germans and the British Authorities* (Norristown, 1939).

68. Bridenbaugh, *Mitre and Sceptre,* pp. 251-252; Thomas Stewardson, ed., "Extracts from the Letter-Book of Benjamin Marshall, 1763-1766," *Pennsylvania Magazine of History and Biography 20* (1896): 207.

69. William Allen to Thomas Penn, October 21, 1764, quoted in Hutson, *Pennsylvania Politics,* p. 171.

70. Bonomi, *A Factious People,* pp. 26-27.

71. Archdeacon, "Age of Leisler," p. 78.

72. Nash, "Transformation of Urban Politics," p. 611. Figures for 1769 compiled from *Copy of the Poll List . . . MDCCLXIX.*

73. Bridenbaugh, *Mitre and Sceptre,* p. 262; Bonomi, *A Factious People* pp. 248-254.

74. Quoted in *Mitre and Sceptre,* p. 263n.

75. Herbert L. Osgood, ed., "The Society of Dissenters founded at New York in 1769," *American Historical Review* 6 (April 1901): 498-507. Votes taken from *Copy of the Poll List . . . MDCCLXIX.*

76. Nathaniel Bouton et al., eds., *Documents and Papers Relating to New Hampshire* (Concord and Manchester, 1867-1941), 13: 63. See also ibid., *12: 148, 433-435, 447-449.*

77. Tiverton church membership lists are printed in James N. Arnold, *Vital Records of Rhode Island, 1636-1850* (Providence, 1896), 8: 49-62. Tiverton votes in Deputies and Freemen, RISA.

78. *Connecticut Colony Records, 8:* 512n.; Grant, *Democracy in Kent,* pp. 123-124; William Samuel Johnson to John Beach, January 4, 1763, quoted in Christopher Collier, *Roger Sherman's Connecticut* (Middletown, 1971), p. 37.

79. Bruce E. Steiner, "Anglican Officeholding in Pre-Revolutionary Connecticut: The Parameters of New England Community," *William and Mary Quarterly,* 3d ser., 31 (July 1974): 369-406. The quote appears on p. 386. See also Zeichner, *Connecticut,* pp. 117-120.

80. "Essex County Presbyterians," *William and Mary Quarterly,* 1st ser., 26 (1917-1918): 65. Essex poll list for 1758 and 1761 are found in Essex County Deed Book, 28: 95-99, 29: 1-7, VSL.

81. Lancaster Presbyterians compiled from names in "Journal of Col. James Gordon," *William and Mary Quarterly,* 1st ser., 11 (1902-1903): 98-112, 195-205, 217-236, 12 (1903-1904): 1-12. Voting lists for 1761 and 1765 are found in Lancaster Deed Book, 16: 222-223, 18: 42-43, VSL

82. Quoted in Wesley M. Gewehr, *The Great Awakening in Virginia, 17* *1790* (Durham, 1930), p. 89. See also George W. Pilcher, *Samuel Davies, Apostle of Dissent in Colonial Virginia* (Knoxville, 1971).

83. *New York Review of Books,* August 5, 1976.

EPILOGUE

1. This theme is emphasized in Bernard Bailyn, *Origins of American Politics* (New York, 1968), chap. 2.

2. Quoted in William L. Sachse, *The Colonial American in Great Britain* (Madison, 1956), p. 207.

3. James Otis, "Considerations on Behalf of the Colonists," *Boston Gazette,* July 22, 1765.

4. "To the Author of Common Sense," in Peter Force, comp., *American Archives* (Washington, D.C., 1837-1853), 4th ser., 4: 1498. See also "Petition from New Brunswick," ibid., p. 1594.

5. *Pennsylvania Packet,* April 29, 1776.

6. *The People the Best Governors: or a Plan of Government Founded on the Just Principles of Natural Freedom* (n.p., 1776), p. 9.

7. *Massachusetts Spy,* July 5, 1775.

8. Jackson T. Main, "Government by the People: The American Revolution and the Democratization of the Legislatures," *William and Mary Quarterly,* 3d ser., 23 (July 1966).

9. Merrill Jensen, "Democracy and the American Revolution," *Huntington Library Quarterly* 20 (August 1957): 321-341; Gordon S. Wood, *The Creation of the American Republic, 1776-1787* (Chapel Hill, 1969).

Bibliographical Essay

★★★★★★★★★★★★★★★★

The sources for the history of voting in provincial America are not concentrated in a small number of books and archival depositories but are scattered far and wide. Each item available yields only a tiny fraction of the total story so that one must consult voluminous amounts of written matter in order to piece together a full picture of the election process in the thirteen colonies.

Of the numerous sources employed, perhaps the most useful for this study were the large published collections of official documents and records that in many cases contain detailed descriptions of elections, petitions by candidates, correspondence of governing officers, and, occasionally, a few voting results. These sets include: James H. Trumbull and Charles J. Hoadly, eds., *Public Records of the Colony of Connecticut, 1636-1776,* 15 vols. (Hartford, 1850-1890); Allen D. Candler, ed., *Colonial Records of the State of Georgia,* 26 vols. (Atlanta, 1904-1916); W. H. Browne et al., eds., *Archives of Maryland,* 72 vols. (Baltimore, 1883-1972); *Journals of the House of Representatives of Massachusetts,* 43 vols. (Boston, 1919-); Nathaniel Bouton et al., eds., *Documents and Records Relating to New Hampshire,* 40 vols. (Concord and Manchester, 1867-1941); W. A. Whitehead et al., eds., *New Jersey Archives,* 30 vols. (Newark, 1880-1906); Edmund B. O'Callaghan and Berthold Fernow, eds., *Documents Relative to the Colonial History of the State of New York,* 15 vols. (Albany, 1853-1887); William L. Saunders, ed., *Colonial Records of North Carolina, 1662-1776,* 10 vols. (Raleigh, 1886-1890); Samuel Hazard et al., eds., *Pennsylvania Archives,* 119 vols. in 9 series (Philadelphia and Harrisburg, 1852-1935); H. R. McIlwaine and J. P.

Kennedy, eds., *Journals of the House of Burgesses of Virginia, 1619-1776,*
13 vols. (Richmond, 1905-1915); John R. Bartlett, ed., *Records of the
Colony of Rhode Island and Providence Plantations,* 10 vols. (Providence,
1856-1865).

While less pertinent than each colony's official documents, local records
provide a good deal of data on voting. Various county, parish, and town
meeting records often have accounts of local contests as well as important
statistical information. The bulk of this material is still in manuscript in city
halls, county offices, and state archives, but some is in print. Many of the
published volumes of these records are listed in vol. 1 of Frank Freidel,
ed., *Harvard Guide to American History,* rev. ed., 2 vols. (Cambridge, 1974).
In addition, town and county histories, though often dated and filiopie-
tistic, can be a storehouse of vital information, printing tax and officeholding lists, plus other enlightening factual matter.

Another significant group of sources are the several compilations of
colonial laws. The legal statutes of that time not only spelled out the rules
and regulations for voting but also presented commentary on the conditions surrounding their passage. Major collections of early American laws
are Abner C. Goodell et al., eds., *Acts and Resolves, Public and Private, of
the Province of the Massachusetts Bay,* 21 vols. (Boston, 1869-1922);
Samuel Allinson, ed., *Acts of the General Assembly of the Province of
New Jersey, 1702-1776* (Burlington, 1776); *Colonial Laws of New York
from the Year 1664 to the Revolution,* 5 vols. (Albany, 1894-1896); J. T.
Mitchell and Henry Flanders, eds., *Statutes at Large of Pennsylvania from
1682 to 1801,* 18 vols. (Harrisburg, 1896-1915); Thomas Cooper and
D. J. McCord, eds., *Statutes at Large of South Carolina,* 10 vols. (Columbia, 1836-1841); William W. Hening, ed., *The Statutes at Large . . . of Virginia,* 13 vols. (Richmond, 1809-1823).

Besides official documents and laws, newspapers provide a wealth of
information about provincial voting. Every major colonial newspaper carried political essays pertaining to upcoming elections. Some of them published advertisements favoring certain candidates. A few even printed
voting results from time to time. The weeklies I used most frequently were:
the *Boston News-Letter,* the *Boston Gazette,* the *Boston Evening-Post,*
the *Connecticut Courant* (Hartford), the *Connecticut Gazette* (New London), the *New York Gazette,* the *New York Weekly Journal,* the *New York
Gazette or Weekly Post-Boy,* the *New York Journal or General Advertiser,*
the *New York Gazette and Weekly Mercury,* the *American Weekly Mercury*
(Philadelphia), the *Pennsylvania Gazette* (Philadelphia), the *Pennsylvania
Journal* (Philadelphia), the *Maryland Gazette* (Annapolis), the *Virginia
Gazette* (Williamsburg), and the *South Carolina Gazette* (Charleston). All
titles and existing copies of newspapers from the provincial period are noted

in Clarence Brigham, comp., *History and Bibliography of American News-papers, 1690-1820,* 2 vols. (Worcester, 1947), and many are available on microfilm or on microcards through the *Early American Imprint Series.*

In conjunction with newspapers, pamphlets and broadsides form a key source of voting material. Pamphlets generally discussed political theories, contemporary issues, or sometimes the qualities to look for in prospective candidates. Almost all titles are now on microcards and are indexed in Charles Evans, comp., *American Bibliography: A Chronological Diction-ary of All Books, Pamphlets and Periodical Publications Printed in the United States of America . . . 1639 . . . 1820,* 14 vols. (Chicago and Wor-cester, 1903-1959), or in Roger P. Bristol, comp., *Supplement to Charles Evans' American Bibliography* (Charlottesville, 1970). Much of this same literature is listed alphabetically in Clifford K. Shipton and James E. Mooney, comps., *National Index of American Imprints through 1800: The Short-Title Evans,* 2 vols. (Barre, 1969).

Personal papers, memoirs, and letters of notable figures, both in print-ed and in manuscript form, make up another fruitful source. Only private accounts can provide a behind-the-scenes dimension that is often missing from public documents. For Massachusetts, the Jonathan Belcher Letter-books in the Massachusetts Historical Society, Boston, and the *Belcher Papers,* published in the Massachusetts Historical Society, *Collections,* 6th ser., vol. 7 (1894), present a close-up view of the political maneuvering of an eighteenth century royal governor. Charles F. Adams, ed., *The Works of John Adams,* 10 vols. (Boston, 1850-1856), and Lyman H. Butterfield et al., eds., *Diary and Autobiography of John Adams,* 4 vols. (Cambridge, 1961), give several insights into the nature of elections in the Bay Colony. The Hutchinson Papers, the Israel Williams Papers, and the Winthrop Papers at the Massachusetts Historical Society also contain some pertinent ma-terial. Rhode Island has the most complete inside view of the election pro-cess seen anywhere, at least for the decade of the 1760's, because of the abundant collection of the Brown Family Papers at the John Carter Brown Library, Providence, together with the Ward Manuscripts and the Moses Brown Papers at the Rhode Island Historical Society, Providence. Much private correspondence concerning Connecticut elections have been pre-served in Robert J. Taylor, ed., *The Susquehanna Company Papers,* 11 vols. (Ithaca, 1962-1971). A few items can also be found in Franklin B. Dexter, ed., *Extracts from the Itineraries and Other Miscellanies of Ezra Stiles, D.D., L.L.D., 1755-1794, with a Selection from His Correspondence* (New Haven, 1916), and in the Stiles Papers, Yale University Library, New Haven, and the Joseph Trumbull Papers, Connecticut State Library, Hart-ford. The personal papers of New York's leading political figures have not been published in most cases. Two collections that are in print, however, prove extremely valuable for understanding that colony's elections. The two are James Sullivan and Alexander C. Flick, eds., *The Papers of Sir William Johnson*, 14 vols. (Albany, 1921-1965), and *The Letters and Papers of Cadwallader Colden*, New-York Historical Society, *Collections* (1918-1937), vols. 50-56, 67-68. Also worth examining for the contests of the 1760's are the Livingston Papers and the James Duane Papers at the New-York Historical Society, and William H. W. Sabine, ed., *Historical Memoirs of William Smith*, 2 vols. (New York, 1956). Fewer collections of letters of New Jersey political leaders are easily available, but the thin volume *Papers of Lewis Morris*, ed. by W. A. Whitehead, New Jersey Historical Society, *Collections* (1852), vol. 4, has a number of interesting items regarding elections. Pennsylvania has many more materials to look at, most notably Edward Armstrong, ed., *The Correspondence of William Penn and James Logan*, 2 vols. (Philadelphia, 1872), for the early period; the Isaac Norris Letterbooks and the Penn Papers at the Historical Society of Pennsylvania, Philadelphia, for the middle period; and Leonard W. Labaree et al., eds., *The Papers of Benjamin Franklin*, 19 vols. (New Haven, 1959-), for the later provincial years. Another mine of information on Quaker colony politics is the Shippen Family Papers at the Historical Society of Pennsylvania, many of which are printed in Thomas Balch, ed., *Letters and Papers Relating Chiefly to the Provincial History of Pennsylvania* (Philadelphia, 1855). For Delaware, George Ryden, ed., *Letters to and from Caesar Rodney, 1756-1784* (Philadelphia, 1933), offers much about the voting process there. The Stephen Bordley Letterbooks and the Daniel Dulany Papers at the Maryland Historical Society, Baltimore, are vital sources for Maryland politics, as are the printed *Calvert Papers* (Baltimore, 1894), vol. 2, and "The Correspondence of Governor Horatio Sharpe, 1753-1771," *Archives of Maryland*, vols. 6, 9, 14. The most illuminating personal papers for Virginia elections are John C. Fitzpatrick, ed., *The Writings of George Washington*, 39 vols. (Washington, D.C., 1930-1944), and Stanislaus M. Hamilton, ed., *Letters to Washington and Accompanying Papers*, 5 vols. (Boston and New York, 1898-1902). Jack P. Greene, ed., *The Diary of Colonel Landon Carter of Sabine Hall, 1752-1778*, 2 vols. (Charlottesville, 1965), is very revealing. The correspondence of two provincial governors can also be used with profit: *The Official Letters of Alexander Spotswood*, 2 vols. (Richmond, 1882-1885), and R. A. Brock, ed., *The Official Records of Robert Dinwiddie*, 2 vols. (Richmond, 1883-1884). Few political papers of Carolinians and Georgians have been collected, though some valuable letters have been printed in the already cited *North Carolina Colonial Records*, and others are available in the unpublished South Carolina and Georgia records located in their respective state archives.

Many general secondary works, while not devoted primarily to the election process, provide fundamental background to the political life and thought of the provincial period. Most important are three fairly recent books: Bernard Bailyn, *The Origins of American Politics* (New York, 1968), a comprehensive analysis of many aspects of early American political culture; J. R. Pole, *Political Representation in England and the Origins of American Democracy* (London, 1966), which traces the growth of English political ideas and their manifestation in this country; and Jack P. Greene, *The Quest for Power: The Lower Houses of Assembly in the Southern Royal Colonies, 1689-1776* (Chapel Hill, 1963), an exhaustive study of the rise of the colonial assemblies and their relationship to royal authority. Certain older volumes are still useful, especially Clinton Rossiter, *Seedtime of the Republic: The Origin of the American Tradition of Political Liberty* (New York, 1953), and Leonard W. Labaree, *Royal Government in America* (New Haven, 1930). The English connection with provincial politics is emphasized in Alison G. Olson, *Anglo-American Politics, 1660-1775: The Relationship Between Parties in England and Colonial America* (New York, 1973), while the English political scene is the subject of many writings such as Sir Lewis B. Namier, *The Structure of Politics at the Accession of George III*, 2d ed. (London, 1957), J. H. Plumb, *The Growth of Political Stability in England, 1675-1725* (London, 1967), and Caroline Robbins, *The Eighteenth-Century Commonwealthman* (Cambridge, 1959). Crucial, too, for an understanding of provincial politics are several major articles including: Richard Buel, Jr., "Democracy and the American Revolution: A Frame of Reference," *William and Mary Quarterly*, 3d ser., 21 (July 1964): 165-190; Roy N. Lokken, "The Concept of Democracy in Colonial Political Thought," ibid. 16 (October 1959), 568-580; J. R. Pole, "Historians and the Problem of Early American Democracy," *American Historical Review* 67 (April 1962): 626-646; and John M. Murrin, "The Myths of Colonial Democracy and Royal Decline in Eighteenth-Century America: A Review Essay," *Cithara* 5 (1965): 53-69. Much of this literature is ably summarized by Jack P. Greene, "Changing Interpretations of Early American Politics," in Ray A. Billington, ed., *The Reinterpretation of Early American History* (San Marino, 1966), pp. 151-184. A number of studies of the Revolutionary and early national periods also cast a good deal of light on the provincial picture. Most noteworthy are Jackson T. Main, *Political Parties before the Constitution* (Chapel Hill, 1973), Gordon S. Wood, *Creation of the American Republic, 1776-1787* (Chapel Hill, 1969), William N. Chambers, *Political Parties in a New Nation: The American Experience, 1776-1809* (New York, 1963), and Richard Hofstadter, *The Idea of a Party System: The*

Rise of Legitimate Opposition in the United States, 1780-1840 (Berkeley, 1969).

In addition to those works on the provinces in general, there are a vast number of studies of the political life of individual colonies, which are indispensable for a survey of voting. Many of the following books and articles deal mainly with the inner workings of the government, the conflicts between royal officials and local assemblies, and the internal factional struggles, but almost all of them touch upon the election process at least to some degree. A few of these volumes analyze voting in greater detail and are classics. They are: Charles S. Sydnor's *Gentlemen Freeholders: Political Practices in Washington's Virginia* (Chapel Hill, 1952), a pathbreaking assessment of the political culture of the largest colony, stressing the aristocratic though benevolent leadership of the planter class, Robert E. Brown's *Middle-Class Democracy and the Revolution in Massachusetts, 1691-1780* (Ithaca, 1955), and Robert E. and B. Katherine Brown's *Virginia, 1705-1786: Democracy or Aristocracy?* (East Lansing, 1964), which argue that Massachusetts and Virginia were democratic in their political framework since a majority of adult males could vote.

Among the secondary accounts of each colony are many important studies of Massachusetts besides Brown's *Middle-Class Democracy*. Michael Zuckerman, *Peaceable Kingdoms: New England Towns in the Eighteenth Century* (New York, 1970), supersedes the former work in several ways, especially in its more detailed analysis of local attitudes and institutions. Best of the recent volumes on the early provincial era are Timothy H. Breen, *The Character of the Good Ruler: A Study of Puritan Political Ideas in New England, 1630-1730* (New Haven, 1970), and Richard S. Dunn, *Puritans and Yankees: The Winthrop Dynasty of New England, 1630-1717* (Princeton, 1962). For the later period, Robert Zemsky, *Merchants, Farmers, and River Gods: An Essay on Eighteenth-Century American Politics* (Boston, 1971), has an excellent discussion of the leadership pattern in the Bay Colony. Other valuable contributions are: John A. Schutz, *William Shirley: King's Governor of Massachusetts* (Chapel Hill, 1961); John J. Waters, Jr., *The Otis Family in Provincial and Revolutionary Massachusetts* (Chapel Hill, 1968); and Ellen E. Brennan, *Plural Office-Holding in Massachusetts, 1760-1780* (Chapel Hill, 1945). A number of penetrating works on the political life in other New England colonies must be mentioned. The leading study of New Hampshire is Jere Daniell, *Experiment in Republicanism: New Hampshire Politics and the American Revolution, 1741-1794* Cambridge, 1970). Still helpful in some ways are William H. Fry, *New Hampshire as a Royal Province* (New York, 1908), and Richard F. Upton, *Revolutionary New Hampshire* (Hanover, 1936). Sydney V. James, *Colonial Rhode*

Island: A History (New York, 1975), provides the first modern synthesis
of that colony's politics. David S. Lovejoy, *Rhode Island Politics and the
American Revolution, 1760-1776* (Providence, 1958), together with Mack
E. Thompson, "The Ward-Hopkins Controversy and the American Revolution: An Interpretation," *William and Mary Quarterly,* 3d ser., 16 (July
1959): 363-375, give an excellent view of Rhode Island elections in the
pre-Revolutionary era. A thorough discussion of Connecticut politics, especially for the later provincial period, is Oscar Zeichner, *Connecticut's
Years of Controversy, 1750-1776* (Chapel Hill, 1949). Richard L. Bushman, *From Puritan to Yankee: Character and the Social Order in Connecticut, 1690-1765* (Cambridge, 1967), skillfully traces changing attitudes toward the leadership class in the eighteenth century. Robert J.
Dinkin, "Elections in Colonial Connecticut," *Connecticut Historical Society Bulletin* 37 (January 1972), offers a brief survey of its subject.
Among the middle colonies, the most sophisticated study of the political culture in New York is Patricia U. Bonomi, *A Factious People: Politics and Society in Colonial New York* (New York, 1971), succeeding
the older and more simplified "progressive" view of Carl Becker, *The
History of Political Parties in the Province of New York, 1760-1776*
(Madison, 1909). Bonomi's book may be supplemented by Michael G.
Kammen, *Colonial New York: A History* (New York, 1975), and by the
knowledgeable articles of Milton M. Klein, which are collected in *The
Politics of Diversity: Essays in the History of Colonial New York* (Port
Washington, 1974). Other volumes worth noting are Stanley N. Katz,
Newcastle's New York: Anglo-American Politics, 1732-1753 (Cambridge,
1968), Jacob Judd and Irwin H. Polishook, eds., *Aspects of Early New
York Society and Politics* (Tarrytown, 1974), and Thomas A. Archdeacon,
New York City, 1664-1710: Conquest and Change (Ithaca, 1976). New
Jersey politics are well treated in Donald L. Kemmerer, *Path to Freedom:
The Struggle for Self-Government in Colonial New Jersey, 1703-1776*
(Princeton, 1940); Richard P. McCormick, *New Jersey from Colony to
State, 1609-1789* (Princeton, 1964); and John E. Pomfret, *Colonial New
Jersey: A History* (New York, 1973). An extensive literature exists for
provincial Pennsylvania. The best examination of political life in early
Pennsylvania is Gary B. Nash, *Quakers and Politics: Pennsylvania, 1681-
1726* (Princeton, 1968). Also noteworthy are Roy N. Lokken, *David Lloyd,
Colonial Lawmaker* (Seattle, 1959); Frederick B. Tolles, *James Logan and
the Culture of Provincial America* (Boston, 1957); and Thomas Wendel,
"The Keith-Lloyd Alliance: Faction and Coalition Politics in Colonial
Pennsylvania," *Pennsylvania Magazine of History and Biography* 92 (July
1968): 289-305. For the subsequent period, the broadest survey is Theodore G. Thayer, *Pennsylvania Politics and the Growth of Democracy,*

1740-1776 (Harrisburg, 1953). Several more specialized studies help round out the picture. These include: William S. Hanna, *Benjamin Franklin and Pennsylvania Politics* (Stanford, 1964); James H. Hutson, *Pennsylvania Politics, 1746-1770: The Movement for Royal Government and Its Consequences* (Princeton, 1972); Benjamin H. Newcomb, *Franklin and Galloway* (New Haven, 1972); and David Hawke, *In the Midst of a Revolution* (Philadelphia, 1961). A full-length portrait of Delaware politics has yet to be written, but significant articles telling some of the story are Robert W. Johannsen, "The Conflict between the Three Lower Counties on the Delaware and the Province of Pennsylvania, 1682-1704," *Delaware History* 5 (1952): 96-132; Richard S. Rodney, "Delaware under Governor Keith, 1717-1726," ibid. 3 (1948): 1-25; and Harold B. Hancock, "Thomas Robinson: Delaware Loyalist," ibid. 4 (1950-1951): 1-36. Maryland politics is well covered in Charles A. Barker, *The Background to the Revolution in Maryland* (New Haven, 1940), and David C. Skaggs, *Roots of Maryland's Democracy* (Westport, Conn., 1973), the latter devoting considerable space to elections. Aubrey C. Land, *The Dulanys of Maryland: A Biographical Study of Daniel Dulany, the Elder (1685-1753) and Daniel Dulany, the Younger (1722-1797)* (Baltimore, 1955), further enhances our knowledge of the colony's politics. For Virginia, in addition to the works by Brown and Sydnor, a well-researched investigation into the nature of the political practices in the Old Dominion is Lucille B. Griffith, *The Virginia House of Burgesses, 1750-1774*, rev. ed. (University, Ala., 1970). Two valuable surveys of the entire period are Thomas J. Wertenbaker, *Give Me Liberty: The Struggle for Self-Government in Virginia* (Philadelphia, 1958), and Richard L. Morton, *Colonial Virginia*, 2 vols. (Chapel Hill, 1960). The full-length narrative by Douglas S. Freeman, *George Washington: A Biography,* 7 vols. (New York, 1948-1957), is also helpful on many points. There is no single study devoted entirely to North Carolina politics, but Hugh T. Lefler and William S. Powell, *Colonial North Carolina: A History* (New York, 1973), provides an up-to-date synthesis of existing writings on the subject. Two works dealing more directly with the election process are Julian P. Boyd, "The Sheriff in Colonial North Carolina," *North Carolina Historical Review* 5 (April 1928): 151-181, and John S. Bassett, "Suffrage in the State of North Carolina (1776-1861)," American Historical Association, *Annual Report, 1895* (Washington, D.C., 1896). South Carolina politics is thoroughly treated in M. Eugene Sirmans, *Colonial South Carolina: A Political History, 1663-1763* (Chapel Hill, 1966). Older but still useful are Roy H. Smith, *South Carolina as a Royal Province* (New York, 1903), and Edward McGrady, *The History of South Carolina under the Royal Government* (New York, 1924). For the period prior to independence, Robert M. Weir, " ' The Harmony We Were Famous For,': An Interpretation of Pre-Revolutionary South Carolina Politics," *William and Mary Quarterly,* 3d ser., 26 (October 1969): 473-501, offers many new insights. Political life in the province of Georgia is covered in William W. Abbot, *The Royal Governors of Georgia* (Chapel Hill, 1959), and Kenneth Coleman, *Colonial Georgia: A History* (New York, 1976).

On specific aspects of the subject of voting, the most authoritative work on the franchise is Chilton Williamson, *American Suffrage from Property to Democracy, 1760-1860* (Princeton, 1960), which uses previously untapped land and tax records to substantiate many of its conclusions. Many older studies still provide some crucial data, beginning with J. Franklin Jameson, "Did the Fathers Vote?" *New England Magazine,* n.s., 1 (January 1890): 484-490, and "Virginia Voting in the Colonial Period, 1744-1774," *The Nation* 56 (April 27, 1893): 309-310. Cortlandt F. Bishop, *History of Elections in the American Colonies* (New York, 1893), and Albert E. McKinley, *The Suffrage Franchise in the Thirteen English Colonies in America* (Philadelphia, 1905), contain extensive material on the suffrage but often mistakenly accept laws as synonymous with practice. Kirk H. Porter, *Suffrage in the United States* (Chicago, 1918), makes a few good points about the electorate in the provincial period. Besides Robert Brown, several other scholars have questioned the idea of a severely limited franchise in early America. Their works include: Richard P. McCormick, *The History of Voting in New Jersey: A Study of the Development of Election Machinery, 1664-1911* (New Brunswick, 1953), chaps. 1-2; Charles S. Grant, *Democracy in the Connecticut Frontier Town of Kent* (New York, 1961); and the previously cited volumes of David S. Lovejoy and Milton M. Klein. Recent writings that take issue with those of the broad suffrage disciples are Jackson T. Main, "The Distribution of Property in Post-Revolutionary Virginia," *Mississippi Valley Historical Review* 41 (September 1954): 241-258; Benjamin W. Labaree, *Patriots and Partisans: The Merchants of Newburyport, 1764-1815* (Cambridge, 1962); Kenneth A. Lockridge, "Land, Population and the Evolution of New England Society, 1630-1790," *Past and Present* 39 (April 1968): 62-80; and the aforementioned David C. Skaggs, *Roots of Maryland's Democracy.*

There is no full-scale study of provincial officeholding and not much literature at all on why men sought office. However, several recent articles contain a great deal of valuable information. The most substantial inquiry is Jackson T. Main, "Government by the People: The American Revolution and the Democratization of the Legislatures," *William and Mary Quarterly,* 3d ser., 23 (July 1966): 391-407, part of which analyzes the make-up of half the assemblies in the pre-Revolutionary era. Other essays on individual towns or colonies include Bruce C. Daniels, "Large Town Officeholding in Eighteenth-Century Connecticut: The Growth of Oligarchy," *Journal of American Studies* 9 (April 1975): 1-12, and "Democracy and Oligarchy in Connecticut Towns: General Assembly Officeholding, 1701-1790," *Social Science Quarterly* 56 (December 1975): 460-475; William F. Willingham, "Deference Democracy and Town Government in Windham, Connecticut, 1755-1786," *William and Mary Quarterly,* 3d ser., 30 (July 1973): 401-422, all of which emphasize a strong tie between wealth and officeholding, while Patricia U. Bonomi, "Local Government in Colonial New York: A Base for Republicanism," in Judd and Polishook, eds., *Aspects of Early New York,* demonstrates that in the town of Kingston local officeholders were generally middle class. Wayne L. Bockelman and Owen S. Ireland, "The Internal Revolution in Pennsylvania: An Ethnic-Religious Interpretation," *Pennsylvania History* 41 (April 1974), 125-159, explore another important aspect of the subject. Two books that provide a comparative element are Robert Lane, *Political Life* (New York, 1964), part of which tries to explain why men seek office in America today, and Sir Lewis Namier, *The Structure of Politics,* which attempts to show why eighteenth-century Englishmen sought seats in Parliament. Perhaps the most illuminating source concerning the attitudes of provincials seeking office is the contemporary play by Robert Munford, *The Candidates; or, the Humours of a Virginia Election,* ed. Jay B. Hubbell and Douglass Adair (Williamsburg, 1948).

The material on the development of the nomination process comes from a wide variety of sources. The first modern secondary account is Robert J. Dinkin, "Nominations in Provincial America," *The Historian* 36 (November 1973): 66-86, now revised and enlarged as chap. 4 of the present work. Frederick W. Dallinger, *Nominations for Elective office in the United States* (New York, 1897), devotes just a few pages to the period before 1776. Carl Becker, "Nominations in Colonial New York," *American Historical Review* 6 (January 1901): 260-275, supplemented by Nicholas Varga, "Election Procedures and Practices in Colonial New York," *New York History* 41 (July 1960): 249-277, give much information on nominations in that colony. On the local level, only the Boston caucus has been subjected to careful scrutiny in G. B. Warden, "The Caucus and Democracy in Colonial Boston," *New England Quarterly* 43 (March 1970): 19-45, and in Alan and Katherine Day, "Another Look at the Boston 'Caucus'" *Journal of American Studies* 5 (April 1971): 19-42.

Some of the best material on electioneering is located in manuscript sources such as the Brown Papers in the John Carter Brown Library and the Penn Papers in the Historical Society of Pennsylvania. A good deal of information on vote-getting techniques in particular colonies, however, can be found in such secondary assessments as Sister Joan de Lourdes Leonard, "Elections in Colonial Pennsylvania," *William and Mary Quarterly*, 3d ser., 11 (October 1954): 385-401, and in the previously cited works of Sydnor, Brown, and Griffith on Virginia, Bonomi and Varga on New York, Lovejoy and Thompson on Rhode Island, and Zuckerman and Zemsky on Massachusetts. An excellent account of campaign methods used in Boston, New York City, and Philadelphia is Gary B. Nash, "The Transformation of Urban Politics, 1700-1765," *Journal of American History* 60 (December 1973): 605-632. Nash expertly discusses the emergence of many new aspects of urban campaigning such as the widespread use of the press, the intercession of the clergy, and the holding of mass public meetings. The short summary on urban politics in Carl Bridenbaugh, *Cities in Revolt: Urban Life in America, 1743-1776* (New York, 1955), is also helpful.

Much of the information on formal voting procedures comes from the several sets of colonial laws, official records, and newspapers cited above. The only secondary volumes that treat this subject extensively are the early work by Bishop, *History of Elections,* which must be used with caution, and parts of the well-researched monograph by Mary P. Clarke, *Parliamentary Privilege in the American Colonies* (New Haven, 1943). Some of the already noted studies of individual colonies present a good many details about the actual process of voting. These include: Sydnor, *Gentlemen Freeholders,* chaps. 2-4, the best single-province assessment of the procedures involved in the casting of votes; McCormic, *History of Voting,* chap. 2; Zuckerman, *Peaceable Kingdoms,* chap. 5; Leonard, "Elections in Colonial Pennsylvania"; and Boyd, "The Sheriff in Colonial North Carolina." A brief but valuable survey of the various methods of balloting employed in the provincial era appears in Charles S. Sydnor and Noble E. Cunningham, Jr., "Voting in Early America," *American Heritage* 4 (Fall 1952): 6-8.

No systematic collection of provincial voting returns has ever been made, though McKinley, *Suffrage Franchise,* among others, has offered a calculated guess as to how many voted based on rather limited data. The chief sources of voting statistics are very widely scattered. Most of the known Virginia totals are printed in Griffith, *Virginia House of Burgesses,* appendix 1, and are derived primarily from materials in the Virginia State Library, Richmond. New York and Pennsylvania figures are found mainly in the local newspapers, though a large number of Philadelphia returns are recorded only in vol. 2 of John F. Watson, *Annals of Philadelphia, and Pennsylvania,* rev. ed., 3 vols. (Philadelphia, 1887), and in the Isaac Norris Journals, Rosenbach Foundation, Philadelphia.

Rhode Island results are located in the Brown Papers, John Carter Brown
Library, and the file Deputies and Freemen, Rhode Island State Archives,
Providence. Many Connecticut figures are preserved in Statistics on Elec-
tions, Connecticut Historical Society, Hartford, some of which are pub-
lished in Dinkin, "Elections in Colonial Connecticut." For Massachusetts,
Boston totals prior to 1715 are in *The Diary of Samuel Sewall,* Massa-
chusetts Historical Society, *Collections,* 5th ser., 5-7, and after that date
in *Reports of the Record Commissioners of the City of Boston,* 39 vols.
(Boston, 1876-1909), 8, 12, 16, 18. A few Salem results are noted in
Fitch E. Oliver, ed., *The Diaries of Benjamin Lynde and Benjamin Lynde,
Jr.* (Boston, 1880), and some Lynn results are available in vol. 5 of *Rec-
ords of Ye Towne Meetings of Lyn,* 5 vols. (Lynn, 1949-1966). Several
New Hampshire returns are found in vols. 11-12 of the *New Hampshire
Town Papers,* while the fairly complete Portsmouth figures are in the
Portsmouth Town Records, Portsmouth City Hall. The available New
Jersey statistics are compiled in Donald L. Kemmerer, "The Suffrage
Franchise in Colonial New Jersey," New Jersey Historical Society, *Pro-
ceedings* 52 (1934): 170.

The analysis of voting behavior in provincial America is based in part
on the application of a number of modern voting studies to developments
in those early years. Most useful were Angus Campbell et al., *The American Voter* (New York, 1960), Seymour M. Lipset, *Political Man* (Garden
City, 1960), the previously mentioned Robert Lane, *Political Life,* and the
summary essay by David O. Sears, "Political Behavior," in Gardner Lindzey and Elliot Aronson, eds., *The Handbook of Social Psychology,* 2d
ed. (Reading, 1969). Edward M. Cook, "Rhode Island Voters in an Era
of Partisan Realignment, 1760-1800: Towards a Model for the Study of
Individual Voting Behavior" (Paper delivered at the American Historical
Association Annual Convention, San Francisco, December 28, 1973),
attempts to apply recent analytical techniques to the eighteenth century.
Further assessment of voting behavior in the provincial period appears
in Brown and Brown, *Virginia,* and in two articles, Patricia U. Bonomi,
"Political Patterns in Colonial New York City: The General Assembly
Election of 1768," *Political Science Quarterly* 81 (September 1966):
432-447, and Roger Champagne, "Liberty Boys and Mechanics of New
York City, 1764-1774," *Labor History* 8 (Spring 1967): 115-135. Several historical studies of voting in later periods are extermely enlightening too. Among the most relevant are Lee Benson, *The Concept of Jack-
sonian Democracy: New York as a Test Case* (Princeton, 1961); Richard
P. McCormick, *The Second American Party System* (Chapel Hill, 1965);
and Ronald P. Formisano, *The Birth of Mass Political Parties: Michigan,
1827-1861* (Princeton, 1971).

Index

★★★★★★★★★★★★★★★

About the Author

Robert J. Dinkin, associate professor of history at California State University, Fresno, specializes in early American history. He has written articles for numerous journals, including *The New England Quarterly* and *The Historian,* and is presently doing research on voting in revolutionary America.